Kimberley
Best as Always,
Jeff Grout

Murder
Without
Motive?

88 Days that Shocked a Nation

Jeff Grout and Liz Fisher

shoehorn
www.shoehornbooks.com

Dedication

To Philip Grout.
A wonderful father and an exemplary police officer.

Acknowledgements

Many people have helped us in researching and writing this book and it is true to say that it would not have been possible without their skill and dedication.

We are particularly grateful to retired Detective Superintendent Jim Dickie QPM for his endless advice on police procedure and for his unfailing enthusiasm (and many entertaining stories). And to Anita Cox, who spent many painstaking hours researching the family history of the Goodmans. Thanks also to Simon Warne for his support and advice.

Alan Wall, a North London accountant with a long-standing interest in local history, began researching the Raven case for a book in the 1990s and it was thanks to him that many of the files at the National Archives relating to the case were opened. Alan died in 2005 and we are enormously grateful to his daughter, Amanda Wall, for sharing his unfinished manuscript with us.

Thanks also to the many experts in their field who took the time to talk to us and give us advice: Alan McCormick, curator of the Crime Museum at New Scotland Yard; Detective Superintendent John Sweeney and the rest of Homicide and Serious Crime Command; DCI Howard Groves and the murder team at Barnes, south-west London; Kathryn Dagnall of the Directorate of Forensic Services, New Scotland Yard; Maggie Bird of the Metropolitan Police Archive; Bev Baker, senior curator at the National Galleries of Justice in Nottingham; Ann Taylor at Barnet Local Studies Archive; Gina Zammitt at the Governor's Office in Pentonville; barristers Chris Sutton-Mattocks, Alan Edge and Kara Chadwick; and the excellent staff at the National Archives, Kew, and the British Library's newspaper archive in Colindale.

To our families and friends who supported us throughout the project, offered excellent advice along the way and pretended to be interested in the minutiae of police procedure in the 1940s, even if they weren't: Sarah Everall, Huw Fisher, Beth Holmes, Sarah Owens and Caroline Wood.

Finally, we would like to thank the many former and current residents of Edgware who shared their memories with us and read early drafts of the book, especially Bernard and Netta Elliston, Dennis Signy, Stephen Newing, Ronald and Esther Paradise, Ashleigh Brilliant, Wendy Farron and Ariane Mil. Any errors or omissions are ours alone.

Shoehorn Current Affairs & History Books

Published by
Shoehorn Media Ltd
4 Great Marlborough Street
London W1F 7HH
England
www.shoehornbooks.com

First published in 2009.

A CIP catalogue record for this book is available from the British Library.

ISBNs: 978 1 907149 03 0 (hard back) 978 1 907149 05 4 (paper back)

Printed in the UK by LSUK, Milton Keynes.

Cover design by Alexander Cornes.
Cover photograph courtesy of The National Archives.

Contents

Foreword 7

Introduction – 1949 11

Chapter 1 – Day One: Monday 10 October 1949.................................... 13

Chapter 2 – Day Two 27

Chapter 3 – Edgware 33

Chapter 4 – Danny and Gertrude..41

Chapter 5 – Days Three to Nine 51

Chapter 6 – Days Ten to Seventeen...61

Chapter 7 – Day Forty-three 65

Chapter 8 – Day Forty-four 77

Chapter 9 – Day Forty-five 91

Chapter 10 – Days Forty-five to Sixty-five...105

Chapter 11 – Day Seventy-one 113

Chapter 12 – Days Seventy-two to Eighty-six....................................... 117

Chapter 13 – Day Eighty-seven...127

Chapter 14 – Day Eighty-eight..133

Chapter 15 – Life and Death 137

Chapter 16 – Beyond Reasonable Doubt 141

Chapter 17 – Forensic Investigation 151

Chapter 18 – A Guilty Mind 163

Chapter 19 – An Unfashionable Affliction.. 171

Chapter 20 – Defect of Reason 179

Chapter 21 – Why and How? 189

Chapter 22 – What Happened Next 197

Significant Participants 204

Photographs and Diagrams.. 206

Bibliography and References 213

Index 214

Foreword

On the night of Monday 10 October 1949, Leopold and Esther Goodman, a well-off, middle-aged Jewish couple, were found beaten to death in their home in Edgware, North London.

The murders are particularly significant for me because my father, Philip Grout, was the most junior of the three detectives assigned to the case. My father left school at the age of 14 and joined the Metropolitan Police in May 1936. He joined the CID in October 1940 before spending four years with the Navy during the War. He resumed his career with the CID in 1946 and was promoted to Detective Sergeant in 1947 and transferred to Hendon, and later to Scotland Yard. Between 1957 and 1960, as a Detective Inspector, he lectured at Hendon Detective Training School, before returning to the CID. By the time he retired from the Met in 1968 he was a Detective Chief Superintendent and was in charge of the Criminal Records Office at Scotland Yard.

During his years as a Detective with the Met my father worked on many high-profile cases including the Great Train Robbery, the Hanratty case and the Profumo affair. He rarely talked about his work but when my wife Sarah asked him one day to tell us about one of his cases, it was the Goodman murders that he chose.

A few months later he died and while going through his personal papers I found a neat file containing original papers and scene-of-crime photographs from the case. He had kept no other records from his police career. Above all I longed to ask him, why? Why keep this file and no other? Why did the Goodman murders make such an impression on him?

The murders of Leopold and Esther Goodman have warranted a passing mention in a number of books over the past 60 years. While murder was relatively rare in London in 1949, it seems that even a horrific double murder such as this was destined to keep the newspapers occupied for only as long as the investigation lasted, and subsequently to be consigned to the curios of local history as nothing more than a string of facts and half-truths. A book that mentions the case in more detail than most is *The Murders of the Black Museum 1870-1970* by Gordon Honeycombe. He sums up the case as follows:

> *Among the murderers who kill without apparent motive are a number of sons who for some reason or other cannot exist without extinguishing members of their families, frequently a mother or father or both. Such inimical offspring tend to plead guilty or to be found insane, and so no explanation or motive is ever officially put forward for their fatal deeds.*

The truth is, though, that no event such as the murder of the Goodmans can be dismissed so easily. The murder had a devastating impact on the family and friends of the victims, but its effects were felt much wider and for far longer than anyone can imagine – on the family of Daniel Raven, on the community of Edgware, on the authorities investigating the case and beyond. During our research we spoke to friends and neighbours of Daniel Raven and the Goodmans, to a newspaper reporter who remembered covering the investigation and to many people who lived in or near Edgware at the time and who have never forgotten what happened. It was clear that to all of them, the Goodman murders meant so much more than a tale of local tragedy.

Our aim was to look again at the murders and the subsequent investigation and trial, in an attempt not only to form a better understanding of what happened and *why* it happened, but also to examine whether the investigation was, in effect, a product of its time. During my father's 32 years with the police force he witnessed enormous developments in police investigative techniques and forensic technology, but also a corresponding increase in administrative and procedural requirements. The explosion of modern communication, too, has meant that almost every detail of the murders would be national news within hours today and forgotten by most days later. In Edgware in 1949, few people owned a television set. The social context within which the murders took place has all moved on beyond recognition over the past 60 years, as has the legal framework within which it was tried. Are we any better off for these developments? If the murders took place today, 60 years on, would the outcome be any different?

We have reconstructed the events of 1949 and 1950 from a wide number of sources including witness statements, police reports, correspondence unearthed in files relating to the case that were opened for us under the Freedom of Information Act, trial transcripts, newspaper reports and eyewitness accounts. Anything reported as conversation has been taken directly from these sources.

Jeff Grout
London, April 2009

Introduction – 1949

The year a US Airforce plane made the first non-stop flight around the globe. Mao Tse Tung declared the creation of the People's Republic of China. The US President Harry S Truman began his second term of office with a promise of a Fair Deal between the people and their government. The North Atlantic Treaty was signed by 12 nations, marking the creation of NATO. Vinyl LPs went on sale for the first time, marking the beginning of the end for old 78s. The Democratic Republic of Germany and the Federal Republic of Germany were established. Crowds at the Wimbledon Lawn Tennis Club were scandalised by Gussie Moran's frilly knickers. Chancellor of the Exchequer Sir Stafford Cripps announced a 30% devaluation of the pound from $4.03 to $2.80, resulting in a rise in the cost of a loaf of bread from 4d to 6d. Clothes were off rationing for the first time in eight years. And the USSR tested its atomic bomb.

In 1949 £1 had the purchasing power of about £25.45, using the Retail Price Index as a conversion rate. This would mean, for example, that a television set costing £36 15s in 1949 would be the equivalent of £935 today, and the £750 of electrical goods that Danny Raven sold to Samuel Vosper would be worth about £19,086.

In terms of average earnings, £1 in 1949 would be equivalent to £76.63. So a Sainsbury's shop assistant earning £4 a week would be the equivalent of a salary of £16,000 a year. Danny's wage of £20 a week from Premier Advertising would be worth in the region of £80,000 a year today. (With thanks to www.measuringworth.com).

Chapter 1 – Day One: Monday 10 October 1949

The sun was setting over an unusually warm London as thousands of commuters worked their way with purpose along the busy pavements. Just after 6pm Leopold Goodman, a short, bespectacled Jewish immigrant who had lived more than half his life in London, locked the front door of his radio dealership, just off Tottenham Court Road. He climbed into a dark grey Bedford van outside, driven by his employee and brother-in-law, Alfred, a 44-year-old salesman.

It had been an exciting week for Leopold because, at the age of 51, he had just become a grandfather. His only child, Gertrude, had given birth to her first baby four days earlier. The extended family were close and Gertrude's new baby was a great cause of excitement for everyone. The two men chatted as they set off through the light traffic – Leopold was rarely short of petrol rations. They drove along Marylebone Road before skirting Regent's Park towards Hampstead, where Leopold planned to make a quick visit to his doctor, before heading home to the new suburb of Edgware.

Four years after the end of the Second World War, London was free of the nightly bombing raids that had terrified its population but life was still a daily grind. The immediate euphoria that the declaration of peace had brought had steadily worn away as Londoners struggled with continued rationing, food, clothing and fuel shortages, and faced the enormous rebuilding task ahead.

'Dreariness is everywhere,' wrote a north London schoolteacher, Gladys Langford[1], at the end of 1948. 'Streets are deserted, lighting is dim,

---

[1] Direct quote from *Austerity Britain* by David Kynaston

people's clothes are shabby and their tables bare.' The small signs promising that the country was at last getting back on its feet seemed to be followed inevitably by a step backwards. By the Spring of 1949 the street lighting was beginning to improve and after dark many of the shop lights shone more brightly than they had in years. In April it seemed that the good times were at last back when sweets and chocolate came off rationing for the first time in 10 years. But by August demand had overtaken supply to such an extent that they were placed, to the bitter disappointment of the country's children, back under rations again.

Great areas of Central London were a construction site – the damage caused by the endless bombing and fires had been cleared away, leaving great swathes of wasteland, waiting for the building to begin. Some exciting projects had already begun – in three days the Prime Minister Clement Atlee was due to lay the foundation stone of a new concert hall on the South Bank, next to Waterloo Bridge – but much of the building work that had begun only confirmed to many Londoners their suspicion that the capital would grow upwards rather than outwards. Huge concrete blocks of residential flats were springing up in some of the areas that had been most heavily bombed during the war, particularly in the East End of London where Leopold had first lived when he arrived in the country as an Austro-Hungarian immigrant more than 20 years earlier. The new high-rise blocks were popular with youngsters but the outbreak of war 10 years earlier had persuaded Alfred and Leopold to move their families to one of the safer (and fashionable) 'garden suburbs' that had begun to spring up to the north and north-west of London.

The London borough of Edgware, eight miles north-west of Marble Arch, had blossomed from a small coaching village, where Handel had once played the organ in the village church, to a busy and bustling new suburb of new family homes during the 1920s and 1930s. Much of its sudden expansion and development was due to the extension of the Morden-Golders Green underground line to Edgware, which was completed in 1924. In the space of just 15 years the fast transport links to Central London had transformed a sleepy village, surrounded by farmland, into a sprawling tangle of residential roads and estates. Edgware's reasonably-priced family homes, its newly-built shops, hotel and cinema, and the parkland that had survived the development boom to the west and north of the area, made it an attractive choice for newly-prosperous young families looking for a better life in London. They had often privately blessed their choice during the previous 14 years, as Edgware had miraculously escaped much of the devastating bombing London suffered during the war.

Less expensive than the more desirable Golders Green a few miles down the road, Edgware had seen a huge influx of Jewish families moving into the area during the late 1920s and 1930s. Many of these were some of the tens of thousands of Jewish immigrants who had flooded into London's East End in the first part of the century. They had worked hard to establish themselves in their adopted country and to escape the grinding poverty of their first few years in Whitechapel, and were now well-established and wealthier than their parents could have ever dreamed they would be. By 1949 it was estimated that one in five of Edgware's residents was Jewish.

As Alfred and Leopold continued on towards home, the streets of Edgware were quiet. Station Road, the busy main shopping street, bustling with women during the day as they hurried from shop to shop to collect their family's food rations, was deserted apart from the occasional group heading towards the bar in the new Railway Tavern, an imposing Tudor-style building on the main street. The Ritz cinema was reporting good business and the Doris Day film *My Dream is Yours* had drawn a good crowd. The lights were on in many homes in the maze of streets as families cleared away their dinner plates and the children crowded around the wireless set to hear the latest episode of *Dick Barton: Special Agent*. A few of the wealthier and luckier households who owned a new television set (the cheapest on the market cost £36 15s plus tax, still out of reach of many families) would have to wait another two hours for the BBC's evening programmes to begin, when the nightly newsreel would report on the maiden voyage of the P&O liner *Himalaya*, and the bumper potato crop on the Isle of Arran.

In the newly-built police station on Whitchurch Lane, the night shift was getting itself organised. Serious crime was a rare event in Edgware but burglaries had become a considerable problem in the area in recent years and residents were frustrated at the apparent lack of action from the police. The small number of police cars that patrolled the area, newly-equipped with wireless radios, had gone some way towards appeasing the residents, although apparently had done little to deter the increasingly imaginative and brazen thieves that continue to plague the area.

Just before 8pm the Bedford van carrying Alfred and Leopold turned off the Watford Bypass and into Ashcombe Gardens, a short, crescent-shaped residential street lined with unprepossessing semi-detached houses. A few yards off the main road, Alfred pulled up outside number eight. Alfred, his wife – the younger sister of Leopold's wife Esther – and their children were frequent visitors to the Goodman's home and the families would often sit down for dinner together in the evening at Ashcombe Gardens or at Alfred's home less than half a mile away. But that evening, as they had done each evening since the baby was born, Leopold and Esther planned to visit Gertrude at the private nursing home in Muswell Hill where she had given birth, a few miles away.

As was his habit, Alfred called in at the Goodman's home for a few minutes to say hello to his wife's sister. The house, only a few years old, was compact but well-furnished and comfortable. Attached to the left of the house was a garage, where Leopold's Pontiac saloon was parked. The house itself followed a layout similar to the thousands of new homes that had been built in Edgware over the past 20 years: the porch led through to a hallway corridor, with two doors leading off on the right – the first, a formal sitting room at the front of the house, and second, a dining room behind. The stairs ran up the left of the hallway, with a cupboard underneath in which was carefully concealed, as Alfred was one of the few to know, a large safe. Another door on the left, tucked in behind the stairs, led outside to the front of the locked garage and between that and the entrance to the dining room was the door to the large kitchen with the scullery and coal store beyond. The Goodmans tended to use the kitchen as a second living room and, since it was big enough to hold a sofa and a table and four chairs, spent a great deal of their time there. The gas cooker, sink and a most impressive new gadget – a fridge – had all been relegated to the scullery to make way for more comfortable furniture in the kitchen.

Esther Goodman, a small but well-built 51-year-old, was preparing supper when the two men arrived. It had been a long day, said Leopold, and he was tired. He wasn't sure he had the energy to drive to Muswell Hill again that evening. But Esther was insistent because her daughter had developed mastitis since the birth: 'Danny came by this afternoon and he said Gertrude isn't feeling so well today. We've got to go. We've got to go.' Danny was Gertrude's husband of just over a year and since the baby had been born Danny had eaten most of his meals at Ashcombe Gardens, occasionally staying at the house overnight even though he and Gertrude lived only 500 yards away. Alfred left Leopold to his supper, promising to call in later that evening for the latest news on the baby.

At about 9.45pm, Alfred's 17-year-old daughter finished her homework in the kitchen of their home and packed away her books. Eager to hear the latest news of Gertrude's baby, she climbed into the Bedford van with her parents for the short journey to Ashcombe Gardens. Alfred parked the van on the quiet road opposite number eight and ignoring the front door the family made their way, as usual, to the side door near the garage, which led into the end of the hallway next to the kitchen. The hallway light was shining through the frosted glass panels in the door. Alfred rang the bell, which echoed only faintly inside. With no signs of movement from the kitchen and assuming that Leopold and Esther had only just returned from visiting Gertrude and were upstairs, Alfred banged loudly on the door. Nothing. Perplexed, the two women went to the front door and knocked loudly. There was still no movement from inside.

Alfred walked from the side door to the front and back again with a growing sense of unease. He knew the habits of the Goodmans well and if Leopold and Esther went out, they always closed the kitchen door to the hallway and checked that the kitchen window, which looked out over the small back garden, was closed. But Alfred could see through the glass in the side door that the fluorescent light was on in the kitchen. They must be in. He knocked on the side door again and leant close to the door, listening for any movement from the house. He could hear something; an occasional sound that seemed almost like quiet snoring, but was not quite familiar enough to be recognisable.

His anxiety increasing by the minute, Alfred left the women and walked around the front of the house and down the pathway between number eight and its neighbour, through the gate that led to the garden and the back of the house. At the back of the house he tried the scullery door, which was locked, but the kitchen window was open about nine inches, the lever hanging loose from its bracket. The curtain was drawn across the window. As he moved closer to the window, Alfred could hear the same sound they had heard through the side door – an intermittent, deep rasping breath. Gathering his courage, he pulled the kitchen window wider, pulled himself up and climbed over the ledge, clambering over the sofa on the other side.

The kitchen seemed unchanged from two hours before, although Esther had apparently cleared away the couple's supper dishes before they left to see Gertrude. Through the doorway to his right, the scullery light was on. Alfred walked through the kitchen and into the hallway. The dining room was in darkness; maybe they were watching television? But there was no sound apart from a clatter in the kitchen as his daughter climbed in through the same window, following her father. As Alfred peered closer at the dining room, in the darkness of the doorway he saw a pair of stockinged legs on the floor, the feet encased in blue leather slippers.

In a daze, Alfred rushed to the front door, turned the lock and let in his wife, running quickly back to the dining room. He reached around the door and crouched low to switch on the overhead light, which was on the skirting board only five inches from the floor. At his feet lay the body of a woman, only recognisable as Esther from the flowered dress and brown cardigan he had seen her in earlier that evening. Her skull was split open from the nose to the back of her head, her eyes bulging open on either side of her exposed brain. A large pool of dark blood had poured onto the wooden block floor and the rug, stretching across to the corner of the room.

His wife sobbing hysterically at his feet, cradling her sister's battered face, Alfred's gaze turned to Leopold, who was lying on his right side further into the room, in front of the fireplace. His friend's head was covered in blood that was pouring from several deep gashes across his scalp, forehead and face. But he was breathing – the slow, rattling breaths that were heard from outside.

Alfred turned and gently pushed past his horrified daughter. He picked up the telephone in the kitchen and dialed 999, asking the operator to connect him to the police. When a male voice told him he was through to the Information Room at Scotland Yard, he blurted out that there had been a burglary and that people were badly hurt. After repeating the address, he put the receiver down and dialed his doctor, who lived in Edgwarebury Lane, a few hundred yards away. Dr Cairns' wife answered and, forgetting to give his name, Alfred stayed on the telephone only long enough to say that the doctor had to come at once to 8 Ashcombe Gardens: 'There are two people lying on the floor. There's a lot of blood. I think they've been murdered.'

Unsure of what to do next, Alfred took Leopold's jacket off the peg in the hallway where he had hung it a few hours earlier and crouched beside his friend, gently placing the folded jacket under his head and loosening his collar. In a daze he moved again to Esther's side and felt her hand; it was warm. His wife and daughter, who were holding each other in the hallway, could take no more and ran out onto the street.

It was just after 10pm. PC Claude Jose answered Alfred's 999 call two hours from the end of his eight-hour shift at the Information Room in Scotland Yard. The man sounded shocked and dazed and in the background, he could hear a woman sobbing. Within a minute PC Jose radioed the closest wireless car to attend the scene, before sending a teleprint message to the police station in Edgware: 'Two people found at 8 Ashcombe Gardens, believed dead.'

Inspector John Harvey, the senior uniformed officer on duty at Edgware that night, left immediately with Sergeant Worth, his driver, for the scene. Before he left the station he asked the desk sergeant to telephone Dr Matthews, a police surgeon who lived nearby in Grange Hill Road, to ask him to go to Ashcombe Gardens.

On Edgware high street, PC Charles Hill and his wireless operator, PC Nabbs, were slowly driving through the town's quiet streets. The pair pulled up near the Ritz Cinema, where in a few minutes hundreds of people were due to spill out of the art deco building onto the streets.

The silence was interrupted by their wireless radio: 'M2MP to Sierra One. Police requested at 8 Ashcombe Gardens, please respond'. PCs Hill and Nabbs were barely half a mile away. The car bell ringing loudly, they drove quickly along the almost deserted Edgwarebury Lane, turning onto the Watford Bypass for 50 yards before pulling into Ashcombe Gardens. Most of the shared driveways on the quiet residential street were without a car – a sign that this was not one of the most affluent areas of Edgware where those lucky enough to own a car were able to get hold of petrol rations on the black market. PC Hill pulled up on the road opposite number eight, which at first seemed peaceful and quiet with no lights on at the front of the house. Another burglary, thought PC Hill. Or maybe someone heard a noise, got the jitters and dialed 999.

As he reached the gate of number eight the front door flew open and a smartly-dressed middle-aged woman half-ran and half-staggered towards him, her eyes wide and face pale with shock. She was closely followed by an equally distraught young woman. PC Hill caught the older woman by the shoulders, trying to make sense of what she was saying. Eventually he made out: 'There are two people in there. Badly hurt.' He left the women leaning heavily on the gate and hurried down the short, steep path to the porch. A stocky, balding man, agitated, pale and shaking, rushed from the hallway to meet him. 'I think there's been a robbery,' he said. 'Mr Goodman is badly hurt.'

A gas lamp lit the hallway with an orange glow. PC Hill tried the handle to the front drawing room as he passed; it was locked. In front of him, the kitchen door was open and the light was on. He could see that the light was also on in the dining room, throwing a harsh florescent glow into the hallway.

As PC Hill turned sharply right into the dining room he saw a pair of feet; a woman was lying on her back with her head facing into the room. She was wearing a multi-coloured floral dress, a brown cardigan and light-coloured thick stockings. Her face and head were so distorted and battered that PC Hill knew she could not be alive. A bald, middle-aged man was lying on the hearthrug in front of the electric fire, a pair of round, black-rimmed spectacles lying beside him and his head resting on a folded-up jacket. He was wearing brown herringbone trousers and waistcoat over a white shirt. His face, too, was covered in blood that was pouring from several deep wounds. PC Hill crouched beside him; he was alive, but only just.

'Who are they?' he asked the man he had passed in the hallway. 'Leopold and Esther Goodman,' said the man, still trembling with shock. PC Hill quickly surveyed the room. A table and chairs was near the wall opposite the fire place; there was a large pool of blood on the table and more blood on the chair nearest the door. 'My wife is Mrs Goodman's sister,' continued the man. 'I've called an ambulance and a doctor.'

PC Hill found the telephone in the kitchen and dialed Edgware police station, curtly confirming that he was at Ashcombe Gardens and that there were two victims. As he put the telephone down, an ambulance pulled up outside, followed almost at once by a man who identified himself as Dr Cairns, of 25 Edgwarebury Lane. The doctor bent over Esther, shaking his head and stepping over her almost at once to crouch beside Leopold – PC Hill moved the dining room table closer to the wall to give him more room. Leopold's breath was shallow, with a weak pulse. Dr Cairns opened his bag and prepared an injection of coramine, a stimulant often used in the treatment of a heart attack. He pushed back the sleeve of the man's white shirt and injected him in the left forearm. The man breathed again. A few more seconds and he took another faint breath.

By the time Inspector Harvey pulled up in Ashcombe Gardens at 10.08pm the road had come to life. Lights were on in several houses, the neighbours roused by the cries of the women and the unusual sight of police cars and an ambulance on their quiet street. Inspector Harvey passed the two distraught women at the gate and nodded to Doctor Matthews, who had arrived just moments before him. He followed the doctor through the open front door and into a house that was buzzing with suppressed horror. He stopped at the dining room door, momentarily taken aback by the appalling injuries of the woman lying at his feet. Doctor Matthews and another man were crouching beside a second body further into the room. As he watched, both turned to him, indicating the death of the man with a shake of his head.

Ordering the growing number of people in the house not to touch anything, Inspector Harvey and PC Hill began to methodically search the rooms. The kitchen was large, big enough for a table and four chairs. On the left was a dresser, next to a coal-fired stove. On the far wall, to the right of the door to the scullery was a glass door which led to the garden and a casement window, which was open. The scullery at the back of the kitchen contained a gas cooker, a sink, a decent-sized larder and, PC Hill noted, a fridge. He tried the back door – it was locked and bolted, as was the door leading from the house to the garage.

In the scullery sink was a large, heavy piece of metal with a solid oval base and a hollow pole about an inch in diameter and 15 inches long rising out of its centre. PC Hill recognised it as the base of a television aerial. It was wet, as if it had just been washed, and a wet rag was in the sink beside it. He looked closer – there were distinct spots of blood on the metal.

PC Hill and Inspector Harvey continued upstairs, where the house was in darkness. Every door was closed but not locked, and they checked each in turn. There were four bedrooms off the small landing; a large master bedroom with a bay window at the front, which had a connecting door to a much smaller bedroom next to it, above the hall. A large bedroom was at the back, above the dining room and the fourth room, next to it and above the kitchen, was clearly used as a workroom. The bathroom was at the back of the house, above the scullery. All of the rooms were neat and nothing seemed out of place, but in the master bedroom the mattress on one of the two single beds, nearest the door, had been pushed diagonally to one side by about 15 inches. A blue eiderdown and two blankets had slipped onto the floor at the end of the bed, and next to them were lying a woman's handbag and coat. The other bed appeared to be untouched and on the table between the two beds a small pile of bank notes sat under an alarm clock.

Within half an hour of the bodies being discovered, word of the murders was spreading quickly throughout the area. News of a possible murder had reached the local newspaper, the *Hendon and Finchley Times*, within minutes of the call to Edgware police station. The paper was on good terms with the police and one of their young reporters, Dennis Signy, would often go in the police station in the evening for a game of cards with the team. If their game was interrupted by an emergency call, it was not unusual for him to tag along for the ride. But a murder was big news and a number of reporters from the local and national press arrived at Ashcombe Gardens within two hours of the Goodman's bodies being discovered, watching the comings and goings of CID officers and relatives and gleaning whatever information they could from the Goodmans' neighbours.

The first plain clothes CID officer, Detective Inspector Jack Diller, a 46-year-old Essex man with 24 years of service with the police force, arrived at 8 Ashcombe Gardens at 10.15pm with two of his team, Detective Sergeant Erskine and Detective Thomas. The reporters waiting outside on Ashcombe Gardens noted his arrival, his dark suit, mackintosh and trilby easily identifying him as a member of CID. After a quick briefing from PC Hill and Inspector Harvey, DI Diller steadily completed the same tour of the house, beginning with the blood-soaked dining room. Just inside the doorway, on the right hand wall, he noticed a light switch at shoulder height. He flicked the switch – nothing happened. Searching around the doorway, he eventually found the light switch behind the door, low down on the skirting board. On the opposite side of the doorway he noticed a spray of blood on the wall, at hip-height.

At 10.30pm PC Hill answered a knock at the door of number eight. Outside stood a young, slight, red-haired man who identified himself as Danny Raven, the Goodmans' son-in-law. With him was his sister, Sylvia, who had heard of the commotion at the house and had gone to Danny's home to warn him of it. The woman looked pale and shocked and the young man, who was wearing a grey pinstripe suit, a yellow pullover, a cream poplin shirt and brown shoes, appeared to be deeply upset and tears were running down his cheeks. PC Hill suggested that he sit down and so Danny slumped heavily at the bottom of the stairs. 'Why didn't they let me stop?' he said, over and over. 'Why did they tell me to go?' Later, PC Hill heard him say, 'I brought them back about 9.30pm.'

The young man was still sitting there when Inspector Harvey finished his examination of the upstairs of the house a few minutes later. As he came down the stairs the man was sitting on the bottom step, his angular face in his hands. Through his sobbing he was repeating 'Don't tell my wife, don't tell my wife.' A handful of people were crowded around him; a young woman was attempting to comfort him but Alfred was less sympathetic. He snapped at the young man in exasperation: 'Pull yourself together, man, you're like a bloody woman!'

PC Hill took Inspector Harvey aside and told him that the young man was Daniel Raven, the Goodman's son-in-law and father of their new grandchild. Inspector Harvey ushered him into the front room, where he slumped into one of the armchairs. 'Now,' said the Inspector, 'what's the trouble?'

'I only brought them back here at twenty past nine – no, it must have been half past,' said the young man. He began sobbing again, dropping his head into his hands and repeatedly running his fingers through his hair. 'You really need to pull yourself together,' said the Inspector. After a while, the man continued: 'We had all been to the nursing home – they came back first and I followed just behind in my car. I asked them to let me stay the night as they had burglars. They pushed me out and said I should go home, in case I was burgled. I went home, put the heater on and had a bath. I felt lonely so I went to my sister's.'

Word spread rapidly that Daniel Raven had been the last person to see the Goodmans alive that evening. Detective Inspector Diller introduced himself and asked the young man to follow him to the kitchen, where he and Detective Sergeant Erskine questioned him more closely. Danny told the detectives that his wife, Gertrude, had had a baby the previous Thursday at a nursing home in Muswell Hill and he had visited every day since then, usually with her parents. They had all visited Gertrude that evening and he and the Goodmans had left together at ten minutes past nine. They had arrived at Ashcombe Gardens at about 9.30pm in separate cars, he said, and he had got out to talk with the couple at their front door. He wanted to stay the night but the Goodmans were not willing. Danny said that he then left, went home and had a bath. Later, his sister and brother-in-law had called at his home and said that something was going on at the Goodmans' house, so they had come straight over to find the police already there.

'Did you get on with your father and mother in law?' asked DI Diller.

'Oh, I didn't get on with Mr Goodman too badly,' said Danny, 'although we had quarrelled at times, but me and Mrs Goodman did not get on at all well.'

'How do you mean?' asked DI Diller.

'Well, she didn't like me and I didn't like her much. Neither did I like Mr Goodman, although he's been very good to me.' He was becoming increasingly agitated. 'But what's this got to do with it? I don't know anything about it.'

Increasingly suspicious, DI Diller told Danny that he would need to come to the police station to make a statement, as he was an essential witness. Danny agreed to go, but added that he knew nothing important. With several of the residents of Ashcombe Gardens watching, Danny was led out of the house and into a police car.

At 11pm Detective Chief Inspector Albert Tansill arrived at Ashcombe Gardens. The tall, 45-year-old Welshman had been transferred to S Division, which covered Hampstead and the surrounding boroughs, only three months earlier but was already a well-known face in the district. Previously with the fraud squad, Tansill had been promoted to DCI only two weeks before transferring to Edgware. The local newspaper reporter Dennis Signy remembers Bert Tansill as 'a real old-time copper' who liked to entertain the younger officers and local reporters with stories from his earlier career. The unmarried detective shared a home with his elderly mother but had a habit of decamping a few times a week to the nearest pub at the end of his shift with as many companions as he could find. Tradition dictated that they would stay and drink as long as Bert remained when, abruptly, he would stand up, brush cigarette ash extravagantly off his lapels and announce to the crowd: 'Right! Home to mother!'

This was Tansill's first murder case since arriving at S Division as head of CID and his role was to lead the investigation, reporting regularly back to his superiors. At Ashcombe Gardens that evening DCI Tansill carefully noted the position of the bodies. Esther was lying with her feet slightly apart and her head towards the fireplace, three and a half feet away from the wall that divided the dining room from the drawing room next door. A pool of blood stretched from her head almost to a recording machine that was in the right-hand corner of the room as Tansill looked in from the doorway. On the carpet near Esther he saw small fragments of bone and part of her dentures.

In front of the fireplace, Leopold was lying in another pool of blood with his head on a folded jacket. His hands were resting on his stomach and his legs were slightly bent, the left resting on the right. His dentures had also been broken in the attack and were lying nearby.

DCI Tansill examined the room for bloodstains, which he noted in his statement. There were spots of blood on the right wall and skirting board as he entered the room, near to Esther, as well as on the sideboard that stood alongside the wall. There were more blood spots on the front of the dining room door, mostly on the lower section. Further into the room, on the wall between the dining room and kitchen, Tansill found more blood spots on the skirting board and wall.

The dining room table was against this wall, with an empty fruit bowl in the centre and two ashtrays at the far end. The centre leaf of the table was covered in a large irregular pool of blood. There were several small pear-shaped areas of blood on the floor around the table, and on the legs and supports under it. At the far end of the table were two dining room chairs, with a third in front of the table, its back pointing towards the French doors at the far end of the room and its seat facing the door. There was a pool of blood on the chair's leather seat, towards the back, and more blood on the woodwork. The fourth dining room chair was directly in front of the television set, its back facing the room.

In the front bedroom Tansill recorded six £1 notes beneath the alarm clock on a table between the two beds. He examined the woman's black handbag that was lying on the floor at the end of the bed nearest the door: it contained a purse, a powder compact, two combs, a small mirror, a calendar, lipstick, a handkerchief and a cheque book.

DI Diller and DS Erskine arrived at Edgware police station with Danny at 11.15pm. DI Diller asked Danny for the keys to his house, at 184 Edgwarebury Lane. Danny handed over three keys on a ring, insisting there was nothing to find in the house and he had only had a bath. As Diller took the keys, Danny tried to snatch them back. 'Why should you have them?

Give them back!' Diller said calmly that he would need the keys as, no doubt, it would be necessary to search Danny's house. According to police procedure, the search would be carried out in the presence of an independent witness.

Just before midnight, Jack Diller, accompanied by Detective Thomas and Danny's father, 42-year-old Edward Raven, arrived at 184 Edgwarebury Lane. The house was quiet but a bright light shone in the garage on the left hand side of the house. Diller pushed Danny's key into the lock and opened the front door.

The lights were on in the hall and in the kitchen and the house felt warm. The roar of the coal boiler, faintly audible from the hall, was much stronger in the kitchen. The small stove, reaching waist height, stood on the floor in the far corner of the kitchen. A gas poker, a long thin rod with holes along its length – a standard piece of equipment in many homes and used to speed up the lighting of coal fires – was sticking out of the front door of the boiler. The poker was still attached to the hose that led from the gas tap on the wall nearby. DI Diller opened the top of the boiler: something was burning inside and an acrid smell filled his nostrils, much stronger than the familiar musty smokiness of burning coal. Quickly, he disconnected the gas tube from the wall socket and extinguished the poker, closing the boiler flues to prevent any drafts rushing into the fire.

Looking through the rest of the kitchen, Diller saw that the stainless steel sink was wet as though it had been recently used and a wet flannel was placed between the taps. The back door was slightly ajar and outside the door, on the concrete floor, was a wet piece of pink cloth. Diller checked the garage; Danny's car, a black Vauxhall Ten, was inside and the front garage doors were secured with a padlock and chain. The back door of the garage was closed and fastened with a rusty padlock, but not locked. Upstairs, nothing seemed out of place. He checked the bathroom; there was little evidence that anyone had had a bath recently. Leaving Detective Thomas to guard the house, he returned with Edward Raven to Edgware police station.

Chapter 2 – Day Two

At 12.30am, DCI Bert Tansill and DI Jack Diller sat down with Daniel Raven at the police station.

'I understand you left the Goodmans at 9.30pm and went home, is that right?' asked Tansill. Danny replied that it was. 'Can you tell me what suit you were wearing last night?' continued Tansill. 'Was it the one you have on now?' Danny said it was not.

'When I got home I had a bath and left my suit on the floor in the upstairs front bathroom. I left it on the floor by the window. When my sister called I put this suit on,' he said, indicating his grey pinstripe double-breasted jacket.

'Will you tell me if you did anything else when you got home?' asked Tansill. 'No,' said Danny. 'I have told you all.'

Jack Diller told him that he had been to his house and did not remember seeing a suit on the floor in the bedroom. 'It's there,' said Danny. 'I'm not a liar.'

'Did you see anyone last night after you left the Goodmans?' asked Tansill. Danny said he had not. 'If you have told me everything you did at home, how do you account for the gas poker being on in the kitchen boiler?' asked Tansill. Danny, increasingly emotional and agitated, said: 'I don't know anything about that. Do you think I murdered them?'

On Tansill's orders, DI Diller returned with Edward Raven to 184 Edgwarebury Lane at 12.45am to check Danny's story; there was no suit on the bedroom floor. Just over an hour later the pair returned again with Superintendent Cuthbert of the Police Laboratory and DCI Tansill. They watched as Cuthbert reached into the cooling boiler with a pair of metal tongs and removed some badly burned brown material – still recognisable as part of a man's jacket and trousers. 'There appeared to be blood spots on the front of the trouser leg', Tansill would write later.

They searched the house again. In the garage, Diller found a pair of brown men's shoes with crepe rubber soles. They were soaking wet, inside and out, and Diller noted in his report 'a small blood clot on the instep of the left shoe and a small blood mark on the toe of the right shoe'.

Back at Ashcombe Gardens, a clutch of newspaper reporters remained outside the house, gathering material for the next day's paper. 'Throughout the warm night police and press swept up and down Edgwarebury Lane,' wrote a reporter for the *Hendon & Finchley Times* the following morning, going on to describe the scene outside the house during that long night:

'Police stood on guard outside the house from which, every now and again, a shaft of light broke across the darkness as the front door opened and closed. There was a continuous coming and going from the house; yet a deathly hush hung over the scene. A muted whisper of conversation, the crunch of a boot on the gravel of the road surface, were the only sounds. Police were seen to carry some medicine bottles from the house, and then cups, saucers, plates and cutlery.'

At 3.15am Tansill and Diller arrived back at the police station and 15 minutes later they interviewed Danny again, this time in the presence of a duty solicitor, Alan Clark. DCI Tansill told Danny that he had reason to believe that he had something to do with the injuries suffered by the Goodmans. The solicitor advised Danny to make a statement. Tansill cautioned Danny: He did not have to say anything unless he wished, but anything he did say would be taken down and given in evidence. Danny signed the written caution and dictated his statement to DI Diller. When he had finished, DI Diller read it back to him:

> *On Monday evening I went to the nursing home to see my wife. She is a patient there. While I was there, at about half past eight or a little earlier, Mr and Mrs Goodman arrived. They stayed there with me and later left with me, travelling in our respective cars to go to the Goodman's house at 8 Ashcombe Gardens.*
>
> *We left there at about ten past nine, that is the nursing home. When we got to the house we drove in and we spoke for a couple of minutes in the front garden. I then left and drove to my home.*

I went in and switched on the immersion heater so that I could have a bath. Then I went round to my cousin's house in Glendale Avenue, Edgware, but no-one was in. I wanted him to come and stay the night with me. I then drove back to my house and put the car in the garage and went into the house and went upstairs.

I went into my bedroom, took off my trousers and jacket and went into the bathroom and started the water. While this was running I heard a knocking downstairs, so I went into my bedroom, slipped on a pair of trousers hanging on the wardrobe and went downstairs. There I found my elder sister at the door. She told me there had been a burglary at the Goodman's, or words to that effect. I said to her, "Let's get down there." I said I would first go upstairs to get my jacket. After I got my jacket I went with my sister and her husband to the Goodman's house. When I got there I was told that something had happened to Mr and Mrs Goodman. I can remember nothing else happening beyond what I have said and have no knowledge of having gone to the Goodman's house at any time since I went there for a few minutes at about a quarter to two that afternoon and saw Mrs Goodman prior to going to the nursing home in the early afternoon.

Danny signed the statement and was told to empty his pockets. He placed on the table in front of him two £1 notes and just over 10 shillings in change, his identity card, a handkerchief, a propelling pencil and fountain pen, a comb, his leather wallet and cheque book, and a small leather folder containing a few letters.

While Tansill and Diller watched, scrapings were taken from underneath Danny's fingernails. He was then led away to spend his first night in a police cell.

At 9.20 the next morning DCI Tansill returned to 8 Ashcombe Gardens, where the bodies of Leopold and Esther Goodman were formally identified by their brother-in-law, Alfred.

Tansill carefully searched the bodies, listing everything found on Leopold: One £5 note, 15 £1 notes and seven 10 shilling notes in the fob pocket of his trousers; and in his back pocket a wallet, cigarette lighter and two bunches of keys. In Leopold's wallet were his identity card and alien registration certificate, eight petrol coupons, an AA membership card and another for the Palestine Farm City Association, a wireless licence in Leopold's name, a cheque for £453 payable to ME Angel, five business cards from various people including one, Tansill noted with surprise, from an Inspector Herbert Hannam of Scotland Yard, and £7 10s in notes. In Leopold's left hand trouser pocket was a handkerchief and some small change. The search complete, the bodies were taken to Hendon Mortuary. It was time for the forensic work to begin.

The 61-year-old Dr Henry Smith Holden, head of the new forensic laboratory at Scotland Yard, arrived at Ashcombe Gardens shortly before 10am. With DCI Tansill watching, he examined the sink in the scullery, where he noted 'obvious traces of human blood'.

While Dr Holden worked DCI Tansill collected evidence from the scene – it was the responsibility of the local police force to identify, collect and label pieces of evidence, which were then officially handed over to the police laboratory that covered their area. Tansill carefully removed the aluminium TV aerial base from the sink, along with the wet floor cloth that was alongside it, and a piece of blood-stained tissue. He added to the collection a towel that was hanging over the back of a chair in the scullery. He then unscrewed the 'U' bend from beneath the sink in the scullery and poured the water and sludge that had collected in it into a jar.

From the dining room he removed and recorded a piece of artificial denture and fragments of bloodstained bone from the floor and Leopold's bloodstained spectacles from the table – PC Hill had seen these on the floor when the bodies were discovered and at some point in the evening someone had moved them to the table.

DCI Tansill examined the table more closely. The large pool of blood spread out from the central leaf, almost two foot long and over a foot wide at its widest point. About two inches from the edge of the table that faced the room, he noticed a large crack about nine inches long. Halfway along this crack was a sharp indentation, almost an inch deep 'as if', Tansill wrote in his statement, 'it had been struck a heavy blow with an instrument'.

Later that morning Dr Holden moved on to Danny's house in Edgwarebury Lane with DI Diller, where he examined Danny's Vauxhall saloon. Dr Holden noted traces of blood on the upholstery of the front edge of the driving seat and on the handbrake. He also found 'faint traces of blood' on the garage door near the off side front door of the car. Inside the house, he found traces of human blood in the sink in the kitchen and on the draining board. As well as the burnt suit that had been recovered from the boiler, bagged and labelled the night before, DI Diller had also collected and labeled the dishcloth from the kitchen sink, the pink cloth from the floor outside the back door and the wet brown shoes he had found in the garage.

At 1.25pm that afternoon DCI Tansill again interviewed Danny under caution. He showed him the remains of the burnt suit and the brown shoes DI Diller had found at his house. 'Yes, they are mine,' said Danny. 'I wore them last night. How the blood got on them I don't know.'

An hour and a half later, at Hendon Mortuary, Dr Teare began a post-mortem of Esther Goodman. He recorded a 'well-nourished adult woman, five feet in height'. The left side of her face was 'grossly lacerated, distorted and smashed in'. A lacerated wound 10" long ran from the tip of her nose to her forehead and into her scalp on the left side of her head, exposing the brain. A cleaner wound ran from laterally her right upper lip, with another about an inch and a half long on the mid line of her chin. Her top lip was badly cut. There were more wounds around Esther's left eye.

Dr Teare's post-mortem report added that the front left quadrant of Esther's skull was 'completely shattered, the bone being broken into dozens of fractures and several fragments were missing'. Apart from her extensive brain injuries, examinations of the internal organs showed that Esther had been in good health with no heart disease or other sign of illness. Her stomach contained a large, completely undigested meal. Dr Teare recorded the cause of death as 'laceration of the brain due to multiple fractures of the skull'. She had suffered, he wrote, at least seven violent blows to the head and face.

Dr Teare's examination of Leopold concluded that he had suffered at least fourteen blows to his head and face. A wound four and a half inches long ran from his right temple backwards, exposing brain tissue. There was an H-shaped wound on the back of his head, two inches long, and a similar wound in the centre of his forehead. There was another two-inch cut on the left of Leopold's forehead and another, slightly longer, on the right running towards his eye. There were numerous other smaller, relatively superficial cuts on his cheeks and chin. The front half of Leopold's skull was shattered and his nose and both cheekbones were broken. His jaw was also broken and a fracture ran down the back of his skull.

Leopold had defensive wounds on his right hand; bruising on some fingers and his little finger was broken at the tip. Dr Teare concluded that the cause of death was again 'laceration of the brain due to multiple skull fractures'.

At 6.25pm that evening, DCI Tansill sat down with Danny for the last time. Danny's father Edward Raven had engaged Sydney Rutter of Rutter & Co, a small firm based in Great Winchester Street in the City of London, as his solicitor. Rutter, a well-built man in his early 40s with a round face and dark receding hair that was swept sharply back from his face, sat next to Danny as Tansill began: 'From the enquiries I have made you are now going to be charged with the murder of Leopold Goodman and Esther Goodman at 8 Ashcombe Gardens on 10th October, 1949.' Tansill cautioned him again that anything he said could be used in evidence.

'I didn't kill them,' said Danny. DCI Tansill formally read out the charges.

'I did not kill them.'

Chapter 3 – Edgware

Although Leopold Goodman consistently told the British authorities that he was a Russian immigrant, he was born Leopold Gutmann in Prague on 25 April 1898, one of two sons and four daughters born to Simel Gutmann, a *schaechter* (or Jewish butcher) and his wife, Jittel. Leopold, or Polda as he was known by the family, was young enough to miss the worst of the First World War but he was drafted into the army in 1917, just before his 20th birthday and served as a private in Bavarian Infantry Regiment. After the war Polda worked in Cologne as a jewellery dealer and then in Frankfurt before arriving in London in the first few months of 1921 in search of a better life.

In London, Leopold joined the ranks of the estimated two million largely Ashkenazi Jews that had fled from Central and Eastern Europe in the wake of increasing persecution and economic hardship between 1881 and 1914, when the First World War brought immigration almost to a halt. Most headed to the United States but some 150,000 settled in the East End of London, near the docks where they arrived.

By 1910 more than 125,000 Jews were living in a state of gross overcrowding in the two square miles around Whitechapel and Spitalfields. A thriving community was established in the East End of London and particularly around Petticoat Lane and many enterprising businesses soon emerged, mainly small-scale manufacturing and street trading.

Jews were almost the only immigrants entering the UK during this period and generally they made huge efforts to integrate with the British community – partly due to necessity thanks to the wave of anti-Semitism that had greeted their arrival in London – learning English and avoiding traditional dress. A Board of Trade report in 1894 said that Jewish children were leaving the Jews' Free School in Bell Lane 'almost indistinguishable' from English children. A proliferation of clubs for young people also played its part in encouraging young Jews to become 'good British citizens'. In common with many other Jewish immigrants, soon after arriving in London, Leopold Anglicised his surname.

East End residents during this time remember a vital and bustling community, albeit one that was steeped in poverty. Large families were crammed into two-room apartments in huge tenement blocks and work was hard to come by. Even so there was a strong sense of community among the Jewish immigrants and on a Friday after their evening meal and again on a Saturday afternoon, thousands of people would stroll along Whitechapel Road. A number of synagogues had quickly been established in the area, often converted from existing buildings, and became the centre of Jewish life there.

Many marriages were made during this time. On 23 February 1926 in Stepney, Leopold married Esther, another Jewish immigrant who had been born in Poland on 1 October 1898. Their only child, Gertrude, was born in 1927. At the time of his marriage Leopold was described as a 'traveller in the provision trade' but he had ambitions to bring his new family out of the grinding poverty of the East End and to take advantage of the promise of his new country.

In 1931 Esther's younger sister married the British-born Alfred, who quickly became part of the family and would later work for Leopold at his radio dealership. As their families grew and their fortunes began to prosper, the two families made the decision to move from the East End to one of the new suburban developments that had grown around London in the 1930s. Many Jewish families moved out of the East End as they became more affluent, settling in Hackney and Tottenham, and further into north west London, particularly Golders Green and the new 'garden suburbs' of Finchley and Edgware.

It was the extension of the London Underground to Edgware that transformed the former coaching village into one of the shiniest and most promising new suburbs that sprang up around London in the 1930s. While a Tube station at Edgware had been under discussion for some time, a lack of capital investment delayed the building until the Trade Facilities Act of 1921 offered a guarantee of interest and capital from the Treasury for any approved building project that would relieve unemployment. Work on the Underground extension from Golders Green to Edgware began in 1922.

Edgware's new Underground station opened on 18 August 1924 – an 'Italian in style' building with high-pitched tiled roof and ornate columns designed by the Underground Company's architect, SA Heaps. Heaps said at the time he hoped the station, which remains largely unaltered today, would be 'sufficiently dignified to command respect and sufficiently appealing to promote affection'. The first services ran every eight minutes to Moorgate in the rush hour, and Edgware's relatively few residents could reach Charing Cross in 35 minutes, compared with 58 minutes on the overground LNER train service. With the Tube up and running, half-hourly bus services were introduced from Edgware Station to Pinner Green, South Harrow and Watford.

With the transport services so improved, it was inevitable that housing developers would soon set their sights on the area and began buying up the farmland and fields surrounding the village. An enterprising young estate agent, George Cross, had bought the 54-acre Edgware Manor Estate in 1919 for £175 an acre, adding a further 16 acres of poor quality farm land to his portfolio in the same area over the next few years. At first there was little interest in the building plots that Cross put up for sale on the Manor Estate and he was obliged to build a few houses at his own expense in an attempt to stimulate demand. These semi-detached, three bedroom houses were advertised for sale in November 1924 for £1,100 each. By the end of 1925 Cross had sold most of his land to housing developers, netting himself a fine profit of £44,000.

Just a month after the opening of the Underground station, another 274 acres of land, Broadfields Manor, was offered for sale. While it failed to sell in a single lot, the land sold in smaller sections for around £960 an acre – land that would have struggled to reach £150 an acre just five years earlier.

And so the development of Edgware continued. Another estate agent and surveyor, Walter Raymond, built The Mall, a Georgian-inspired parade of 29 shops and flats opposite the new station in 1927. George Cross, who had already constructed and sold Premier Parade, a row of eight shops next to the new station, was still reaping the benefits of a booming area and bought 85 acres of local grounds, Canons Park, overseeing the development of a number of detached and semi-detached houses, with garages and large gardens, of between three and six bedrooms. These went on sale in the late 1920s for prices ranging between £1,425 and £3,500. The rest of Canons Park was sold in 1928 to another developer and to the local council, which retained part of the land for a park.

In 1926 the developers Jarvis and Streather started construction on a series of four-bedroom houses with two reception rooms, a 'lounge hall', kitchen, scullery and garage on Edgwarebury Lane. These went on sale for £1,450.

Inevitably, there were mixed views of the speed and nature of Edgware's development. In 1926 the *Daily Express* predicted a building boom in Edgware that would exceed 'anything known in this country, even Golders Green, and more on a parallel with the land rush at Miami, without the risk of loss or hurricanes'. The *Golders Green Gazette* noted that 'within the last two or three years, a considerable change has taken place, and a beautiful garden suburb has sprung up. Handsome shops are already erected, and good wide roads have been constructed, or are in the course of construction.' But the following year the first annual report of the Edgware Ratepayers' Association took a different view. '[We] have long viewed with grave concern the indiscriminate expansion of inartistic building enterprise,' it said. 'Various commercially minded builders and building speculators are gradually but surely obliterating the rural delights which gave Edgware its chief charm. Instead of a beautiful village, we may, ere long, be gazing on an ugly township.'

Even so, the marketing of Edgware as a desirable suburban location began in earnest. Slightly concerned by an increase in traffic on the Underground extension that was smaller than predicted, a number of estate agents and builders joined forces in 1927 to form the Edgware Publicity Association. Its intention was to boost the image of the borough 'to the skies' and soon adverts began to appear in newspapers and at railway stations emblazoned with the Association's slogans: *Edgware – Live There* and *Live Where? Edgware*.

In 1932 the Ritz cinema opened on The Mall in the centre of Edgware. The building was seen as evidence that Edgware had 'arrived' and the *Edgware Gazette* announced that it would establish the area as 'the pivotal centre of a large and increasing district'. While the Ritz initially failed to meet the £36,000 a year in takings that had been predicted, it quickly became an important social landmark, as did The Railway Hotel, a large Tudor-style public house that had been constructed on the opposite side of the road.

By the mid 1930s the borough was well established. The Watford Bypass (now the A41) cut through the northern end of the town, bringing the Green Line coach service through the area and into Central London for the first time (the stretch of the M1 motorway between junctions 2 and 3, which now borders Edgware to the east and north, would not be constructed until 1967). Arthur Curton, later to be a council member and Mayor of Hendon, had developed a number of 'uniquely designed Tudor Houses' along the west side of Edgwarebury Lane and building of other developments had continued apace.

The scale of the expansion of Edgware is best illustrated through the rise in the number of passengers using the Underground. In 1929 the *Daily Mail* reported that the number of passenger journeys to or from Edgware station had grown from 75,000 a month in 1924 to 233,000 a month within five years. It was during the 1930s, though, that the population began to expand apace, with the Edgware parish alone seeing an increase from 5,353 in 1931 to 17,523 in 1939.

The high price of many of the new houses in Edgware suggested a reasonably affluent suburb that was, thanks to the excellent transport links into central London, attracting young professional families. A local paper, reporting a derailment at Edgware in 1934, spoke of 'ladies in evening dresses and their silk-hatted escorts' waiting at the station – by now the Underground was running late-night services to and from the station and many residents were taking advantage of the service and heading into town to see an evening show. During the 1930s though, developers such as Taylor Woodrow and Wimpey moved into the area and began building more modestly-priced houses. Laings began to build an estate near Canon Park, the new station in western Edgware feeding the newly-extended Metropolitan Line into Baker Street, with prices from £610, while Taylor Woodrow's Broadfields Park Estate offered three-bedroom semi-detached houses from £735.

Edgware's expansion placed enormous strain on its public services, which struggled initially to keep up with the population explosion. In 1927, for instance, the old Hendon Poor Law Institution at Red Hill was converted into a hospital with 175 beds (the Redhill Hospital, now Edgware General Hospital). Between 1930 and 1938 the population within the 63 square miles covered by the hospital grew from 185,000 to 500,000. A large extension was put up in 1939 to cope with the extra demand. A new police station opened in Edgware in 1932 – too late, in the view of many residents as the area had been under-policed for some time. Two years later the Metropolitan Police introduced radio-equipped police cars to cover the area, which did a great deal to reassure residents that Edgware was being properly patrolled, although apparently did little to reduce the growing number of burglaries in the area.

The Goodmans moved to Edgware in the early 1940s, Leopold and Esther buying a three-bedroomed semi-detached house in Ashcombe Gardens on one side of the Watford Bypass for just over £1,000. By 1935 Leopold had set up his own business as a dealer in radio and electronic products and in April 1940 converted the business into a private company with a premises on Percy Street, off Tottenham Court Road in the west end of London – a convenient commute from Edgware along the Morden-Edgware Tube line.

Middle-class Jewish families had begun to settle in the new suburb of Edgware from the late 1920s onwards. In the summer of 1929 an advertisement in the *Jewish Chronicle* suggested that Jews in the district should come together to form a congregation. Two years later, a local paper estimated that there were 120 Jewish families in the district – which would account for about 10% of the new residents of Edgware. At the end of 1933 a fund was set up to finance the building of a synagogue (the congregation had until now been meeting at a local church hall) and the United Synagogue on Mowbray Road, which cost £3,000 to construct on land donated by a Golders Green estate agent, was consecrated in September 1934.

While some local residents remember a level of friction between the growing Jewish population and the gentile remainder – mainly caused by a popular but not necessarily accurate view that Jewish families were wealthier than their London-born counterparts – the two communities seemed to have lived relatively harmoniously together. A local councillor remarked in 1939 that 'in no other district around London did Jew and Gentile live together so amicably', but perhaps that was a somewhat rose-coloured view. Local Jewish residents do remember tensions in the area during the 1940s and 1950s and some took part in regular civilian patrols that were organised in order to protect the Edgware synagogues from vandalism.

Life for the Goodmans continued quietly in Edgware as the war approached. The time was characterised by a transition from the old to the new, with the United Dairies horse-drawn milk float and delivery boys from Brills' bakery on their bicycles weaving around the small number of motor cars that were beginning to appear on the streets. A large collection of small shops filled Station Road, as well as the more established retailers such as the Co-op, Woolworths and Home and Colonial. Two Stanley J Lee department stores had opened on Station Road, one selling fabrics and clothing, the other furniture to meet the demand from the many new homeowners. At the smart white-tiled Sainsbury's', shoppers chatted as they queued at the cooked meat, butchery or dairy counters, where butter was carefully weighed out from a large block and patted out for each customer.

Edgware was fortunate to escape the worst of the Luftwaffe's attention during the Second World War. It was not a target for the V1 and V2 flying bombs, which tended to fall onto east and south-west London, and was far enough away from the docks and munitions factories to avoid the worst of the Blitz. Many bombs did fall on the area, most frequently jettisoned by bombers returning to Germany from overnight raids north and west of London – among the worst incidents in the area were the 1,000kg bomb that destroyed four streets in Hendon in February 1941, killing 80 people, and the flying bomb that hit the Standard Factory in East Barnet on 23 August 1944, killing 33 people and injuring more than 400. Throughout the war residents remember the searchlights sweeping the night skies and the barrage balloons overhead by day, and watching the red glow of fires in Central London, just eight miles away, during the terrible nights of the Blitz. Later, on D-Day, the skies above Edgware were filled with Allied aircraft, many towing gliders, heading towards France.

By the end of the war Leopold's business was solid and well set-up for the technological boom that would soon arrive. The demand for radios and other electronic equipment had continued throughout the war – the radio, especially, was one of the most important features in most homes. A survey of domestic evening activities in a range of homes that was completed in 1947 showed that there were never less than 20% of homes (and often more than 30%) that had the radio on for half an hour or more during the evening. The most common evening activities cited by respondents to the survey during that time were 'radio and reading', 'radio and conversation' or 'radio and resting' and the series *Dick Barton – Special Agent* was regularly attracting 15 million listeners a night during its 15-minute slot at 6.45pm. The future for Leopold's business, although he may not have fully realised it, looked even rosier thanks to the new television sets that would become a feature of the most affluent family homes in the early 1950s.

Gertrude was approaching 19 and an attractive and smartly-dressed young woman, with a striking head of red hair. Leopold and Esther may well have had ambitious plans for her – maybe even beginning to think of likely future husbands from the close-knit community of Jewish families in the area. Some time after the summer of 1946, though, Gertrude introduced them to her new boyfriend – a 20-year old, slightly built young man called Daniel Raven.

Chapter 4 – Danny and Gertrude

Netta and Bernard Elliston, who were friends of Danny and Gertrude Raven in the years before October 1949, remember a fun-loving couple who were a regular feature of the large group of young Jewish friends in Edgware who often socialised together. With money short, the group often met in each other's homes for an evening of card games or a dinner party, as long as rations allowed. In the months and years after the end of the war, evenings out were limited to regular trips to the Ritz cinema, or the occasional gathering at one of the new Edgware hotels and pubs. Restaurants were in short supply and heavily restricted by both rationing and legislation – *The British Restaurant* in Hale Lane in Edgware was one of the few available in the area and was an unprepossessing option where diners sat on long benches to sample the cheap, subsidised food. Other restaurants were constrained in the amount they could charge in the post-war years and so tended to resort to imaginative pricing structures. One, which charged the specified five shillings a head for a meal, charged diners four times as much to sit on a chair.

Netta remembers Danny as an average young man (in the sense that there was nothing out of the ordinary about him), likeable and reasonably outgoing. Two things she remembers above all: that Danny would not eat fish unless it was boned, and he always went to sleep with the light on. These two facts hint at an aspect of Danny's personality that would become a topic of heated debate later – while he seemed friendly and outgoing in public, in private he was prone to deep-rooted anxiety and nervousness.

Danny Raven was born Daniel Ravech on 18 August 1926 in Stoke Newington, the middle of three children. The family – Danny, his parents Edward and Betty, and his sisters Sylvia and Muriel – moved frequently during his childhood as his father Edward lurched from one short-lived business enterprise to another. Edward, a highly-strung man with a mercurial temper, had a colourful career that began as a travelling salesman and soon moved onto to a huge range of business enterprises, not all of which were successful. For the first few years of Danny's life the family travelled the country as Edward moved from one employer to the next, rarely staying in one place for more than a year or two.

Danny began his schooling in Stoke Newington but at the age of six Danny moved out of London with his family to Cardiff, and from there to Newcastle and later Hull. Before the family left Hull, when Danny was 11, he was awarded a scholarship to attend secondary school and when the family returned to London soon afterwards, he was enrolled at the Grocers' School in Hackney Downs after gaining another scholarship. Less than a year later the family moved again, this time to Hendon, and Danny was forced to move school once more. By the time he was 12, Danny had attended at least six different schools. One of his teachers would later say that he was 'a brilliant pupil' but seemed nervous, highly-strung and 'abnormal' and was probably in need of some psychological attention.

War broke out when Danny was 13 and in 1940 the family sought refuge from the bombing in Woodley, just outside Reading. They found the local secondary and grammar schools full, which marked the end of Danny's education and he took a job at a local aircraft company in the drawing office.

Perhaps as a result of his peripatetic childhood, Danny developed some nervous habits early on. He was afraid of the dark and suffered night terrors, bit his nails almost to the quick from a young age and, he was to tell a doctor years later, wet the bed until the age of 10.

In 1941 the family returned to London. Betty, Danny's mother, began working as an advertising agent and within months, the business had taken off and was registered as a limited company, Premier Advertising, with Edward named as a director and Danny as an employee. For the first time, the Raven family was comfortably off.

In 1943, just before his 17th birthday, Danny volunteered for the RAF and was eventually accepted in August 1944. He passed the required medical examination, the report only noting a scar on his forehead, which Danny explained was the result of his falling against a glass door at the age of seven. His career with the RAF would prove to be short but eventful.

Danny trained as an air gunner and reached the rank of temporary sergeant. In November 1944 he was stationed at el Ballah in Egypt, moving to RAF Aqir in Palestine in March 1945 and Abu Suier in Egypt in July 1945. Danny later told some family members that he had been involved in a plane crash while in the Middle East in which the rest of his crew were killed, although there were suggestions later that Danny had embellished this story somewhat and that he was not in the plane at the time of the accident.

In August 1945 Danny was in Abu Suier and working outside in the afternoon sun and complained of a severe headache, dizziness and a throbbing in his head to his superior officer. He had only been outside for 20 minutes but told the RAF doctor he suffered from sunstroke as a child. The doctor could find no evidence of sunstroke and assessed in his report that the sudden illness was down to anxiety and nothing to do with exposure to the sun. As a result, Danny was removed from flying duties with immediate effect.

Danny was referred to an RAF neuro-psychiatrist, would found no evidence of any disorder in his central nervous system. The verdict was that Danny was suffering from anxiety and that he had a long personal history of being unduly nervous and anxious. Danny was brought before an RAF medical board, who agreed with the psychiatrist's report and he was invalided out of the service on 14 September 1946 due to 'anxiety neurosis'. The board's view was that Danny's level of disability due to this condition was 15% and might last at least six months.

So, in late 1946 Danny found himself back in north west London. His first two weeks back in London were spent in Finchley Memorial Hospital, recovering from a bout of malaria he had picked up in Egypt. He was to have recurring attacks of the illness over the next 18 months.

Danny did not return to a happy home life. His father Edward had gone to Ireland on business the previous year and during a day at the races had lost just over £3,400, an extraordinary sum. A friend he was with had lost £600 on the same race and according to their bookmaker, Edward had given the impression that he would also cover this debt. Edward had failed to pay and as a result the bookmaker pursued him through the courts. In

October 1946 Edward was declared personally bankrupt while the family's various businesses, including Premier Advertising and Raven Publicity, continued on their chaotic way. A few years later Edward would be described by the detectives and legal professionals who met him as 'fly' in his business dealings.

For Danny, things were beginning to look up. Premier Advertising was reasonably healthy and Edward employed Danny as a director of the firm on the impressive salary of £20 a week (at a time when a shop assistant at Sainsbury's earned around £4 a week). While Danny was not particularly comfortable with the level of responsibility required by the job, the wage was far better than he could expect anywhere else. And he needed it because he was in love and hoping to get married to his new girlfriend, Gertrude Goodman. On 31 August 1947 he asked Gertrude to be his wife.

The winter of 1947 was extraordinarily harsh. The freeze set in on 23 January, the beginning of the longest and most severe cold spell for more than 50 years. Fuel was already expensive – coal had reached 4s 10d a bag – and was in dangerously short supply. High snow drifts that blocked many of the main roads across England, Wales and Scotland added to the problems and on 29 January electricity cut out across almost the entire country as the power stations ran out of coal. The domestic gas supply was at a quarter of its normal pressure in most of the large cities and factories were forced to close because of the lack of fuel and materials. At the beginning of February the government announced that for the foreseeable future homes in London, the Midlands and the north west of England would have to do without electricity for three hours every day from 9am, and for another two hours from 2pm.

February 1947 was a tough month for the nation even by the decade's standards. Temperatures barely reached above freezing for the first half of the month and unemployment soared from 400,000 in mid-January to 1.75 million by the end of February. Television broadcasts and many magazines and newspapers were suspended and no electricity was available for any recreational activity from the theatre to greyhound racing, or most forms of outside lighting. Shops stayed open as best they could, with many resorting to opening under the dull glow of as many gas lamps and candles as staff could lay their hands on.

The thaw eventually set in late in March and workers began returning to the reopened factories, but restrictions on the use of domestic electricity would continue well until April. As a final blow to the nation's morale, sudden heavy rainfall poured into rivers that were already swollen by the thaw, destroying 80,000 tons of potatoes and 70,000 acres of wheat across southern England.

The end result of the flooding was that potatoes were put on rationing for the first time. In the mid to late 1940s rationing became, if anything, more restrictive than it was during the war. Bacon and meat rations had already been cut in the autumn of 1946 and rations for an adult were now once ounce of bacon, two ounces of butter, three ounces of margarine, one ounce of cooking fat, two ounces of cheese, three pounds of potatoes, one shilling worth of meat a week, half a pound of bread a day and one pound of jam or marmalade a month.

Protected by Danny's job from the worst of the hardship, Danny and Gertrude happily continued with the preparations for their wedding. They married on June 22, 1948, in Marylebone and spent their honeymoon at the Strathmore Hotel in Torquay. But during their stay Danny's tendency to lose his temper surfaced and one evening, during one of the regular dinner dances held at the hotel, he flew into a rage in front of other guests when Gertrude danced with another man. A couple who had befriended the newlyweds at the hotel remember an argument between the couple, with a red-faced Danny berating Gertrude as guests turned away in embarrassment.

The couple returned to London and settled into a comfortable married life. Leopold and Esther had presented their daughter and son-in-law with a house as a wedding present, which would remain in the Goodman's name but Danny and Gertrude would live in it rent-free after their marriage. Danny's well-paid job meant that they were one of the few families in the area who could afford a car. Quickly they settled into a routine, with Danny heading off to work for his father each morning and Gertrude looking after the housework, walking into Edgware to pick up rations, and spending time with her parents.

The house, number 184 Edgwarebury Lane, was one of a new development of three-bedroom detached homes built by AW Curton. The property was a comfortable distance from the busy Watford Bypass and close to the green open space of Edgwarebury Park, giving it a much less claustrophobic feel than the Goodman's home in Ashcombe Gardens less than half a mile away. While smaller than the Goodman's home, the new house was well laid out and stood on the corner of a side road, which gave the impression of space. Downstairs the front door opened into a large hall, 12 foot long. The drawing room was at the front of the house, with a large bay window overlooking Edgwarebury Lane. This room was separated from the dining room behind by a set of folding doors which, when opened, formed one long room from the front of the house to the back. The kitchen was at the back of the house, next to the dining room. Upstairs were two large bedrooms above the drawing room and dining room, a bathroom and separate toilet, and a small room, nine by seven and a half feet, which would be perfect as a nursery. Attached to the left of the house was a garage with a small storeroom behind. Danny and Gertrude named the house 'Auburns' in honour of their red hair.

There were signs, though, that Danny's mental state was beginning to unravel as his responsibilities as a husband, and head of what he expected to be a growing family, increased. About six months after their marriage, he suffered a nervous breakdown. He was unable to carry on working for his father and, on his doctor's advice, he and Gertrude moved to Bournemouth for a few weeks, away from the stresses of London, to help him recuperate. By the time he returned to London, though, Edward Raven's advertising agency was struggling and he was no longer able to offer his son any work.

Salvation came from his father-in-law, Leopold, who offered Danny a job at his radio dealership in Percy Street. For the next few months, Danny commuted daily to Tottenham Court Road, often driving to Edgware Station to catch the underground train to the Goodman shop. He would sometimes pass his neighbour, Mrs Paradise, walking down Edgwarebury Lane towards the shops and always stopped to offer her a lift. She remembered a kind and pleasant young man.

Danny's career with Leopold, though, was not going smoothly. He was paid considerably less than the wage he earned from his own father's business, and perhaps felt his fall in status and living standards keenly. There were rumours later that he might have had gambling debts but whatever the reason, in the months he worked for Leopold, Danny began stealing stock from the shop and selling them to a shady collection of acquaintances.

One of these acquaintances was Samuel Vosper, a radio valve dealer who ran a shop in Queen's Road, Peckham. A native Australian with a history of petty crime, he had been deported from Australia while still a minor after being convicted of stealing a bicycle. Within 18 months of arriving in London he had been convicted of embezzlement and sentenced to 18 months in prison. Between 1930 and 1941 he gathered a string of further convictions, including stealing bicycles, willful damage to plate glass, burglary, attempting to obtain cash by deception, and theft of a car.

Vosper first met Danny Raven in early December 1948, when Danny had called at his shop with radio components to sell. Over the next two months the pair conducted fairly regular business and Danny sold him around £750 of electrical goods, about a third of which were lampholders. Vosper was one of the first witnesses to be interviewed in the days after the murder of the Goodmans – for reasons that would soon become apparent.

Vosper told police that early one morning at the end of January 1949, Danny had called at Vosper's shop in Peckham and asked him if he had realised that there was 'something funny' about the lampholders Danny had sold him. Vosper told Danny he certainly did not (which, given his record, was unlikely), and Danny told him that he had stolen them from his father-in-law, Leopold Goodman. Until this point, Vosper told police, he had assumed that the relationship between Danny and Leopold, which Danny had discussed with him, was one of employer and employee and no closer.

'I then questioned him at length and he told me that practically all the stuff he had sold me had been obtained in that way,' Vosper told police. 'I asked him why he had done this and he said words to the effect that he meant to get the money somehow and didn't intend to scrape along all his life. Then he asked me would I help him and I said I would, if I could.'

It appears, from what Vosper told police after the murders, that Danny had had a showdown with Leopold the day before he turned up at Vosper's shop and was trying desperately to limit the damage. Vosper said Danny gave him the impression that Leopold himself was not averse to buying stock from dubious sources – adding that Leopold had been 'implicated in a lorry load of valves and had only just got out of it'. If Vosper hinted that he knew this, said Danny, he felt that Leopold would drop the matter. Vosper said he was non-committal about Danny's request and Danny then left the shop.

As Danny predicted, a few hours later Leopold arrived at Vosper's shop. Vosper told Leopold that Danny had called at the shop that morning, and showed him the receipts and invoices from his transactions with Danny over the past two months. At this, Leopold broke down. 'A crook in the family! I can't believe it. What am I going to do?' was how Vosper described his reaction to police. Leopold then began trying to add up his potential losses, but gave up and left.

A few days later, according to Vosper, Leopold returned to his shop with Gertrude. Gertrude, he said, was upset and was refusing to believe that Danny had sold the stolen goods to Vosper, and Leopold asked Vosper to relate to Gertrude what he had told him earlier that week. In an unlikely burst of honesty, Vosper offered to call in the police but the pair refused. As they left, Leopold, ever the businessman, told Vosper that if he was looking for a supplier, he, Leopold, was probably cheaper than anyone else. Vosper did later write to Leopold asking for a price list but Leopold replied saying he did not give out written lists and asking him to call in. The pair did no further business with each other.

Probably because of this incident, Danny stopped working for Leopold early in 1949. Gertrude was by now pregnant with their first child and Danny had to find a new source of income quickly. In March 1949 he approached the *Hendon and Finchley Times*, and told the newspaper that he was setting up a recording studio from his home. A young reporter duly interviewed Danny for a small feature in the paper, during which Danny said that he had bought recording equipment (costing £200) and planned to offer his services to local singers and musicians, as well as recording wedding parties and barmitzvahs for a fee. Danny also took out a six-inch advert in the paper to announce the opening of the Raygood Recording Studios (a combination of his and Gertrude's surnames) in Edgwarbury Lane, where recordings could be made by anybody.

There are suggestions – although some of this evidence was provided later with the benefit of hindsight – that Danny and Gertrude's relationship came under increasing strain during 1949, probably as a result of his dealings with Leopold. After the murders a neighbour of Danny and Gertrude's approached the police and told them that she had frequently heard the couple arguing late at night.

Nellie Muir lived next door to the newly-married Ravens, across the side street that separate their homes, with her sons Roy and Trevor between January 1948 and August 1949. For some months the Ravens seemed to live peaceably enough, she told the police, 'but one evening, I heard quarrelling late one night. From that time onwards at frequent intervals – sometimes two or three times a week – I heard them quarrelling. It was always late at night, between 11pm and 12pm.'

The rows were never considered particularly serious but sometime in July 1949, Danny and Gertrude's quarrelling spilled over into public. At about midnight one evening, they had a heated argument, loud enough to wake Nellie. She was worried enough (or curious enough) to put on her dressing gown and told police that she went into the street and found there Danny's sister, who lived opposite Danny and Gertrude, as well as several other neighbours, watching the house.

The lights were on at the Raven house and the front room curtains were open. 'I could see Danny Raven with his hat and coat on, moving about,' said Nellie. Then, she said, she heard him shout, 'I'll strangle you.'

According to Nellie, at these words Danny's sister and some of her family went to the front door and banged on it repeatedly. Danny opened it, none too pleased, and yelled at them to mind their own business. After more shouting, he shut the door on his relatives and the quarrelling inside stopped almost at once.

Recollection of other neighbours, though, do not support Nellie's story. The Paradise family lived directly next door to Danny and Gertrude and remember a quiet couple. They do not recall hearing of any argument between Danny and Gertrude, public or otherwise.

On 6 October 1949 Gertrude went into labour and Danny drove her to the Strathlene Nursing Home in Muswell Hill. Just after 10pm that evening, their baby was born.

Chapter 5 – Days Three to Nine

During 1949 London would see 57 murders in a city with a population of 8.4 million. While many of the national newspapers were still enthralled by the case of Sydney Setty, a second-hand car salesman whose body was found on the marshes of Essex after apparently being thrown from a plane, the discovery of two bodies in north-west London was still front-page news. In Edgware itself, the news spread quickly, the residents of the quiet suburb horrified that an ordinary residential street, so similar to the hundreds of other developments that covered the area, could be the scene of such horror.

Ashleigh Brilliant, a 15-year-old schoolboy, interrupted his recording of the ongoing saga of the cancellation of the annual County School Carol Festival in his diary to write:

'News! A gruesome double murder has been committed in Edgware. A Jewish man and his wife were murdered in their home in Ashcombe Gardens. I thought I would like to see the murder house but I didn't know where the street was. I went out for one and a half hours looking for it but did not find it. I discovered later that I had been quite close to it.'

The following day Ashleigh went out again and this time found Ashcombe Gardens. 'It was being guarded by two policemen, but apart from some broken flowers in the front garden, I could see nothing unusual,' he wrote in disappointment. 'It was just an ordinary house.'

Elsewhere in Edgware, Bernard Elliston and his wife were eating breakfast when they read in the local paper of the murders of Leopold and Esther Goodman, the parents of their friend Gertrude. Bernard immediately sent off a telegram to Danny, sending their deepest sympathies to him and Gertrude and adding, 'I hope the police soon catch the man who did this'. A few hours later, Bernard heard on the radio that Danny had been arrested and charged with Esther and Leopold's murder.

By the time Danny appeared in front of two local Magistrates at an Occasional Court at Wealdstone on the morning of Wednesday 12 October, charged with murder, the case was attracting enormous press interest, in both local and national newspapers. The normally quiet courtroom, used to hearing petty arguments over property and perhaps, the occasional case of theft, struggled to cope with the number of people, mainly locals, who turned up to see Danny for the first time. The *Hendon & Finchley Times* noted 'a full public gallery comprised mainly of men' in the courtroom, as well as 'a knot of people who stood outside the court hoping to catch a glimpse of the accused man'. Danny, who stood throughout the hearing, was 'smartly dressed in a brown bird's-eye suit,' said the paper. He only spoke to refuse legal aid – an innovation that had been introduced only three months previously and which was viewed with scepticism by most – and was remanded in custody for a week before being taken away to Brixton Prison.

A few miles away, Danny's wife Gertrude was the subject of intense press interest and newspaper reporters stood outside the nursing home, hoping to catch sight of her. On the Friday after the murders, a *Daily Express* reporter filed a breathless account of the first sighting of Gertrude: 'With two blue blankets around her shoulders and supported by a nurse, Mrs Raven left the nursing home where her baby was born five days earlier,' he wrote. 'Against doctor's orders and despite urgings by the nursing home's matron, she left her cream bedroom on the second floor, looking out on a copse of pine trees.' According to the reporter she got into a black Standard car driven by Edward Raven. Danny's mother was also in the car. 'An hour and a half later she was at Brixton Prison talking to her husband.'

The reporter added that the matron of the nursing home, Miss Flett, had said of Mrs Raven: 'The poor body was so distraught that I could do nothing to detain her. I thought it best to let her go to her man.'

In the days after the gruesome discovery at Ashcombe Gardens, while the press scrambled around for details, the CID team – DCI Tansill, DI Diller, DS Grout and Detective Constable Thomas – set about interviewing witnesses and taking formal statements. Dr Matthews, Dr Holden and all of the police officers that had attended the scene the previous evening provided formal statements, and the detectives took detailed statements from Alfred, who had discovered the bodies, and from Dr Cairns. All were hand-written, usually by DS Grout or Constable Thomas, and later typewritten with carbon paper, producing three copies.

The Goodman's brother-in-law Alfred was the key witness and spent hours with DCI Tansill and DI Diller, going through the events of 10 October and providing background on the Goodman family and their relationship with their son-in-law.

DCI Tansill and DI Diller began by questioning Alfred closely about his business relationship with Leopold. He told the detectives that even though he was nominally a director of Leopold's company, he was effectively employed as a travelling salesman. He had been given one share in the company in 1948, which he did not pay for, and played no part in the control of the company. Leopold, he said, signed all of the cheques and made all of the business decisions. Alfred was paid £8 15s a week.

Alfred told Tansill and Diller how he had left the shop in Percy Street with Leopold at about 6pm on the evening of the 10 October and driven him to see his doctor in Hampstead, where Leopold had stayed about 30 minutes. He described how he had dropped his friend off at his home in Edgware and discovered their bodies two hours later. He added that he had seen a television aerial similar to the one found in the scullery sink at the Goodman's home lying in the hall of the house in the days before the murders. It looked like an aerial base sold by Leopold's business, he said, known in the trade as a Di-Pole. The versions sold at Leopold's shop, though had a bakerlite insulator at one end, and the one found in the sink did not have this attachment – he had looked around the house for the attachment but had not been able to find it.

Asked about the Goodmans' son-on law, Alfred told the detectives how, when Gertrude had first introduced him to Danny, the young man had been working for his father's advertising business. From conversations with Danny he knew a few details of his background – he knew that Danny had spent time in the RAF, he said, and had told him that he had been involved in an aircrash while in Egypt.

Alfred told the detectives that Danny had had a breakdown shortly after his marriage and Leopold had taken him on as a salesman after his father's business had collapsed. He told them how Leopold had discovered that Danny had been selling stolen stock to Samuel Vosper (who was called into the police station to confirm the story) and had sacked him from the business. But that, he said was not the only argument that Danny had had with Leopold.

'A few months ago Lew [Alfred's affectionate name for Leopold] told me that he had had a terrible row with Danny because he had taken a bill of sale on the furniture at 184 Edgwarebury Lane, for £500,' he said. He added that the Goodmans had bought much of the furniture at the house and that Danny and Gertrude were living there rent-free.

Tansill asked him what he knew of Danny's personality. 'He's a young man of moods and I understand he has a terrible temper,' Alfred replied. Tansill asked if Danny had ever spoken against Leopold to him. Alfred replied that he had never heard Danny express any resentment for his father-in-law, even after he had been sacked by him. Tansill asked if Leopold would have been likely to defend himself if attacked: 'Lew was robust and enjoyed good health,' said Alfred. 'If given the opportunity he would put up a good fight against an assailant'. Esther, he added, was 'a frail woman' but in good health.

While Diller and Tansill interviewed the immediate witnesses, the rest of the team gathered statements from others who could corroborate the movements of Leopold and Danny.

DS Grout took statements from two nurses at Strathlene nursing home where Gertrude, who had not been told of the death of her parents and the arrest of her husband until the evening of Tuesday 11 October, was still a patient. Linda Thomas told DS Grout that she had been on night duty at the home for the previous month. Gertrude Raven, she said, had been admitted the previous Thursday, 6 October, and had given birth at 10pm that evening. Daniel Raven and Mr and Mrs Goodman had been to visit every evening since then, she said.

'I can remember Mr Raven very well, because he usually stayed after visiting period, which ended at 9pm, and I had difficulty in getting him to leave,' she said. 'He was usually in Mrs Raven's room when I took a cup of tea in, which would have been around 9.10pm.' But on the evening of the 10 October, she had taken Gertrude a cup of tea at about 9.10pm as usual, and was surprised to see that her husband had already left. 'Mrs Raven mentioned something about her visitors having left early,' she said, adding that she saw neither Danny Raven nor the Goodmans on that Monday evening.

Another nurse, Phyllis Conquest, told DS Grout that she had been on duty at Strathlene from 5pm until 9pm during the evening of 10 October. She had been looking after six patients that evening, including Gertrude Raven, under the supervision of a Sister. She had come to know the Goodmans over the previous few days during their visits to Gertrude and their new grandchild, but did not see them arrive on that particular evening.

Nurse Conquest continued that at about 7.45pm that evening Daniel Raven had come to find her and had asked for some advice about the baby. He seemed, she said, 'a bit fidgety' but otherwise normal. She did not go into Gertrude Raven's room while the Goodmans were there but at about 9pm was in the hallway when they left, without Daniel Raven, at about 9pm. The couple wished her a goodnight as they passed. 'I was in the hall for about 10 minutes after that but didn't see Daniel Raven leave,' she said.

DS Grout and DI Diller then interviewed Danny's aunt, Esther, who lived in Glendale Avenue in Edgware with her husband, son and daughter. She told them that Danny had stayed with them on the night of Thursday 6 October, after his child was born, and on the following evening. On the Saturday evening her son Dennis, Danny's cousin, had stayed with him at 184 Edgwarebury Lane. On the Sunday afternoon Dennis, his sister and Danny had all visited Gertrude and the baby at the nursing home in Muswell Hill.

Esther told the detectives that on the following day, Monday 10 October, Danny and his mother had collected her by car from her home at about 1.50pm and they had all visited Gertrude and the baby. They left shortly after 4pm and Danny had dropped his mother back at his parents' home in Gurney Drive, Hampstead. Danny then drove Esther back to Glendale Avenue, arriving at about 5.45pm. She asked him to stay for dinner but he told her that his mother-in-law was expecting him for dinner that evening and left in his car. He was wearing, she said, a brown herringbone tweed suit. That evening Esther and her children went to the Ritz cinema in Edgware to see the Doris Day film, leaving the house empty, and did not arrive home until 10.30pm.

The Goodman's neighbours in Ashcombe Gardens were able to provide little information of use. Betty Cowan, who lived opposite the Goodmans at number five, said she and her husband had gone out for a walk at about 9.45pm on the evening of the 10 October but as far as she recalled the Goodman's home was in darkness and there was no car outside or in the driveway. She added that Leopold normally left a light on if the house was empty.

Winifred Bayes, who lived next door to the Goodmans at number six, had returned home with her husband Eddie from a night out in London at about the same time, and had passed Mr and Mrs Cowan as they turned into Ashcombe Gardens. She said they had noticed no cars on the road and when she went indoors to prepare supper, she could see that there were no lights on in the kitchen of number eight. She said she heard nothing until she saw two policemen in the garden of the house at about 11pm that evening.

Elizabeth Rogers, who lived at number ten, said she was at home during that evening and spent most of it listening to the wireless with her husband. *Ladies' Night* was just coming to an end (which would have been shortly before 10pm, although Mrs Rogers felt it was closer to 9.30pm) when she thought she heard a scream. 'At first I thought it was the children upstairs but the screams continued so my husband switched off the wireless and put the lights out. I looked out of the window and saw a woman running up and down shouting 'murder!' and screaming. Shortly afterwards the police arrived.'

At the house in Ashcombe Gardens, the police team removed the Goodman's safe from the cupboard under the stairs. The safe was tucked away at the far end of the cupboard, with several coats hanging in front of it and a floor sweeper leaning against its door. There was no sign that anything had been disturbed in the cupboard and the detectives were confident that it had not been touched on the night of the murders. The keys to the safe were in the bunch found in Leopold's pocket and when it was opened the police team found several pieces of photography equipment and a large amount of cash: £1,426 in £1 notes, £1,045 in £5 notes and £50 in 10 shilling notes.

By the end of the week, DCI Tansill had received a summary of the official report from Dr Henry Smith Holden at the scientific laboratory. It was brief but, as far as Tansill was concerned, conclusive. Dr Holden's report noted that the blood samples taken from Leopold and Esther Goodman were, unusually, both of the type AB, 'the least common of the blood groups'.

Dr Holden reported that he had found 'a number of blood splashes' on the outside of the left leg of the burnt trousers that had been recovered from the boiler at 184 Edgwarebury Lane. 'There was a smear of blood along the bottom of the turn-up,' he added. 'This blood is human blood belonging to Group AB.'

On the shoes found in Danny's garage Dr Holden had found a 'blood crust' on the upper of the left shoe at the base of the tongue and 'additional blood was present on the welt of this shoe'. This blood, he said, was also of type AB. The dishcloth taken from the house was 'faintly bloodstained'.

From the items gathered from the house at Ashcombe Gardens Dr Holden noted that there were traces of blood present in the sludge collected from the sink, and on the floor cloth found in the sink. A 'small irregular flat flake of human bone' had also been found in the sink. There were traces of blood on the towel found in the scullery. The base of the television aerial, he said, 'showed considerable blood stains' which were of the type AB. The aerial base, he added, weighed two and a half pounds.

Dr Holden had also examined the scrapings taken from Danny's fingernails on the night he was arrested but had found 'nothing significant' – in other words, there were no traces of blood. DCI Tansill was to comment directly on this point in his official report: 'The prisoner's nails, when the scrapings were taken, were cut to the quick and with the presumption that the prisoner had washed his hands immediately after the attack, traces of blood may well have been washed away,' he wrote.

The visiting card of Detective Inspector Herbert Hannam, found in Leopold's wallet, could not be ignored and Tansill tracked Hannam down to Golders Green police station. Hannam told him that he had met Danny Raven, his father Edward and Leopold Goodman.

He had first met Danny, he said, in June 1947, while he was interviewing Edward at his place of business in Oxford Street. Hannam was vague (or was not asked directly) what he was interviewing Edward about but said he was 'seeking information' from him. He had not seen Danny again until early 1949, he said, when Danny had got in touch with him and asked him to help his father-in-law, who wanted to apply to become a naturalised British citizen. 'I told him what Goodman needed to do to start the process,' said Hannam. Danny asked if he would meet Leopold personally, and Hannam agreed. They met shortly afterwards at the Brent Bridge Hotel, where he had told Leopold that all the forms he needed to apply for naturalisation could be bought from the Stationery Office. He advised the older man to consult a solicitor before filling them in.

But this was not the first time he had met Leopold. Hannam told Tansill that he had first met Leopold in the middle of the previous year, in connection with enquiries he was making into currency offences. 'Leopold Goodman was one of the many people who were able to assist me,' said Hannam, 'and he did, in fact, give me assistance at that time and subsequently.'

During their meeting at the Brent Bridge Hotel, Leopold asked Hannam if he would be prepared to put a good word in for him in his naturalisation application. 'I said I would be happy to, as he had been of assistance to me in my official capacity,' Hannam told Tansill, 'but that it was dealt with by a different department from mine.' After that meeting, he said, he did not see Leopold again.

Danny, though, proved to be more persistent and rang Hannam at his home six or seven times, asking if he could do anything to speed Leopold's application up. 'He rang me on a Sunday morning in September this year and said he hoped I was going to do something for his father-in-law and said it had been going on for a very long time,' Hannam told Tansill. 'He said to me "the old chap is a very good scout to me, and I would like to see this done to put his mind at peace." I said I understood Leopold had been interviewed and it was only a matter of waiting for the Home Office decision.'

Two or three days before the murders, said Hannam, Danny rang again. 'He said "Have you any good news for my father in law yet? He is a very good chap to me and I really want to do everything I possibly can for him about his naturalisation. Could you possibly find out anything about it and give me a ring and let me know?" I told him I would let him know if I had any news.' He did not hear from Danny again.

A week after the Goodman's murder, DCI Tansill sat down at a typewriter to begin his official report on the case to his Chief Superintendent. The report would stretch to 18 pages and took him almost two days to complete.

Daniel Raven, wrote Tansill, an advertising agent aged 23 of 184 Edgwarebury Lane, was on remand to appear at Hendon Magistrate's

Court at 10am on 20 October on a charge of murdering Leopold and Esther Goodman.

Tansill began by setting out the facts of the case. The Goodmans, he wrote, were a 'comfortably off' Jewish family. He set out the details of how Esther and Leopold had arrived in the UK, met and married, but he was unable to provide similar details for the accused man. 'We have not got the full history of the prisoner by reason of the non-co-operation of the relatives and the solicitor for the defence,' wrote Tansill. There were sketchy details available on Danny's RAF career and Tansill said he was hoping to receive more information from the Air Force before too long. 'There may be a medical history,' he wrote, 'for [family members] state that the prisoner was in an Air Crew during the war and was involved in an air crash in the Middle East'.

Tansill continued that Danny was described by a family member 'as a man of moods and has a terrible temper,' and noted Danny's breakdown after his marriage. 'We know that the prisoner was not altogether on friendly terms with the Goodmans,' continued Tansill, 'and the reason for this may have result from incidents described in the statement of Samuel Vosper.'

'There is no evident motive for this crime,' concluded Tansill, 'but the prisoner's actions after its committal tends to show that he was in possession of his full faculties because of the way he tried to cover up his tracks. He may have anticipated that the crime would not have been discovered until the following day but the discovery [of the bodies by Alfred] was his undoing. It would seem that after he had changed and taken steps to destroy the blood-stained suit and wash his shoes he called at his cousin's house, with the intention of inviting him to stay at 184 Edgwarebury Lane that night to prove an alibi, expecting that the bodies would not be discovered until the next day. The cousin was not at home.

'No robbery was attempted, but the prisoner was open to financial gain with the deaths of his father and mother-in-law, for their properties would come into the hands of their only daughter – the prisoner's wife.

'The violence used in the assaults was brutal' continued Tansill, describing the blood and indentation found on the dining room table. 'The indentation coincides with the pointed edge of the aerial base found in the sink,' he wrote.

In Tansill's view, it was clear that Danny was the murderer: 'That the prisoner is the assailant there is no doubt,' he wrote, 'for the crime has certain salient features pointing to the individual having a knowledge of the house.'

The most damning points, as far as Tansill was concerned, that pointed to Danny being involved were that the light switch in the dining room was almost impossible to find unless you had knowledge of the house; that the aerial base had been washed, which could only mean that the attacker was anxious to remove his fingerprints; and the level of violence used which, said Tansill, 'is presumptive that the assailant was known to them.'

Tansill set out his theory: 'In our view the crime was carried out in this way. Raven arrived at the house at 9.30pm – as admitted by him. He went inside, Goodman removed the jacket he was wearing, and went into the dining room with the prisoner. Simultaneously Mrs Goodman went upstairs to her bedroom. While the prisoner and Mr Goodman were in the dining room a quarrel developed. In a raging temper the prisoner got the aerial base and attacked his father-in-law, who shouted out. On hearing the noise downstairs Mrs Goodman, who had put on her indoor shoes, leaving her coat and handbag on the divan bed, which was then made, rushed downstairs. The prisoner continued to batter the man. Hearing Mrs Goodman coming downstairs he stood behind the door and, as she entered the dining room he struck her a blow on the head and continued to rain blows on his victims with the aerial base. Having done this he went to the sink in the scullery, washed the instrument and his hands. He returned to the dining room and switched off the fluorescent lighting.

'To make it seem that a burglary had occurred he went upstairs, entered the front bedroom, disarranged the bed, threw the eiderdown and other property on it onto the floor. He then switched off the light in the bedroom and closed the door. He left the house through the front door by pulling the lever of the Ingersoll lock. The attempted disposal of the suit and the washing of his shoes followed immediately on his arrival at his house.'

'It is suggested that this report and copies of the statements be sent to the Director of Public Prosecutions for his information and his consideration,' concluded Tansill. He signed the report and dated it. Now it was a matter for the courts.

Chapter 6 – Days Ten to Seventeen

On the morning of Thursday 20th October, the morning after DCI Tansill finished his report, Danny was taken from his cell in Brixton and led by DS Grout to a police van. The van made its way across the city through the light traffic to North West London. The crowds outside Hendon Magistrates' Court, noted the *Hendon & Finchley Times*, were considerably bigger than they had been the week before when Danny was first remanded in custody: 'Before 9 o'clock a number of men and women – mainly Jewish – stood waiting on the steps of the Court House for the doors to open.

'When the court was opened at 9.20am they all took their places in the public gallery of Number One Court. Twenty minutes before the magistrates took their seats, all places in the public gallery were occupied.

'Raven arrived at the court at 9.25am in a closed police van and was taken to the rear of the court, accompanied by DS Grout. A big crowd gathered at the rear of the court hoping to catch a glimpse of Raven, but the high wooden gates were kept closed.'

The hearing, as expected, was brief since solicitors on both sides were still preparing their case, but it was not without incident. The Magistrate quickly became exasperated with two sets of solicitors who had been engaged by relatives of the Goodmans who were furious that the police had removed the Goodman's safe from the house at Ashcombe Gardens without the family's permission. Maurice Arram, Gertrude's solicitor, objected to the removal of the safe on the grounds that it contained some of Gertrude's belongings. Another solicitor, Alfred Bieber from the well-known West End firm Bieber & Bieber, had been instructed by Leopold's brother-in-law, Alfred, to look after the family business. The two solicitors had already been in contact on several occasions with DCI Tansill, who had told his Chief Superintendent that his inquiries had been 'impeded' by the 'incessant activities between the various solicitors and relatives to gain possession of the keys to 8 Ashcombe Gardens and the premises of the Goodman company'. He told the Chief Superintendent that, because there seemed to be so many clashing interests and because he had had to withdraw the police guard from Ashcombe Gardens, he felt 'it was inexpedient to leave the house and its contents unprotected'. The safe had been removed from the house, he said, and the solicitors had been asked to make a formal application by letter for the keys to the house and to Leopold's shop and office.

At the hearing the situation was complicated still further when Sydney Rutter, who had been hired by Edward Raven as Danny's new solicitor, made an application to inspect the safe and its contents. His request was opposed by the Director of Public Prosecutions. The arguments over for the time being, Danny was remanded in custody for a week and returned to Brixton.

On the same day, a few miles away at Bushey Jewish Cemetery, Leopold and Esther were buried in twin graves. Once again, a reporter from the *Hendon & Finchley Times* was there to watch:

'There were no flowers, according to Jewish custom. About 120 mourners, who travelled in 40 cars, stood by the graveside. Almost all were men. A few yards away with a bowed head stood the father of the accused man. No mourning was worn because this week was the week of the festival of the Tabernacles.

'As a rabbi recited the committal service, the sister of the dead woman, was overcome and cried out.'

By the time Danny appeared at Hendon Magistrate's Court again a week later for the committal hearing, both sides were ready to set out their case. Danny, wearing the same brown suit and a brown double-breasted overcoat, sat in the courtroom while both sides outlined their arguments. The strain of prison life was beginning to take its toll on Danny. When he arrived at Brixton he weighed 144lbs – by now he had lost almost 10lbs and was looking tired and haggard as he sat in the court for six and a half hours as the two sides set out their cases. 'Two or three times during the day,' wrote the *Edgware and District Post*, 'he grimaced at his father, who sat in court, but the remainder of the day he sat impassively listening to evidence.'

This was the first opportunity for the press and public to hear the full summary of evidence in the case, as well as to hear direct from the police officers and witnesses to the case and as a result, places in the small public gallery were in high demand. People queued for more than an hour outside the courtroom before the doors were opened at 9.30am. The gallery was packed once more, and places had been reserved for relatives of the Goodmans, and for Danny's family. On a table between the witness box and the clerk's desk, on a table covered with white paper, were a collection of objects ready to be marked as evidence by the prosecution or defence. Among them, some wrapped in cellophane, were Danny's burnt jacket and trousers, his shoes, the television aerial base, cloths removed from the sinks in Ashcombe Gardens and Edgwarebury Lane, and Leopold's wallet.

On one side of the courtroom sat KS Lewis from the office of the Director of Public Prosecutions, who told the court that no evidence concerning any possible motive would be offered. On the other side sat Danny with Sydney Rutter. Danny listened closely as a succession of witnesses came to the stand to give evidence.

Leopold's brother-in-law Alfred, the first witness to be called, spent three hours on the stand under ferocious questioning by Sydney Rutter, who concentrated his attention on the business arrangement between him and the Goodmans. Under Rutter's insistent probing, Alfred told him that he was in temporary sole control of the business following the death of the Goodmans, but he was answerable to Gertrude Raven's solicitor, Maurice Arram.

Rutter questioned him closely about the evening he had found the Goodman's bodies. How had he got into the house? Why didn't he try the front door? Was the casement window on the catch? Was the kitchen light on? Was the television on in the dining room? Did he go upstairs after finding the bodies?

Rutter asked him what he had done after calling the police and Dr Cairns. 'Lew was still breathing so I got a jacket from the hanger and folded it up and put it under his head,' said Alfred. 'I pulled off his collar and tie – that's all I could do. Then I waited. It seemed like an age before the police came.' Rutter asked him if he had knelt beside the bodies. 'I may have, I'm not sure. I just felt Mrs Goodman's hand. It was cold. I mean, it was warm. I don't remember exactly what I did.' And did you get blood on your clothes? Alfred said he could not recall, but he was wearing the same suit that day as he had on 10 October, so it seemed unlikely. His wife, he added, had been covered in blood when she took Mrs Goodman into her arms.

Rutter changed tack again. Did he know there was a safe in the house at Ashcombe Gardens? Yes, Alfred replied, under the stairs.

'And did you know where Mr Goodman kept the key?'

'I think he kept them on a ring in his pocket.'

The remaining witnesses – PC Hill, Inspector Harvey, DI Diller, DCI Tansill, Dr Cairns, Dr Holden and some of the staff from the nursing home – all came to the stand in turn to give their evidence. After more than six hours the magistrates had heard enough and Danny was committed for trial at the Old Bailey the following month.

As far as the Director of Public Prosecutions was concerned, Sydney Rutter's tactics during the committal hearing suggested that the defence was floundering under the weight of evidence put forward against Danny. KS Lewis, the prosecuting Counsel, felt strongly that the hearing showed that the defence team was hoping that it could suggest that someone else had committed the murders, throwing enough doubt on Danny's guilt to secure his release.

It was also clear to him who their main target had been. Lewis made a note on his file for the Director of Public Prosecutions after the hearing: 'The line of cross-examination made it appear that the defence would like to point to [Alfred] as the murderer'. Rutter seemed to believe, the note continued, that Alfred had as much opportunity as Danny to commit the murders, but also had a motive where Danny did not – to gain sole control of Leopold's radio business. 'Probably they have now realised that they could not hope to succeed in this respect,' added Lewis.

The Director of Public Prosecutions agreed with Lewis' assessment and added another note to the briefing file, saying that it was possible that the defence team would argue during the trial that Danny discovered the bodies and seeing himself bloodstained, had panicked and left the house. 'Theoretically,' concluded the note, 'that might account for everything, except perhaps Alfred taking his 17-year-old daughter along with him – and, of course, the common sense of the thing!'

Chapter 7 – Day Forty-three

On the morning of Tuesday 22 November, London awoke to the news that the BBC was planning to build a 'television city' on an undeveloped, 25-acre site in Shepherd's Bush, West London. A small article on an inside page of the *Daily Express* also noted that the trial of Daniel Raven, accused of murdering his parents-in-law, was due to start at the Old Bailey.

That overcast Tuesday was Danny's second day at the Old Bailey. He had spent the previous day in a cell below the court while another murder case was being heard, in case it finished earlier than expected. But by 4 o'clock it was clear that the court would not be hearing his case that day and he was returned to his cell in Brixton prison for the night.

The trial attracted a huge crowd. A queue of over 250 people, most of them women, snaked along Newgate Street outside the Old Bailey from early in the morning. The first woman to take her place in the queue for the public gallery arrived at 6am.

By the time Danny was led into the courtroom the public gallery was full. Danny's father sat in the back row but was largely ignored by the many reporters in the room thanks to the presence of, to their amazement, a genuine film star. Ann Todd, the popular star of the Oscar-winning *The Seventh Veil*, was spotted in the public gallery by a *Daily Express* reporter, who delighted in adding the snippet to his report the following day. Ms Todd, who was married to the director David Lean at the time, had no connection to either family or to Edgware and was probably at the court to research a future role. In 1950 she appeared in the film *Madeleine*, directed by her husband, in which she played a young Scottish woman from a wealthy family who was accused of poisoning her French lover with arsenic.

In the film, which was based on a true story, the jury's verdict of 'not proven' allowed Madeleine to walk free from the court.

Danny, dressed in the same brown suit and red and white tie he had worn at Hendon Magistrates Court, sat in the dock near his defence team: the lead barrister John Maude KC, and two junior barristers, Gerald Howard and Victor Durand. On the other side of the room sat the prosecuting counsel, Anthony Hawke and his assistant, Henry Elam. Mr Justice Cassels sat behind the raised desk at the front of the court. Danny watched as the 12 men of the jury were sworn in. 'Raven looked flushed and tired but listened intently, looking searchingly at each of the 12 faces' wrote the reporter from the *Hendon & Finchley Times*, 'He kept his brown overcoat on throughout the hearing, although the crowded court became warm towards the end of each day.'

Once the jury were sworn in the Clerk of the Court asked Danny to stand and told him that he was charged with the murder of Leopold Goodman on 10th October 1949. Are you guilty or not guilty?

'Not guilty,' said Danny.

Anthony Hawke got to his feet to introduce the prosecution's case. He described how Alfred had found the bodies at number eight Ashcombe Gardens and how PC Charles Hill had been the first police officer to attend the scene. Upstairs, he said, PC Hill had found that one of the two beds in the front bedroom had been pushed aside. On a table between the beds were a pile of banknotes, clearly visible to the policeman and presumably to anyone else who entered the room. 'I mention that for this reason only,' Hawke told the jury. 'If robbery was the motive for this murder, then it was a very curious robber who committed it, because there for anybody to see, and therefore for himself to see, was a bundle of banknotes which for some reason, he never took.'

'Quite apart from this,' Hawke continued, 'there was no sign in the house of any disorder at all, any indication that the house had been broken into. Besides that, Mr Goodman was wearing a watch and a ring, which were both untouched, and he had upon his person over £30 in notes. Mrs Goodman was also wearing a ring. It does not appear upon the face of it that these murders were the work of thieves.'

Hawke described how Danny had arrived at the house at 10.30pm that evening and had spoken to DCI Albert Tansill. He read out the statement that had been taken from Danny at 3am the following morning at Edgware police station, in which he said that he had left the Goodmans alive and well at about 9.30pm that evening and had gone home to have a bath. This account, Hawke told the jury, 'is the only account that had been given by him. The question for you to consider is whether it fits in at all with any of the facts which can be proved, you may think, quite conclusively to you'.

Hawke recounted how, at Edgware police station that evening, DI Jack Diller had asked Danny for his house keys and Danny had handed them over, only to try to snatch them back moments later. 'You may wonder why, having quite willingly handed over his keys one moment, there was this sudden regret at having done so and a desire to recover them as quickly as he possibly could,' Hawke told the jury. 'You may think that the answer to that question lies in what DI Diller discovered at Raven's house.'

Hawke told the jury that they should not be concerned with the motive for the murder. It was, he said, the responsibility of the Crown to prove Danny guilty, if he was, but not to 'go searching avenues for motives for crimes that are committed. What may have been the motive for this shocking crime is a matter which is entirely outside your inquiry. Motives may spring from a thousand mainsprings of which we who investigate know nothing and can know nothing. Nor is it the duty of the Crown to reconstruct the crime, except in so far as such reconstruction can be said to be consistent with the known and provable facts.

'But you may think, from the presence of Mrs Goodman's coat and handbag in the bedroom upstairs, it may well be that having heard the attack upon her husband going on downstairs, she went down to see what was happening, and as she entered the dining room was struck down – you remember she was found lying just inside the door.

'It does not appear on the face of it to have been the work of people who broke in and stole,' concluded Hawke. 'So far as we, for the Crown, with all such resources as we have at our disposal can show you, the accused person was the last person known to be with them, on his own admission. Their blood is upon his clothes and those clothes he was, you might think, without any doubt, endeavoring to destroy.'

His introduction complete, Hawke called his first witnesses. Phyllis Conquest and Linda Thomas, nurses at the Strathlene home, confirmed that they had seen Danny and the Goodmans there that evening and that the Goodmans had left soon after 9 o'clock. Next to the stand was Leopold's brother-in-law Alfred, who told the quiet courtroom how he and his wife and daughter had called at the Goodman's home just before 10 o'clock that evening, and how he had found Leopold and Esther covered in blood in the dining room.

The prosecution's questioning of Alfred over, Danny's barrister John Maude rose and walked towards the witness stand. He asked Alfred if he knew what was in the safe under the stairs. No, said Alfred, but added that his wife kept some money in there. How much money, asked Maude?

'I never asked my wife what was in the safe. I wasn't interested.'

'Do you have a bank account?' Asked Maude.

'I do, but I only opened it a week after the murders.'

'Where did you keep your money before you had a bank account?'

'At home,' replied Alfred to a ripple of laughter in the court, 'in a wardrobe.'

Maude asked him if he would be surprised to know that when the safe was opened it was found to contain £1,426 in £1 notes. 'Why should it be a surprise?' said Alfred. 'I know Mr Goodman always carried a certain amount of money in his safe.' Leopold was in the habit of attending Ministry of Supply auction sales, he added, where buyers had to pay for goods in cash.

'There was also £1,045 in £5 notes and £47 10s in ten shilling notes in the safe,' continued Maude. 'That is surprising, isn't it?'

'Yes, it is.' agreed Alfred.

Maude asked again if he knew how much money of his wife's was in the safe.

'No.'

'Come! You two people, like my client and the Goodmans, are Jewish people, are you not? You are not telling the jury that you were not interested?'

'Never interested. I do not know what my wife is worth. I am not interested in the slightest. Very peculiar, but true. I can support my wife without touching any of her money.'

Maude switched to a new line of questioning. He asked Alfred whether he had seen the television aerial base – which was on the table in the courtroom and labeled Exhibit 5 – before that day. Yes, Alfred replied, he had seen it in the hallway of Leopold's house a few days before the murders:

'I never gave it any particular interest. Goodman was always messing about with his television set, always trying to change over, always complaining about the picture.'

Maude asked Alfred if it was his habit to call at Ashcombe Gardens every evening to ask how Gertrude and the baby were. Alfred said it was, at about 10pm. That would have been known to Daniel Raven, would it not, asked Maude? Yes, Alfred replied.

Alfred's daughter followed her father into the witness box for a brief appearance. She told the court that she and her parents had left their home at 9.45pm for the short drive to Ashcombe Gardens. She knew the exact time that they left, she said 'because I always look at the clock when I finish my homework.'

Next, Anthony Hawke called the medical men who had attended the scene after the discovery of the bodies to give their evidence. Dr Cairns, the family doctor called to the house, confirmed that Leopold had been alive when he arrived, but died shortly afterwards. Dr Donald Teare, the pathologist called in by the Home Office to carry out the post mortems, then told the court that Mr Goodman had received 14 blows on the face and head, and his wife at least seven. The television aerial base could have caused the injuries, he said.

On the table in front of John Maude were a set of police photographs that had been taken of the house and of the bodies. These, Maude told the jury, would form part of the defence. Four photographs, showing the bodies of Esther and Leopold in the dining room, including two close shots of their mutilated faces, were handed to the jury, with the warning that they should not turn them over until instructed as they would be upsetting to see. Maude then turned to Dr Teare, asking him to look at the photograph which showed Esther lying in the doorway of the dining room, on her back, with her head facing into the room and her feet into the hallway.

He asked the doctor whether he thought Esther was entering or leaving the room when she was struck. Dr Teare replied that he thought she was entering the room when she was struck: 'It is difficult, but I offered the opinion because I thought if she was struck going out of the room she was more likely to fall back parallel to the wall rather than obliquely into the room.'

Maude replied 'politely and humbly' that this was 'really quite hopeless as a theory, because the angle at which she is lying depends entirely on from where she was coming into the room, which way she was walking out of the door, what she was actually doing at the moment the blow struck her, and a hundred and one other things.'

'It would be more difficult to strike her from outside the room in the direction in which she was falling,' said Dr Teare, 'because there is a wall of a passage.' He added that he believed that Mr Goodman was struck first, while sitting at the dining room table, and had staggered to his feet before falling in front of the fireplace. Mrs Goodman had been struck later, as she came through the door.

Maude asked him what force of blows would be necessary to cause the injuries suffered by Leopold. Great violence, said Dr Teare, which would mean raising the weapon at least as high as the shoulder before bringing it down.

'In that event,' said Maude, 'it would be surprising, would it not, if the assailant had not got blood on his coat.'

'Yes,' agreed, Dr Teare, 'it would.'

Maude turned to the blood patterns that had been found in the dining room. Dr Teare told him that he would expect arterial blood – and the injuries suggested that both Esther and Leopold had suffered arterial damage – to be sprayed up to nine to twelve feet from their source. Maude suggested that the blood splatter marks found on the legs and lower crossbars of the table suggested that blood was spraying from Leopold's head while he was on the floor, as well as when he was sitting at the table.

'It is most suggestive,' said Dr Teare. There were also splashes on the wall near Esther's body, he conceded, although he added that most of this blood was low down on the wall, so it did not automatically suggest that blood would have sprayed onto an attacker's jacket.

Maude moved to the table of exhibits and asked for Danny's burned trousers to be taken from their protective covering. The trousers were badly burned and almost all of the right leg had been destroyed. He handed them to Dr Teare. Where could he see blood, he asked? Dr Teare said he had not examined the trousers closely before but it appeared that about 90% of the blood was on the inside of the front crease of the trousers, while only 10% was on the outside of the leg. There was also blood in the bottom of the turn-up.

Maude pointed out that the right leg of the trousers had been burnt away to above the knee, which made it impossible to say conclusively whether the man wearing them had kneeled in blood. 'What I am suggesting to you,' Maude continued, 'is that all the marks you see, the spots on the trousers, might be caused by the wearer kicking into some blood and it splashing up.'

'Yes,' agreed Dr Teare.

Maude said that he had heard that it was common during a post-mortem for doctors to kick blood from the floor onto their clothes. 'You have all had experience of kicking blood, and you know you get marks like that?' Yes, replied Dr Teare. Maude suggested that Dr Teare had looked closely at the trousers to look for any blood marks that contradicted that suggestion.

Yes, said Dr Teare, he had. 'And that's what makes you sure?' asked Maude.

'Yes, that's what makes me agree with you.'

On the parquet floor of the dining room, Maude continued, police had found a mark which looked as thought it had been made by a foot kicking into the blood. Dr Teare said he had seen the mark on the floor, and agreed with Mr Maude's assessment. Maude asked him to examine the trousers again, and to especially look at an area near the crease of the surviving leg, which appeared to show spots of clotted blood. Dr Teare said he could see the marks.

'Is it correct to say that blood clots within a comparatively short time after leaving the body?' asked Maude.

'Yes, on the whole,' replied Dr Teare.

'In between what? Two to ten minutes?'

'Yes, once it is shed from the body.'

'What you have on the trousers is something that would appear to have clotted before it got on the trousers,' said Maude.

'I would not like to say, sir,' replied Dr Teare. 'It is rather bold to say that.' But he added after closer inspection that the shape and depth of the blood marks on the trousers 'would suggest that they were partially clotted before they struck the trousers.'

'And so that means that those spots that you are able to identify reached the trousers at least two minutes after the blood left the body?' asked Maude.

'Yes, that would follow.'

'And possibly longer, anything up to 10 minutes or more?'

'Yes.'

Satisfied, Maude returned to his chair. Anthony Hawke rose and asked permission to ask Dr Teare a few more questions. He asked the doctor to pick up the aerial base and demonstrate to the court how he would aim a blow at someone who was sitting on a chair in front of him. The public gallery stirred, and the many newspaper reporters in the room began writing feverishly. Dr Teare picked up the heavy aerial base and raised it over his head, bring it down two or three times with a straight arm in front of him. The court in silence, Dr Teare handed the aerial base back to the court clerk, who replaced it on the exhibits table.

'Have you been able to confirm where the attacker was standing when he hit Mr Goodman?' asked Hawke.

'No,' said Dr Teare, 'I have not.'

Was it also true, asked Hawke, that there was little or no blood on the front of Leopold's shirt, in spite of the fact that this was a man who had 'bled profusely all over the place'. Dr Teare agreed that that was the case. Anthony Hawke thanked him for his time and Dr Teare stepped down.

Next in the witness box was PC Charles Hill. He told the court how he had found the aerial base, apparently recently washed, in the scullery sink, and examined the bedroom upstairs, where he had seen the mattresses on one of the beds pushed aside – by about six inches, he estimated initially, but later corrected himself and said it could have been closer to 15 inches – and a pile of banknotes on the table between the beds.

He described how he had answered a knock at the front door at about 10.30pm, and let in Danny and his sister and brother-in-law. 'He told me he did not feel well.'

John Maude, cross examining PC Hill, wondered why the mattress in the bedroom had been moved.

'Do you find that many people hide money under mattresses?' asked Maude.

'I have heard of it,' replied PC Hill, 'but I have never experienced it.'

'That room looked, did it not, as though somebody had looked under the mattress?'

'No,' said Hill.

'The bag and coat were not where one would expect a woman to put them down?'

'No.'

'Your wife does not fling her bag and coat on the floor, does she?'

'No.'

Late in the afternoon, Dr Henry Smith Holden, head of the new forensic science unit at Scotland Yard, was called to the witness box. Anthony Hawke began by handing him Danny's burnt trousers and asking him to describe to the jury what he had found. The blood, said Dr Holden, was mostly below the knees and on the front of the trousers and it was of group AB, the least common of the four blood groups.

'What is the percentage of people with Group AB blood?' asked Hawke.

'On my figures, just over 2% on the number I have examined.'

Hawke asked him if he had found any blood on the jacket. No, said Dr Holden, but the jacket had been much more heavily burned. He described how he had also found blood on Danny's shoes, which was also of the type AB, and on the aerial base. Hawke asked him if he had tested the blood taken from Leopold and Esther Goodman. Holden confirmed that both were of type AB.

'That is a rather curious thing, is it not?' said Hawke.

'I was very surprised,' agreed Dr Holden.

Dr Holden said he had found a streak of blood on the driving seat of Danny's car and on the handbrake, and a drop on the garage floor. 'If someone sat in the driving seat with blood on his trousers,' asked Hawke, 'could it have got there from that source?' It could, said Dr Holden.

'You would agree that the fact that you did not find blood on Raven's jacket tells very much in his favour?' asked Maude.

'I do not think it tells either way,' replied Dr Holden. 'In similar cases I have had through my hands there has been no blood on the coat at all.'

Next was DI Jack Diller, who was asked to recount his conversation with Danny at 8 Ashcombe Gardens on the evening of 10 October, and how he had turned off the boiler in Danny's house when he realised something was burning inside.

Anthony Hawke asked him how far it was from the nursing home to Ashcombe Gardens. Seven and six-tenths miles, said DI Diller, adding that he had made the trip and it had taken him 16 minutes to make the journey along the North Circular Road and the Great North Road while driving at 30 miles an hour, although most of the roads on the route had no specified speed limit. It was a quarter of a mile between Ashcombe Gardens and Danny's house, he added.

Last into the witness box that afternoon was DCI Albert Tansill. Hawke began by asking him to describe the position of the light in the dining room of Ashcombe Gardens. 'It is 35 inches away from the door on the skirting and five inches up from the floor,' said Tansill. 'Of course, it would not be readily observable by any person not conversant with it.' He described what he had seen at Ashcombe Gardens that evening, and his conversations with Danny while at the house and later, at Edgware police station.

Rising for cross-examination, John Maude asked DCI Tansill whether he had looked carefully for blood in any other part of the house. Tansill said he had: 'It would be a normal part of my examination as officer in charge of the case.'

'Were scrapping taken from the nails of both Raven's hands?

'Yes.'

'In order to see whether there was any blood?'

'Yes.'

'You are satisfied there was none?'

'The nails were cut to the quick and there was hardly any substance left there...'

'Did you hear what I asked you?'

'Yes'

'What is the answer?

'No, sir.'

There was a short pause as the two men looked at each other keenly. Maude asked DCI Tansill whether it was true that Danny had reported two burglaries at his home during the previous year. Tansill confirmed that Danny had reported that 30 dozen lamp shades, worth about £9, had been stolen from his car in the unlocked garage on 1 January 1949, and on 22 February he had reported the theft of an alarm clock worth £1 10s, which he said had been taken after someone entered the house through an open window.

Maude turned to the exhibit table and picked up the shirt and pullover that Danny had been wearing when taken to the police station that evening. He asked Tansill to confirm that no blood had been found on either. Tansill agreed that that was the case.

Judge Cassels stopped John Maude for a moment. Does that mean, he asked that the accused had not changed his shirt at any point during the evening? He asked Tansill if he had seen a shirt at Danny' house during the search, which could suggest that Danny had removed one he was wearing earlier in the evening. Tansill said he had not looked for a shirt.

'We have heard of two suits, one worn before and one worn afterwards,' said the Judge. 'Is there any shirt other than the one he was wearing when arrested?'

'I should think there must have been,' said Tansill, 'because he has a fine stock of wearing apparel.'

Maude asked for one more question. Had a careful search been made of the boiler in Edgwarebury Lane, he asked, to see if there were any remains of a shirt as well as the suit? The boiler had been carefully searched, said Tansill. 'And there was no sign of a shirt?' No, said Tansill.

Judge Cassels nodded, and announced that court was adjourned for the day. Exhausted, Danny was led downstairs.

Chapter 8 – Day Forty-four

A buzz of excitement surrounded the Old Bailey at the start of the second day of the trial. An even larger collection of newspaper reporters had packed into the crowded public gallery, knowing that this was the day when they would hear two, hopefully dramatic, testimonies – from the accused man, and from his wife.

This was the defence team's chance to put forward Danny's version of events and just after 9.30am, Danny's barrister John Maude got to his feet to set out his argument. He stood in front of the 12 men of the jury and, looking at each in turn, began:

'It seems to me that what you would wish to know, among many other things, is something about this man. You have not been told anything about him at all. You know that he married about 18 months ago the daughter of a businessman in the wireless trade. You know where he lives. You know that a child was born to them. But you know little or nothing of his past history.'

Maude went on to recount in detail Danny's chaotic childhood and education, his early working life, his career with the RAF and his marriage. 'He has never been in any trouble before,' stressed Maude.

The prosecution, he told the jury, had made five main arguments, and he intended to address each in turn. The first 'limb' of the prosecution's case was that Danny was with the Goodmans shortly before the murder. That, said Maude, was entirely true.

The second was that Danny had set out to deceive the police by burning his clothes, washing his shoes and lying about his movements during that evening. There was also evidence to support this, said Maude.

Third, there was the blood, probably Mr or Mrs Goodman's, which was found on Danny's clothes and shoes. Again, it was true that there was definitely blood of a rare group on the clothes, said Maude.

Fourth, the prosecution had argued that Danny was not on good terms with the Goodmans. This was where the prosecution's case began to unravel. Danny, said Maude, had given a frank assessment of his relationship with the Goodmans to the police and had hidden nothing about his relationship with his parents-in-law. But, said Maude, the jury should think carefully about what the prosecution was saying: 'It cannot be suggested that if you do not love your in-laws passionately or strongly you murder them. People do not murder their in-laws because they do not feel particularly fond of them.'

'Mr Hawke was at pains to describe to you that it was not the duty or burden of the Crown to search for motives. What may have been the motive, he had said, for this shocking crime is entirely outside your enquiry. That, of course, may or may not be accurate. For instance, if you can show something is a motive, that is of great importance. If in fact you can show that a man was doing a robbery, and somebody was killed, the motive being gain, that is very important.

'There are motives for murder. They are countless. But where the Crown is unable to show a motive, then it gives, naturally, cause for thought.

'How astonishing is this, how fantastic it would really be if this man, with his wife in the nursing home, who had only just had a baby, who had been sleeping at the Goodman's house from time to time, who had had his meals cooked by Mrs Goodman, had sat and talked with her, had been in their house constantly, without any reason whatsoever, should suddenly murder them. It is not very likely.'

The fifth limb of the prosecution's case, continued Maude, was that there was no sign of a burglary at the house, which suggested that the murders could not have been carried out by any other intruder. But if the murderer was Danny, he knew very well that Esther Goodman's sister and her husband would be visiting at around 10 o'clock, so why would he choose a time to enter the house when he knew someone might turn up at any moment? 'That,' said Maude, 'is hopelessly improbable.'

The prosecution's hypothesis of what happened that night, he continued, had been deliberately vague. 'They said it is no part of their duty to reconstruct the crime. But if in fact they could reconstruct the crime, you need have no doubt that they would have done so. But it is impossible.

'It may be that Mr Goodman's head was on the table and he was struck first; or he may have been sitting on a chair; he may have been by the window; he may have been pushed or pulled and hit or partially stunned, pushed down against the table...all sorts of things. It is impossible now to get any clear picture of exactly what happened in that room. It is possible that the assailant came in when the two were there; it is possible that the assailant came in when one was there; it is possible that Mrs Goodman was on the far side of the room and managed to run round to get to the door. All sorts of things are possible.

'Was there someone in the house besides Daniel Raven?'

Maude paused for a moment before continuing. The jury, he said, should ask itself, what happened in the bedroom? The disorder that the police had described in the front bedroom – the mattress pushed aside and clothing and blankets thrown onto the floor – did not seem to be something that had happened in the ordinary course of life.

'Why was the room in that condition? If this man had done it, would he have done it before the two people were killed? It is a remarkable thing, is it not, that in spite of the disorder it does not look as though it was the act of some person who was behaving carefully. And yet there is no blood at all upstairs, or on the way upstairs.

'Was there somebody else in the house? The mere fact that the man has not stolen does not necessarily mean that he was not there for the purpose of stealing money and was disturbed. It was a good crib to crack; there was a lot of stuff in it.'

If someone was looking for money, argued Maude, Leopold would have been an obvious victim to select. His business was dealing in wireless equipment. He had a habit of paying in cash for goods bought at public auctions, a fact that would have been general knowledge to a great number of people. It would have been obvious to many that he probably had cash in the house.

So, suggested Maude, wasn't it possible that someone else had broken into the house that evening? Someone, he said, could have broken into the house through the back window while the Goodmans and Danny were at the nursing home. He might have heard the two cars arriving back at the house and the three talking outside. 'People were talking outside on the drive and he was trapped for a moment. Where would he go? Into one room or another, hoping to escape detection? Perhaps Mrs Goodman then goes upstairs, and do you suppose it is possible she found the disturbed room and let out a shout?'

Mr Goodman had taken off his coat and hung it in the hall. He had probably then, as usual, gone into the kitchen where he and his wife usually spent the evening. Perhaps, said Maude, he had heard his wife shout out and, as would be your instinct, had gone into the dining room to search it. But the burglar was waiting behind the door and attacked him.

'Someone was disturbed there; and who would that be?'

Maude picked up the six visiting cards that had been found in Leopold's wallet from the exhibits table, selected one and waved it in front of the jury. It was the card of Inspector Herbert Hannam. 'Mr Goodman was not, in fact, a quiet and dull person,' Maude told them. 'He was not so out of touch as people might assume. It may be dangerous to be in constant touch with a police officer where big issues are at stake. It is dangerous to be thought to be an informer. It is dangerous to be thought to be a "squeak". It is dangerous to be thought to be somebody who is in contact with the police, and assisting them to bring big criminals to justice.

'Suppose there was somebody in that house, a murderous person who wanted revenge or wanted to talk to Mr Goodman to stop something happening, and then there was the murder?' Maude placed the visiting card back on the table of exhibits.

So, he said, turning again to the jury. What had really happened that night? He pointed at Danny.

'That night, this man saw something so awful that the photograph of it has been withheld from you as jurymen.'

Maude told the jury that they would now hear what had really happened that evening. He described how Danny had returned with the Goodmans that evening to Ashcombe Gardens and had left them shortly afterwards, heading to his own home to have a bath. Once at his house he turned on the boiler, and while the water was heating, he decided to go to see his cousin, who lived nearby. They were not in and on his way back he passed the Goodman's house again. 'With nothing to do, he stopped outside.' He parked the car in the driveway and when he went in the lights were on in the hall, kitchen and scullery. 'He called out something – "Hallo, is anybody there?" There was no answer.' And in the dining room he found a scene of horror, discovering Mrs Goodman dead with injuries so horrific the jury had so far been spared the sight.

'He moved across to the far side of the body and knelt down – whether he knelt on his knee and it touched the ground, or whether he knelt down close to it, he does not remember, but there on the floor is the mark of a foot in that very position.

'Maybe he did not like his wife's mother particularly but she was dead, horribly dead. And, in the dim light, so was her husband as well.

'He recoiled from that room and stepping back into the full light of the hall he noticed blood on his hands, bright scarlet blood, and it was also on his shoes and it had splattered on his trousers.

'Fear seized him, he was terrified. What he felt is probably past description. Perhaps foolishly, he was frightened. Suppose someone had come in and found him spattered with blood, what do you think would have been the reaction of the person who found him? Would they not think they had found a most appalling murderer?

'He got into his car and drove home as quickly as he possibly could. And once you have run away and got into a car and are on the way home, it is irretrievable. You cannot go back.' He stopped for a moment. The courtroom was silent, everyone straining to hear.

'One thing leads to another when first one practices to deceive,' continued Maude. 'It is impossible, generally, for somebody to evolve a scheme on the spur of the moment. If it had been thought out you would have expected he would have had some intelligible line of conduct, but he had not. He had made no proper arrangements to dispose of his things.'

'There is more behind all this than you would have expected – much more.' An hour and fifteen minutes after he got to his feet, Maude returned to his desk and called his first witness to the stand – Daniel Raven.

Danny stepped down from the dock and walked slowly to the witness box. 'He was a slight figure in a grey lounge suit and a canary pullover,' noted the reporter from the *News Chronicle*. Danny put his hand on the Bible to take the oath, but stopped when he realised that he had nothing to cover his head. 'I do not have a hat,' he told Judge Cassels. From the back of the room, a police sergeant borrowed a brown trilby from a man in the public gallery and took it to Danny on the witness stand. Speaking quietly, Danny repeated the oath.

'You may sit if it is more comfortable,' the Judge told Danny. Danny said he would rather stand, but asked for a glass of water. In a voice that often dropped to a whisper – so low that the Judge on a couple of occasions asked the shorthand clerk to repeat back his replies – Danny began his evidence.

Maude's first question was whether Danny was happy with his wife. Yes, he said.

'Did you murder Mr Goodman?'

'No,' said Danny, shaking his head vigorously.

'Or Mrs Goodman?'

'No.'

Danny described himself as owning an advertising business and was earning between £20 to £22 a week. Leopold, he said, had given him and Gertrude the house at 184 Edgwarebury Lane when they married. He had no financial worries, he said, but had borrowed against the furniture in the house, from an insurance company in Holborn, to cover some additional expenses when he got married. While Gertrude was at the nursing home, he told Maude, Esther Goodman had asked him to eat all his meals at Ashcombe Gardens. On the morning of 10 October, he had also shaved and washed there as there was no hot water at his house. The previous evening, he said, was the first he had spent alone at his own home since the baby was born.

'Do you like being on your own?'

'Not very much.'

Maude questioned him closely about his movements on 10 October. Danny told him that he had gone to Ashcombe Gardens early in the morning and eaten breakfast there, which Esther had prepared for him. Just after 10 o'clock he rang the nursing home to check on his wife and child's progress. He left Ashcombe Gardens shortly afterwards, saying he would let Esther know if he would be back for lunch. He went back home to deal with some 'business and personal things' before going to his elder sister's home, opposite his own, just after 12.30pm. He left there at about 2pm, dropped his watch off at a jewellers in Edgware for repair, and returned to Ashcombe Gardens.

Later that afternoon he picked up his younger sister and mother and took them to the nursing home to see Gertrude and the baby. Afterwards he had returned again to Ashcombe Gardens and had dinner with Esther, before leaving at about 6.45pm to return to the nursing home. He arrived at about 7pm and the Goodmans arrived at about 8.30pm.

Maude asked him to describe what had happened next. Danny explained how he had chatted to the Goodmans at the nursing home and they were all perfectly happy. When the gong went at 9pm to mark the end of visiting time, the Goodmans left the room first and he stayed for a minute to kiss Gertrude goodnight. He then met the Goodmans at the nursery downstairs and they spent a few minutes with the baby. They all left at between five and ten past nine and he followed the Goodmans home in his car, as he had done every evening since the baby was born.

When they arrived at Ashcombe Gardens they both pulled into the driveway and he got out to talk to the couple. Esther asked if he wanted anything to eat, but he refused. 'I mentioned about staying the night,' said Danny, 'but Mrs Goodman said I was foolish to do so as it meant leaving my own house and, as I had already had burglars, I was asking for trouble.'

He told the court how he had left the Goodmans at about 9.30pm and gone home, switching on the immersion heater. While the water heated, he looked through some business papers for about five minutes and then got into his car and drove to his cousin's house. There was no reply and as he had to go past the Goodman's house on his way home, he thought he would call in.

The front door was open and he assumed that Leopold was in the garden or had gone across the road.

'The hall lights were on...I walked to the breakfast room and called out "anybody there?" The light was on in the scullery and I thought possibly someone was there.' Danny's voice dropped again and tears began to roll down his pale cheeks. 'His knuckles showed white as he gripped the side of the box,' wrote the reporter from the *Daily Mirror*.

Danny stopped to wipe his forehead with his handkerchief before continuing. In a whisper, he said that when there was no answer he headed towards the dining room, where the Goodmans sometimes watched television.

'I saw Mrs Goodman's legs and part of the body. I recognised her dress. I walked forward towards her, and I could see there was something wrong. I did not know what it was then. I walked a little further into the room alongside Mrs Goodman and bent down beside her to see, and when I bent down close I saw her face and I could see her eyes were open, and I could see her face was...all messy.' He bowed his head and wiped his eyes.

'What was the effect on you?' asked Maude after a moment.

'I felt sick.'

Maude asked Danny to show the court how he had bent beside Esther. Danny left his seat on the witness stand and as the jury and packed courtroom watched, he stood beside it and then crouched down and rested on his left knee.

The room in silence, Danny returned to his seat. What happened then, asked Maude? 'I was half getting up and I saw something near the fireplace,' said Danny. 'So I got up...' Danny stuttered to a halt again and Judge Cassels asked for a brief pause to allow him to gather himself and have a drink of water. After a few moments, Danny continued: 'I took a couple of steps forward and I could see Mr Goodman's head shining, because he was almost bald, and it showed up.'

'Could you hear any breathing?'

'No.'

'Did you think he was dead or alive?'

'I was sure he was dead. He was completely still.'

'So what did you do?'

'I wanted to get out of the room, first of all,' said Danny. 'I stepped into the hall for a moment and it was then that I saw blood on my shoes and on my trouser legs.'

'What was the effect of that sight on you?'

'If anything it made me feel even worse, and that made me frightened. I do not think I was really frightened until then, but when I saw the blood it did frighten me.'

'What did you do then?'

'I ran away.'

Danny told Maude that he ran straight out of the front door, got into his car and drove away. When he got home, which he thought was about 9.45pm, he was in 'a complete panic'. He took off his shoes, trousers and jacket, put the gas poker into the fire, lit it and put the jacket and trousers in. He thought about putting the shoes in too, but realised that they would not burn.

'Why did you burn the jacket if there was no blood on it?'

'I knew that it would be evident that the trousers were missing if there was just a jacket.'

Danny told Maude how he washed his shoes in the sink and put them in the garage. 'Then I went back into the house and went upstairs. I was sitting in the bedroom, trying to think what to do.'

'What sort of state were you in?'

'I was still terribly frightened and I was worried. I knew I had to do something I knew I had been foolish but it was too late. I could not do anything about it.'

'Did you think about your wife?' asked Maude.

'I was worried about my wife and the effect it would have on her when she knew what had happened to her parents.'

Danny continued that he sat in his bedroom for a few moments, before going into the bathroom and to begin running a bath. He heard a knock at the door and went downstairs, where his sister told him that something had happened at the Goodmans' house. By the time he returned to Ashcombe Gardens a few minutes later with his sister, he said, he was 'in a complete state of fear'.

'And the lies followed?' Maude asked Danny.

Danny bowed his head. 'Yes.'

I think, said Judge Cassels, that we will adjourn for lunch 10 minutes early to give the witness rather a longer break. The courtroom broke into a cacophony of chatter as the jury filed out and Danny was taken back to the cells below the courtroom.

Just over an hour later the courtroom was again full and the jury had returned to their seats. The clerk handed a note to Judge Cassels, which he read out to the court – the jury had asked, he said, at what time the 999 call had been received. According to PC Hill, he told them, it had been received at 10.01pm but he would make sure that that information was checked with the Information Room at Scotland Yard.

Anthony Hawke rose to cross-examine Danny. 'Is your evidence today of what happened on 10 October true?' he asked.

'Yes,' said Danny.

'When did you decide to tell it?'

'I told it to my solicitor on the day after I was accused, in the afternoon or early evening.'

'Up to that time you had given an account of this matter to four or five different people, had you not?'

'Yes.'

'I am to take it, am I, that every one of those versions, with their slight variations, is untrue?'

'Yes.'

'What made you decide to tell the truth to your solicitor?'

'He told me that I was in a very bad position and that I was going to be charged with murder very soon, and he wanted the truth.'

Was it the discovery of your blood-stained clothes in the boiler that had persuaded you to tell your solicitor this version of events, asked Hawke? 'No,' said Danny.

'Why didn't you ring for help from the Goodman's phone?'

'Because I was frightened.'

'Of what?'

'I think it was the sight of the blood on me, just the blood itself. When I first ran out of the house I had not really got the idea I was liable to be suspected. It was not until afterwards, when I had gone out of the house, that I knew I had put myself in a terrible position.'

'Is that what made you try to burn your suit? You thought you might be suspected?'

'Yes. I knew my mother and father-in-law were in the house dead and I was out of the house with blood on my clothes.

'What was the matter with the telephone in the breakfast room?'

'Nothing. I agree with you that that was the logical thing to do and it is quite easy for you to stand there and say I should have done it.' His voice dropped again to a whisper. 'Possibly it is just the fact that I am a coward that I did not do it.'

'What made you think you would be suspected?'

'I had already come out of the house and started away home and I had blood on my clothes. I was outside this house where something dreadful had happened and I had blood on my clothes.'

'Something with which you had nothing whatever to do?'

'Nothing.'

'Two people with whom, you have told us, you were on the best of terms?'

'Yes.'

'And you decided to run?'

'Yes.'

Hawke gave Danny a long look and told the Judge he had no more questions. It was three o'clock in the afternoon.

John Maude stood and called his next witness – Mrs Gertrude Raven. A stir of anticipation shot through the courtroom.

Gertrude was escorted through the court to the witness box by a uniformed policewoman. She was a striking, attractive figure in a grey shawl-collared coat, black gloves and black peep-toed shoes. Her cloud of red hair was covered with a scarf and she had removed the halo-brimmed hat, decorated with a peacock feather, which she was wearing when she arrived at the courtroom with two friends an hour earlier.

The many journalists in the room strained for the best view and any hint of interaction between Danny and his wife. 'Raven, who had been sitting motionless in the dock, leaned forward,' reported the *Daily Mirror*. 'He watched his wife as she took the oath. Mr Justice Cassels asked Mrs Raven to sit – and then the wife looked across the court and smiled at her husband. Raven's eyes hardly left his wife as she answered the questions put to her.'

John Maude passed over the questioning of Gertrude to his assistant, Gerald Howard. He began by asking if she was the wife of Daniel Raven. 'Yes,' replied Gertrude.

'We know that on 6 October, which was a Thursday, you went to a nursing home and had a baby.'

'Yes'

'On that evening, did you see your husband and your mother and father?'

'Yes.'

'Together?'

'Yes.'

'And each evening after that, the 7th, 8th, 9th and 10th, did you see all three of them at some time during the evening?'

'Yes.'

'And was there a time when they were all three together?'

'Yes.'

'And on those evenings were you all happy and friendly together or not?'

'Yes.'

'Were your mother and father and husband happy and pleased about the baby?'

'Yes.'

'Now the last night, the 10th. We have been told that a gong goes in the nursing home at 9 o'clock.'

'Yes.'

'To warn visitors that it is time to go?'

'Yes.'

'Do you remember that Monday evening the gong going?'

'Yes.'

'Was your husband with you in the room then?'

'Yes.'

'And your mother and father?'

'Yes.'

'Can you remember who went out of the room first?'

'First my mother and father went away.'

'Leaving your husband behind?'

'Yes.'

'And about how long do you think after they had gone did he leave?'

'About a minute.'

'And had they been perfectly happy and friendly that evening?'

'Yes.'

'From your room you can hear people who happen to be talking by the entrance door of the nursing home?'

'Yes.'

'After your mother and father had gone, followed a minute later by your husband, did you hear any more of them?'

'I heard them outside, laughing.'

'Could you distinguish their voices?'

'Yes.'

'All three of them?'

'Yes.'

'All together?'

'Yes.'

Gerald Howard thanked Gertrude and said he had no more questions; Anthony Hawke indicated that did not intent to cross-examine. Gertrude had been on the witness stand for just six minutes. 'Raven watched as his wife left the witness box,' wrote the *Daily Mirror*. 'She sat down at the back of the court, out of his sight.'

John Maude called the last witness for the defence; Detective Inspector Herbert Hannam. DI Hannam told Maude that he had first met Danny in June 1947 at Edward Raven's office in Oxford Street. He had not seen him again until early in 1949, when he had asked for his help in advising Leopold on his application for naturalisation.

'From first to last, did you find there was no reason whatsoever to doubt the good character of Leopold Goodman, Mrs Goodman and Daniel Raven?' asked Maude. 'This is true,' replied Hannam.

Hannam continued that he had met Leopold for the first time in the middle of 1947. He had approached Leopold for information about people he was investigating about currency transactions, who were doing business with Leopold. 'He gave me information which was useful,' said Hannam, adding that in one case he gave information which 'was of material assistance to the prosecution.' Maude asked him what had been the result of the investigation. Hannam replied that the man in question had been fined between £10,000 and £12,000 for currency offences and had been recommended for deportation. And has he been deported, asked Maude? Hannam said he did not know.

Maude asked Hannam how his visiting card had come to be among Leopold's wallet. 'In October 1947 I was taken off currency work and transferred to another department. I did not desire to lose contact with people like Mr Goodman. I told him that as he could not contact me at Scotland Yard, if he wanted to get in touch with me on something of importance he could ring me at home.'

Anthony Hawke asked Hannam whether it was important in his line of investigation to keep his sources of information secret. 'It is excessively desirable,' said Hannam.

'Did Mr Goodman ever give you any information which, in your view, was likely to make his life dangerous?' asked Hawke.

'No, sir, not so far as I know.'

'The suggestion here is that Mr Goodman may well have been in danger of his life because of information he gave to you,' said Hawke.

'As far as I know,' replied Hannam, 'no-one living, apart from he and I, knew he gave me that information.'

Hannam stepped down from the witness box. The case for the defence was closed.

Newspaper reporters rushed to reach Gertrude as she was hurried by police from the courtroom. In the following day's papers, one maintained that he had asked her what she would do if Danny was found not guilty. 'Well,' he claimed was her reply, 'I suppose he would come home and I would make him a cup of tea.'

Chapter 9 – Day Forty-five

For the many journalists who sat in the crowded courtroom at the Old Bailey on Thursday 24 November, there was no doubt what stood at the centre of this story. As the Judge opened proceedings on the final day of the trial in the hushed courtroom, the attention of the journalists was firmly on Gertrude Raven and her brief appearance on the witness stand the previous day. 'A beautiful girl of 22, whose pale face under her red hair had haunted the court,' wrote the *Daily Mirror*. 'This tragedy was hers.'

'Not even the oldest Old Bailey official can remember so tragic a figure as petite Gertrude Raven,' added the *News of the World*, 'as she sat, almost doll-like, listening to the story of the tragedy which had brought her whole life crashing about her head.' Only once, added the paper, had she spoken to anyone other than her relatives in court with her, and that was to say: 'I will never believe that Danny murdered my mother and father. Danny could never do such a thing.'

Gertrude sat quietly in the public gallery on the final day of the trial, only able to see the back of her husband's head. 'Hour and hour, motionless and tense,' wrote the *Mirror*, 'she listened to the fight for Daniel Raven's life.'

The long day began with John Maude summing up the case for the defence. 'The case for Raven is a strong and powerful one,' he told the jury. 'Upon the evidence and upon the arguments, it is an overwhelming one.' But, he said, no case should be decided on suspicion alone. If the jury felt that an explanation had been given and it may be true, then that means there is some doubt. 'And where there is a doubt the Crown has not proved its case beyond all reasonable doubt and the man, or woman, must be acquitted.'

Whatever the prosecution had said, the lack of a motive, said Maude, had to be something that the jury should consider. The prosecution may have said, most forcibly, that they had no duty to prove a motive at all but, said Maude, 'if they do not then in many cases they will fail'.

Maude asked the jury to consider the case of a man caught red-handed firing a gun at the King, shouting "Death! Death!". In such a case, he said, there was little point in looking for a motive. But if it emerged that that same man was a faithful servant to the Royal household for many years, someone highly trusted and held in high affection, surely you would want to search for a motive? 'Why on earth should this man suddenly behave in that way? If you have a motive, the crime becomes clear. And so it is with this case.'

The first point he would ask them to consider, he said, was that there was no evidence of motive. In fact, the act that Danny Raven had been charged with was contrary to natural instincts: 'It is contrary to the family ties. It is contrary to the spirit of gratitude for the past and it is contrary to his hopes for the future.' It was accepted by both sides that Danny was a frequent visitor to the Goodman's house, that he was eating most of his meals there, that he had even shaved there on the morning of the murders. And Danny's wife had said they were all happy together that evening. 'Is one to believe in such a state of things that a man is going to murder his father-in-law and mother-in-law within, what is it, three-quarters of an hour? To commit one of the most appalling murders that any of us has ever seen?'

Maude picked up the album of photographs of the murdered couple. 'Would you run if you saw this?' he asked the jury, holding up the photograph of Esther's injuries. 'Alfred did not run away, but Alfred was not alone.' Even so, Alfred had told the court that he arrived at the house at 9.53pm or 9.54pm and the emergency call was not made until 10.01pm In other words, said Maude, eight minutes had elapsed before *he* called the police – 'it did not seem to have occurred to *him* at once.'

There was no suggestion, said Maude, that Danny was prone to violence – 'awful, brutal violence'. In fact he is, said Maude, 'an ordinary, sane man of 23' and as the jury saw the previous day, 'a nervous, shrinking and frightened man. Is that the violent type?'

It was hardly surprising, Maude suggested to the jury, that Danny had been frightened on the witness stand the previous day. 'Put yourselves in a position where you have been a fool and a coward,' he said. 'Put yourself in

Brixton Prison for a month awaiting trial for murder.' He had been subjected to 35 minutes of brutal accusations under cross-examination.

'What was the result? Was there a single answer Danny Raven gave that was shown to be a lie? Not one.' One of the objects of cross-examination is to expose the truth by breaking down a witness, by showing that he has contradicted himself, said Maude. 'It is very powerful, so powerful that until 1898 prisoners were not allowed to go into the witness box because Parliament felt they might be broken down unjustly. It was dangerous to cross-examine an innocent man. But Danny went through it and in no single instance was it possible to show that he lied. He may have lied to the police – but he had good reasons for doing so.'

Maude stressed again that the Crown had offered no motive for the murders. 'There is no evidence of need or greed. Danny was alright financially and getting on with the in-laws.' It may not be part of the Crown's duty to prove a motive, he said, but that does not mean that it is not important to do so. 'People murder for a reason.'

Ordinary experience of London, he continued, would suggest to anyone that the city contains a great number of thieves and robbers, as well as a good many who are murderers. There was a great deal of money in the house at Ashcombe Gardens and Mr Goodman's occupation would have been a clue to many people that it was there. 'There was no possible motive for Daniel Raven, but possibly there was bait in the house for a thief. Wasps are inclined to raid beehives; honey is the motive for people to come and steal, and it was there in the Goodmans' house all right.'

But, he continued, robbery was not the only possible motive. Leopold was giving information to the police, which had resulted in one man being fined and deported. 'When did that man find out that it was Leopold who had supplied the information, if he did? Those of us involved in intelligence during the war know how difficult it is for policemen to keep their mouths shut. If there was an order for deportation, that means utter ruin. And if the man was Jewish, deportation might mean losing more than money – Europe is not a very comfortable place to go back to. But if news had been brought to this man of how Mr Goodman provided information about him, do you not think he would have had a bone to pick with him?'

'The absence of motive is fatal to this case. Quite fatal.'

And that was not all. There were other points where, said Maude, 'the Crown labours in hopeless difficulties'. There was disorder in the main bedroom of the house at Ashcombe Gardens, which was unusual and unexplained. 'Who did it? Not Mrs Goodman, or Mr Goodman. It was not Alfred – he says he never went upstairs. It must have been somebody else. Was it this man? If it was not, then there was somebody else in the house. If it was Danny, then he either went upstairs before or after the murders. Afterwards, he had blood on his trousers and shoes. There was no sign of blood at all upstairs, not a spot. Would not one expect there to be some blood kicked into the carpet somewhere? Because if this man had committed these murders his mental condition must have been beyond belief.'

So, said Maude, the disorder must have happened before the murders. But there was no evidence of friction between the Goodmans and Danny when they left the nursing home. 'What are we to suppose happened? That before the murder when they returned to the house this man goes into the house with the Goodmans, goes upstairs and pulls the bedclothes off? It is a fantastic idea. No. Mrs Goodman went up there to take off her hat and coat.

'Is it not obvious that someone was disturbed there? That is the only possible explanation.'

The fact that the money on the table in the bedroom had not been stolen was only consistent with someone hunting for more than £6, said Maude. And the disorder in the bedroom was only consistent with someone being disturbed and going downstairs. It was not consistent with Danny going upstairs, in any shape or form.

Then, he continued, there was the question of the light switch in the dining room. Mr Hawke, he said, had made a point of asking: Who turned off the light? 'That sounds tremendously good,' said Maude. 'But the answer is: "Would you mind proving that the light was ever turned on?"'

Suppose, he said, that Mr Goodman had taken off his coat and gone into the dining room. Mrs Goodman had gone upstairs and, finding that the bedroom had been disturbed, shouted out that there was someone in the house. 'The unfortunate Mr Goodman is in the dining room where a man is hiding,' said Maude. 'It is perfectly consistent.'

The lack of blood on Danny's jacket, pullover, shirt or hair, said Maude, was another difficult point for the prosecution. 'The Crown cannot explain, and does not attempt to, the absence of blood in places where you would expect to find it.

'When you have fountains jetting blood from several arteries of two people it is peculiar, it is odd, and it is in a man's favour, as Dr Teare said, that no blood is found above the waist – or indeed above the knee.' The fact that the blood on Danny's trousers was clotted, he added, was also of vital importance.

Maude suggested to the jury that the first detectives on the scene, and particularly DCI Tansill, had decided early on that Danny was guilty and that the arguments from then on had been formed to fit that view. 'There was a hideous moment yesterday when I asked DCI Tansill about the nail scrapings taken from Danny,' he told the jury, 'one of those awful moments when instead of the police officer at once saying, "Yes, scrapings were taken," he starts an elaborate explanation as to why the point I am trying to make is no good. It shows, does it not, the slightly biased mind, and no doubt Detective Chief Inspector Tansill has great power to impress upon other persons his own view of what has taken place.

'You understand how ideas get into people's heads, how somebody might have a false view of the case caused by people making up their minds that something is wrong. Every sensible man knows quite well that thieves get into houses when windows are left open. It is a usual thing about which, if this had not been a murder case, everybody would agree. Instead, you find the Crown asking who opened the casement window. It is no use asking how the window got open – it is up to the Crown to show that it was not.'

Finally, Maude asked the jury to think about the timing of events during that evening. Danny left the nursing home at five or ten minutes past nine and said it took 15 minutes to get to Ashcombe Gardens. 'That means he got to the house at 9.20pm or 9.25pm. It would have taken a couple of minutes to put the car away, and another couple of minutes for Danny and the Goodmans to have a conversation. One to two minutes to drive home. That makes 9.30pm the time Danny got home. He turned on the immersion heater and looked at business papers for five minutes, which brings us to 9.37pm. He says he arrived back at Ashcombe Gardens at 9.45pm.

'The two gaps you want to think about is how long Danny has been away from the house, and had he been away long enough for someone else to be hiding in that house. Danny said he had been away from the house for 15 minutes, and that left plenty of time for him to do what he said he did that evening before the Goodman's visitors arrived.

'Your knowledge of your fellow men,' concluded Maude, 'and your ability to see the points, to sit impartially in the way you gentlemen have done suggest, do they not, that my arguments are sound and based upon fact. And the proper verdict here is the only just, right and safe one, and that is that this man must be found not guilty.'

Maude had spoken for almost an hour and a half. He walked back to his seat and the jury settled itself once more for the prosecution's closing arguments. As soon as Anthony Hawke rose to his feet, it was clear that Maude's comments that the prosecution was 'labouring in hopeless difficulties' had struck a nerve. How could Maude say such a thing, he wondered.

'If, when I have put the case to you in just a few words, you think the Crown is labouring in hopeless difficulties, then you can sit back and listen no more.'

The case for the Crown, Hawke told the 12 men in the jury box, was clear. A 9.30pm on the night of 10 October Mr and Mrs Goodman were alive and well and at some minutes past 10 o'clock they were dead. 'The last person known to be with them was the accused man. He gave four separate versions to four separate people of what his movements that night had been. Those four versions are all demonstrably untrue, and are proved to be untrue by the evidence upon his own clothes, evidence which he himself took the earliest possible steps to destroy. Is that a case, gentlemen, labouring under impossible difficulties?'

The question for them to consider, said Hawke, was whether Danny's story – which he had only come up with after his burned clothes had been found – stood up to testing? 'If it is true that Raven came into that house and found what he said he found, does the account of his actions thereafter appeal to your minds?'

He asked the men to put themselves in Danny's place for a moment. What would their first instinct be if they had stumbled onto the horrific scene at Ashcombe Gardens? 'Do you think that you would have rushed from the house except to find a policeman? Or do you think you would have rushed from the house and as you got outside thought: "I shall be a suspect of this murder. I must get home and destroy all evidence that I have been near the place"?

'Why should you at once leap to the conclusion, when you find your mother and father-in-law alone and dead in their house, that you are going to be suspected as the murderer? Does it make any sense to you?

'Is anything more contrary to human instincts and family ties than what this man is telling you? He found his mother and father-in-law, one of them still alive. There was a telephone in the next room. There was, no doubt, a policeman [in the vicinity] and, instead of telephoning the police, instead of calling for assistance for these miserable people, instead of going outside to see if there was any help to be had, he slinks across to his motor car, hides his shoes in his garage and tries to burn his clothes. Would any of you have done that in the same circumstances?'

Hawke allowed a short pause before moving on to the other theories put forward by John Maude. If Leopold had been killed by a thief that he had disturbed in the dining room, he asked, why was he sitting in a chair when he was hit? And if the attacker was someone bent on revenge, perhaps because Leopold had supplied information that had led to his conviction for currency offences, this was a curious man, because why would he come to the house without a weapon?

'I cannot do more than talk about the possibilities and probabilities because we are theorising,' said Hawke. The only evidence of what had really happened had been told to the jury for the first time the previous day by Danny himself, when he told them how the blood had come to be on his clothes. It was true, said Hawke, that there was no blood on Danny's jacket, but 'it is no good theorising about blood unless you know where the person who is likely to become splattered is standing, how near he is to the victim, in what position he is in relation to the victim – all considerations which only two persons could tell us, and one is dead.'

Did Mr Maude's story of an unknown visitor make sense? 'Had this utterly nebulous unknown person, a creature of imagination, who must have been created only to explain the blood on Raven's clothes, displace the known facts? The facts were that Raven was the last person known to be with the Goodmans. He was no stranger to their house, and the jury might think that there was evidence that this was the work of a person who was not stranger to it.

'He endeavored to destroy vital evidence and finally told an entirely different story when he discovered that his attempts to destroy that evidence has been unsuccessful. These are facts.'

Hawke repeated again that it was not the duty of the Crown to prove a motive. 'If you are driven to the conclusion that all the evidence before you points inevitably in one direction, motive is utterly irrelevant,' he told the jury. 'Evidence of motive may assist, of course, in the solution of a crime, but if the solution is at hand, then the absence of motive cannot displace it. Motives may spring from a thousand obscure causes, from some recess of the mind which suddenly comes to the forefront and which has been latent for long years, a motive may come quite suddenly in the space of a second or two. It is not part of a jury's duty to search for motives just for the sake of finding them.'

Hawke's summary was complete in just over an hour. Judge Cassels announced there would be a short adjournment before he began his summing up. In the public gallery, Gertrude had heard enough. 'She raised a tired hand to her forehead and asked a friend to take her from the court,' wrote the *Daily Mirror*. 'She was smuggled out of a side door and driven away by police.' Her seat remained empty for the rest of the day.

By the time Judge Cassels resumed his seat just before 2pm, the atmosphere in the courtroom was electric. Journalists, friends and relatives of the Goodmans, and Danny's family, sat and tensely listened to the Judge's summing up. What he had to say and the points he would pick out from the two days of evidence would, they knew, ultimately seal Danny's fate.

Judge Cassels said he would begin by setting out the events of 10 October, as told to the court. 'The facts are for you; you alone are the judges of them,' he told the 12 men in the jury box. 'If I should say anything in the course of my summing up to you bearing upon the facts, you are entitled to ignore what I have said and to make up your own minds.'

If they were satisfied that two people met a violent death at the hands of the same person on the evening of 10 October,' he said, the question they must then consider is whether the prosecution had proved to their satisfaction, beyond reasonable doubt, that the accused man was criminally responsible.

'The crime is murder, killing with malice aforethought – which refers to the state of mind which immediately precedes, or exists at the moment of, killing,' the Judge continued. 'If the act which causes death is done with the intention to cause death or serious bodily harm, that is murder. Malice aforethought does not mean that a motive has to be shown, or ill-will, or long premeditation beyond that momentary premeditation just before the act.

There is no burden upon the Crown to establish a motive in a prosecution for murder. Men kill for many reasons, and men do not kill and leave a statement of the motive by the body. Counsel for the defence mentioned yesterday among motives passion, revenge and closing someone's mouth. He might have added such motives as jealousy, temper, desire for gain, or even a desire to enjoy a benefit as a result of the death. Motives may be sudden or they may be nursed for a long time.'

Since the timing of events that evening was disputed by both sides, Judge Cassels told the jury that there were only three times that they may think it possible to place absolute reliance – the emergency call received at 10.01pm, PC Hill arriving at Ashcombe Gardens 10.03pm and Dr Cairns arriving at 10.12pm.Otherwise, he said, they should bear in mind that witnesses often underestimate the amount of time that has passed. If you ask some to estimate how long two minutes is and time them on a stopwatch, he said, it is generally found that the witness will say that two minutes has passed after about 45 seconds. 'You must bear that in mind when you come to consider to what extent you can rely upon these approximate times.'

He described the scene at Ashcombe Gardens. 'Photographs have been put before you, picturing perhaps in a not very attractive way, what those bodies must have looked like to anybody who went into that room. There was blood on the bodies, there was blood on the floor, there was blood on the table, there was blood on the wall. It was very nearly a shambles. Somebody in that room, almost with the ferocity of a maniac, had struck the life out of those two persons, wielding some very heavy instrument with great force.'

Judge Cassels described how PC Hill and Inspector Harvey had searched the house and how DI Diller had found Danny's burnt clothes in the boiler at his home. Dr Holden, he reminded the jury, had told the court that he had found nothing significant on the remains of Danny's jacket. 'Observations have been made in the course of this case as to the absence of blood spots on the jacket and, of course, you are not entitled to assume that there were any on it. There is not evidence that there were any blood spots on that jacket.'

As far as the other forensic evidence was concerned, it was right that the jury was told that scrapings had been taken from beneath Danny's fingernails, said the Judge: 'It is right you should be told that scrapings were taken from the prisoner's fingernails and taken to the laboratory, and no evidence has been given about them; nothing was revealed. Detective Chief Inspector Tansill said the prisoner's nails were cut to the quick. Dismiss that observation, that piece of evidence, from your mind. If they were cut to the quick, there would not be much chance to get any scrapings from underneath them, and we do know there were some scrapings which were sent to the laboratory. We have no evidence about them, and that has not established very much.'

Turning to the evidence for the defence, Judge Cassels reminded the jury that no witness had been called on either side to suggest for a single moment that this family was not perfectly happy. 'The newly-married couple had not even had to endure what thousands had had to,' he added, 'and live in the house of their in-laws.'

As far as Danny's version of events was concerned, Judge Cassels stopped at the point Danny said he had made a second visit to the Goodmans after finding that his cousin was not at home. 'It is entirely for you to say how that strikes you but, taking it to be what happened, it is a little curious. He had been in his car at the Goodmans' house up to a little before 9.30pm and here he was back within a very short period of time, a very short time indeed.'

One of the most significant and important parts of Danny's evidence, said Judge Cassels, had come when he talked of how he found the bodies of the Goodmans. 'Remember how he came down from the witness box and stood between your box and the witness box and he knelt down upon his left knee, showing you how he said he knelt down by the side of Mrs Goodman.'

The Judge read out to the jury what he said they might consider to be the most important parts of Danny's evidence while on the witness stand. He had said that after finding the bodies, he was in a complete state of fear and the next sentence in his evidence was 'and the lies followed'. Danny had arrived at Ashcombe Gardens, according to the police officers there, at 10.30pm. 'A great deal had happened – had it not? – in what after all was a very short space of time between 9.20pm, which might be the earliest the Goodmans could have got back from the nursing home, and 10.30pm.'

'No burden rested on the defence to prove innocence or explain how the murder might have happened,' continued the Judge. 'None the less, a fair amount of time and been quite properly occupied on certain theories put forward on both sides. Counsel for the defence had said that Goodman's home was a "good crib to crack". So the possibility was put forward that this brutal killing was the work of a thief, that some people put money under the mattresses and that the mattress here had been shifted.

'The realm of speculation knows no limits. If one side speculates, the other side speculates and everybody speculates, and even you can speculate if you like, if you think it is an advantage and if you think speculation is more important than looking at the actual and real evidence that you have.

'Do not put these theories on one side by any means, but at least approach the suggestions in a reasonable way, as I am sure you will.'

The defence, he said, had built up a picture of a figure of a man making his way through the Goodmans' house seeking revenge, to call upon Leopold Goodman to pay 'the penalty of a sneak'. If this was the case, said the Judge, the jury might think that this man had worked quickly. 'If it was a marauder and if exhibit 5 was the instrument which he used, he was a strange and fortunate marauder. He was a strange marauder who went to carry out such a design as that without any arms or any weapon, and he was a fortunate marauder because in the hall of the house which he was visiting there was a weapon to hand.'

And what of Danny's explanation that he found the bodies and had panicked and left the house? 'In approaching your deliberations it may well be you will ask yourselves, why did the prisoner call for no help? Why did he not use the telephone? Why did he burn his clothes? Why did he tell lies to the police? As he stood in the doorway of the dining room that night, as he knelt by the side of that dead woman and saw across the room the shape of the father-in-law, the man who had been kind to him, is it not a question for you to pass through your minds: Why did he do what he did?'

The explanation that had been offered was that he had left the house because he was afraid, said the Judge, and as a result he had done nothing that could have brought the police to the house, who might have been on the track at once of a thief, or another intruder, if there had been one. 'Instead, he got into his car, backed out into the passageway, and drove home. He burned his clothes and he washed his shoes. Not until he was told at 10.30pm that something had happened did he make his way back to that house of death.'

With that, Judge Cassels concluded his summing-up. John Maude immediately got to his feet. 'I should not be doing my duty if I did not mention that your lordship did not deal with the clotting of the blood and the inferences to be drawn,' he said.

The Judge turned to the jury once more. He reminded them that Dr Teare had told them that some of the blood found on Raven's shoes and clothes might have been caused by his kicking against blood, which had clotted. Dr Teare had also said that blood would clot from two to 10 minutes from coming from the body and it was found clotted on his clothes.

'Dr Teare said that under cross-examination, and you should accept it,' said the Judge. 'Of course blood will clot, we all know that, and I suppose it clots when in the ordinary course of nature it comes out from the body, and I suppose it will clot wherever it may drop. It may well be that it was clotted when it was on the ground and the prisoner walked through it.'

He told the jury to retire to consider their verdict as a quiet murmur broke out in the public gallery. The time was 4.15pm.

The jury had barely left the room before Anthony Hawke rose to his feet and suggested that, in order the save time, the Judge could begin the next trial, another murder case. The Judge agreed. For the journalists in the room it was, as the *Daily Mirror* report put it, 'A moment of tremendous anti-climax as Raven's place in the dock was taken by another young man not dissimilar in age and appearance'. They did not have long to wait – after just 45 minutes a message came that the jury was ready to return.

'The tension which had been broken gripped the court again as the jury filed back,' wrote the *Daily Mirror* reporter. 'Raven once more stood in the dock. A deathly silence fell on the 200 people crammed into every seat and every inch of standing space – a silence only broken by the sounds of a woman sobbing high in the public gallery.'

'Members of the jury, have you agreed on your verdict?' asked the Clerk of the Court.

Alfred Butler, the chairman of the jury, stood. 'Yes.'

'Do you find the prisoner guilty or not guilty of the murder on this indictment?'

'Guilty.'

'You find him guilty of murder, and that is the verdict of you all?'

'Yes.'

Danny stared straight ahead. 'He seemed dazed,' wrote the *Mirror* reporter. 'His white face set his auburn moustache increasingly against the pallor of his skin.' In the public gallery, a woman continued to sob. Outside the courtroom where he was waiting with two friends, Edward Raven took off his spectacles and wept bitterly when he was told of the verdict. 'My boy,' he said. 'Oh, my boy.'

Judge Cassels placed the black cap over his head and looked directly at Danny.

'Daniel Raven, you stand convicted of murder. For that there is only one sentence. Have you anything to say why the court should not give you judgment of death according to law?'

Danny was still for a moment and then, barely moving, he shook his head.

Chapter 10 – Days Forty-five to Sixty-five

The packed courtroom erupted at the judge's words as Danny was led away. The commotion of the Old Bailey and the crowds outside gave way to the silence of a police van for the lonely trip to his new home, a cell for condemned prisoners at Pentonville prison.

The Ville, as it was known locally, was slowly returning to its normal routine after sustaining serious bomb damage during the war to its hospital and to one of the four long wings that formed the prison's distinctive star shape. Danny joined around 750 other prisoners but his routine as a condemned man would be very different from everyday prison life. While other prisoners rose at 6.30am and spent the day sewing mailbags for the Post Office, unravelling ropes and other material for the Ministry of Supply or making basic clothing for government departments, Danny would spend most of his time in his 13 by 8 foot cell, watched day and night by a rota of prison officers.

Danny was driven through the white gatehouse of the prison on Caledonian Road, searched, examined by the prison doctor and weighed (his weight was recorded as 135 pounds, nine pounds less than when he was first arrested). He elected to keep his own clothes rather than wear a prison uniform and was led along one of the three metal walkways that lined the long, three-storey high A wing. His cell, halfway along the wing, overlooked the exercise yard that filled the space between the radiating buildings of A and B wing.

Danny quickly slipped into a dull routine, spending most of his day playing cards with his warders, and taking a solitary walk in the exercise yard once a day. His solicitor, Sydney Rutter, had promised him an appeal and Danny firmly believed that he would soon be a free man. 'I am treated very well,' he wrote to a friend. 'The food is fairly decent although very monotonous. The days pass very slowly. We play cards and I read a lot, but I don't seem to be able to get very interested in anything.'

Visits were permitted between 1.30pm and 3.30pm and were restricted to 30 minutes. When he first arrived at the prison Danny was asked to list the visitors he expected to receive. He wrote down the names of his parents, sisters and brother-in-law, his aunt and uncle and one friend. The first name on his list was Gertrude Raven, but she never came.

Edward, Betty and Muriel visited Danny every day except Sunday, when visitors were not allowed to enter the prison, and his elder sister Sylvia and her husband, Danny's aunt and uncle and a couple of friends also made regular visits. But Edward and Betty were becoming overwhelmed by the press attention that followed them and a week after Danny's conviction Edward, Betty and Muriel moved out of their home in Edgware and checked into the Piccadilly Hotel near Euston Station, less than a mile from Pentonville, under an assumed name. Edward wrote to the prison Governor, saying that 'owing to the publicity and the effect it is causing upon my wife, I have found it essential to be removed from our present house'. From now on, he added, he and his family would visit Danny under the name of Rogers.

Two days after the verdict, a letter was delivered to the Postmaster General in London. Inside the handwritten envelope was another, marked for the attention of Mrs Gertrude Raven but with no address. The letter was postmarked Liverpool. It read:

> *So you believe in your husband – so do I, I'm the only bloke who nos the facts. I'll tell you about it, but this won't help him any as he'll hang like a man – him – not me.*
>
> *About 9.30, 10th of Oct, I spotted your dad's house as easy – no lights no answer to the door, so round to the back I goes. First winder I tries had the catch back so in I goes. I was going up the stairs when all of a sudden the front door opens and someone comes in – more than one there was. I edged up the stairs before they saw me out of harms way and waited, and soon they went out as I thought, as the lights was still on I thought as how it looked like they was coming back again. Anyway I had an idea to get out quik. I got too the front*

door quietly and opened it a bit to look out before quiten, when the dinin door opened and out walked an old guy. He came at me afore I could get out. As I pushed him along the hall he shouted to someone to call 999 so I had to hit him with my stick on the but and boled him over. I went to the old lady and dotted her one and she boled over to. Not liking any blood on my stick I picked up the aerial and hit em with it. The old lady lay quiet, the old man was harder, but I gave im a couple of extras to go on with. I took the aerial into the back kitchen. I was thinking how unlucky the old man was to open that door. That's why I had to do it, no witnesses to testify again me. Dead heroes are better than life witnesses. I then went up the stairs and as I was half way up someone came into the hall and went out quicker. So did I as the hall was lit up. I did not have the heart to put them out. I'm a chap as been in no trouble with the cops, touch wood, and I don't intend to be. I always work alone. That was a phony house to me, when the old man came at me in the hall I had no chance to close the front door. I thought of it when the chap walked in so easy. It could have been a cop for all I knew. Lucky me again.

Don't take this to the cops as they won't help you any. The think-nuts think he did it and you won't turn them from their duty. If you went to them they would say you wrote this. So keep away from 'em. I went to Birmingham after burning my togs. What a mess they were in. I wiped my pants before I came out, so as not to leave a trale. Thoughtful aren't I? No-one knows me here in a pool like Birmingham as I hass the cops innocent like. If they only knew. I sleep well, no dreams or anything like that. Your hubby must feel rotten in jael, wonder if he sleeps well.

When your hubby is hanged I will feel much easier anyway. He is doing me a good turn. I won't be able to attend the funeral either. Funny, isn't it?

I feel OK hope you are keeping the same to.

Good-bye until he is strung up and after.

The anonymous letter was the most dramatic of many pieces of new evidence, theories and confessions that emerged in the days after the verdict. While the Judge and jury at the Crown Court had felt that the case against Danny was hopelessly damning, it seemed that a significant proportion of the general public did not agree.

While many of the national newspapers had reported Danny's death sentence as an inevitable result of the overwhelming evidence against him, as far as the local papers were concerned there were still many unanswered questions. The *Hendon & Finchley Times* asked its readers to consider a number of points which, it said, had still not been properly addressed: What was Danny's motive? Why was the kitchen window of the Goodman's house open? What had happened in the bedroom and why was the money there left untouched? And what was the truth about the clotted blood on Danny's trousers?

The newspaper was not alone in voicing its doubts. Dozens of letters had begun to arrive at the Home Office from members of the public horrified at the verdict. 'Raven may have committed murder but who has proved it?' wrote an irate Donald Watson from Leicester. 'Are we to start a new half century by hanging people even before we have proved them guilty?

He was not alone in doubting the strength of the case against Danny. The Trolley family from Mitcham, South London, spoke for many when they wrote to express their 'horror that a jury could condemn a man to death on the grounds of circumstantial evidence alone, unsupported by motive or character'.

'The evidence on which this young man was convicted is indeed flimsy and certainly circumstantial,' wrote Mrs Fox from St John's Wood in London. 'It appears to me that the crime was committed by a burglar, who was perhaps already in the house when the Goodmans came home.

'I have spoken to many people about the case and not one of them expected the verdict to be guilty,' she continued. 'I understand that Raven is to appeal so I do beg you to spare the young man. He may have acted foolishly in burning his suit, but we do not always do the rational thing when shocked or frightened, as he would have been if innocent.'

'Although everything points to it, there isn't one iota of proof in this case, and I hope you will think hard before you allow such flimsy conjecture to send a man to the gallows,' wrote Josephone Callard from Liverpool. 'Everyone, that I know anyway, is amazed that he should have been found guilty on such slender evidence. Telling lies and unnatural reactions don't make a murderer.'

Donald Dickinson, writing from Wiltshire, said that Danny's only mistake was not to call the police when he found the Goodmans: 'All his lies from that moment sprung from a moment of panic. He sealed his fate, innocent or not. Does a normal man never panic? Is it unthinkable that he would?'

Mrs Willoughby, from Chelsea, felt that 'had this young man had the coolness and calmness, under all these circumstances, to have gone to the telephone and called the police, he would have seemed in my opinion, much more like someone who could do a murder. The jury weighted this against a middle aged man who arrived with two witnesses – to prove that he could not have done the murders – who did call the police.'

For many, enough doubt remained to warrant the Home Secretary granting a reprieve from the death sentence, as Mr Vernon of East London pointed out: 'After reading the case of Daniel Raven I feel, like many people I have discussed it with, the remote possibility that he is not the murderer. It would be a tragedy if this man was to die for a crime he may not have committed.'

The anonymous letter confessing to the Goodman murders and a sudden rush of 'new' evidence that was brought forward in the days after the verdict meant more work for the team of detectives in Edgware. The Liverpool letter was quickly dismissed as a fake but other theories and evidence put forward demanded closer inspection.

An Edgware fishmonger, Frederick Dadd, was convinced that the police were missing an important lead. Dadd had telephoned the police on that day following the murders to report an incident that he and his wife, Louisa, had witnessed the previous evening. The couple had been interviewed by DS Grout and a uniformed police constable at their home the following day but had refused to give a written statement. Dadd was now convinced that police were not taking what he saw seriously. In late November, after reading newspaper reports of the trial, Dadd wrote to Scotland Yard, complaining that the information he had given police had been withheld from Danny's defence team.

Dadd had told DS Grout on 11 October that he and his wife had been walking along the main road in Colindale, about four miles from Edgware, at about 9.30pm on the previous evening, when they saw a woman fall from a passing trolley bus. Two men got off the bus and approached the woman, who was sitting on the pavement, where they began arguing with her. One of them hit her several times across the face. Dadd said they went to the woman to see if they could help, but she told them that the men were her husband and brother and they [the Dadds] should mind their own business. He said the two men pulled the woman to her feet, continuing to argue loudly with her, but shortly afterwards left her alone on the pavement and jumped onto a number 140 bus that was heading towards Edgware.

DI Jack Diller was asked to look again into the incident in the wake of Dadd's complaint. Diller interviewed Dadd again on 4 December and was told the same story. Dadd refused again to provide a written statement and told Diller that he was happy to leave the matter in the hands of the police. In his report, DI Diller said DS Grout had made local inquiries in Colindale but was unable to find anyone who could confirm that the incident had happened and no separate complaint had been made to police.

DI Diller's report to the Chief Superindendent concluded that Dadd was 'a self-opinionated and very talkative type of individual and despite the verdict at the Central Criminal Court, formed on overwhelming evidence, is still firmly convinced in his own mind that Raven is innocent.' This, said Diller, was no doubt why he decided to write the letter.

'The incident referred to by Dadd has no use and little significance in this case,' concluded Diller. 'It appears to have been a family quarrel which occurred some four miles away from the scene of the murder. The only reason Dadd believes it may have some connection with the offence, is that when the two men left the scene of the quarrel they jumped on a bus travelling towards Edgware.'

While the feverish speculation continued, Sydney Rutter set to work on preparing Danny's appeal. Convicted men had the right of appeal against their conviction, but could not appeal against their sentence. If the appeal was successful the murder conviction would be quashed or reduced to a lesser offence. In other words, Rutter had to prove that the Crown's case or the trial was fundamentally flawed.

The immediate problem for the Ravens was how they were going to pay for the appeal. Edward's funds were all but exhausted – he had sold most of the family's belongings to pay the legal fees and had not spent a day's work at his latest business since his son was arrested, with the result that it was close to collapse. It was time to get creative.

On 10 December Sydney Rutter made one of his regular visits to see Danny at Pentonville. He had with him a document for Danny to sign, which instructed Rutter & Co to brief John Maude KC and Victor Durand to appear on his behalf at the hearing of his appeal. Since a prisoner was not permitted to sign any documents without the knowledge of the prison authorities or Home Office, the letter was checked and quickly passed on to the Governor, who read it with rising disgust. The second paragraph continued:

> *I further authorise you to act on my behalf and enter into any agreement or agreements which in your sole discretion may consider desirable for the sale of or granting of sole rights to any person or company, for the publication of my life story in any newspaper or other publication and of any photographs which may be in or come into your possession. I authorise you to give authority on my behalf for publication of the facts which I told you whilst I was awaiting trial in Brixton Prison regarding my life and the matters in connection with my defence, and any facts which you may have ascertained in connection with my defence from other persons.*
>
> *I leave entirely to your discretion the price which you are to ask and receive in connection with the sale of such rights and agree to ratify any arrangements which you may make in that connection. Any monies which you may receive in connection with the sale or granting of such rights shall be retained by you and utilised towards your costs and disbursements in connection with my defence and my appeal.*

Danny's access to his solicitor was already a touchy subject for the prison service because his defence team had asked for the original trial to be postponed on the grounds that Sydney Rutter had not been granted sufficient facilities to see Danny in Brixton prison. The prison Governor had explained that the problem was one of a shortage of staff and Danny's access to Rutter had not been deliberately restricted. Judge Cassels refused the application to postpone the trial but said that facilities would be provided for the solicitor to spend as much time as he liked with the prisoner from then on.

The Governor at Pentonville immediately sat down to write to the Home Office. In his letter he explained that at the time, his counterpart at Brixton prison had suspected that the real reason why the defence had asked for more time with Danny was to enable the solicitors to have ample time to get his life story from him, with a view to selling it to a paper for profit. 'It looks from this letter of authorisation as if this is precisely what happened,' he wrote, 'and that the facilities which were granted to the solicitor were in fact used for Raven to dictate to him his life story for subsequent sale to the newspapers. This is highly objectionable, and I think it is clear that the matter ought to be referred to the Law Society when this particular case has been disposed of.'

He added that since the letter included authority for the solicitors to act on appeal and since the harm had already been done in terms of gathering his life story, Danny should be allowed to sign Sydney Rutter's letter, which he did on 14 December. The Home Office decided not to approach the Law Society unless Danny's life story subsequently appeared in the press. It never did.

Chapter 11 – Day Seventy-one

The appeal in the case of Rex V Raven was lodged within two weeks of the verdict. In his official ground for appeal submission, Sydney Rutter concentrated almost entirely on Judge Cassels' summing up of the trial and evidence to the jury and he listed 17 separate instances where he felt Judge Cassels had misdirected the jury or failed to present the case for the defence adequately.

Starting with Dr Teare's evidence, Rutter argued that the Judge had ignored in his summing up the doctor's assertion that it was possible that Leopold was near the table or seated at it when he was attacked, and that if that was the case, he would expect to see blood on the attacker's coat cuff and on other parts of his clothing. The Judge had also failed to mention Dr Teare's evidence that all or part of the blood on Danny's trousers could have been caused by the wearer kicking into blood on the floor. 'The Learned Judge omitted this important evidence from the summing-up until reminded by the defence,' wrote Rutter, 'whereupon he gave an abbreviated and inaccurate version. Nor did he show that Dr Teare's evidence supported strongly the case that Daniel Raven had got the blood by an innocent visit to the deceased after an attack by a third person.'

Rutter continued that the Judge's summing up failed to put reasonably Danny's explanation that fear and panic cause him to run away from the house after finding the bodies, and had not drawn attention to evidence suggesting a good relationship between him and the Goodmans.

Rutter argued that the Judge had largely ignored the evidence of Detective Inspector Herbert Hannam and his previous dealings with Leopold and had 'wrongly prejudiced that part of the defence which went to show that Leopold Goodman had acted as a police informer, by comparing the evidence to fiction'.

Rutter added that the Judge had consistently failed to give 'proper weight' to evidence in Danny's favour, such as that there was no trace of blood found in the scraping taken from underneath his fingernails. The Judge had also failed to give credence to the defence's argument that another assailant could have committed the murders and got away without being spotted – or that it was possible that this attacker could have entered through the open window at the back of the house. And in adding to his summing up that comment that if there was another attacker he had brought no weapon into the house, the Judge had suggested to the jury that this attacker was extremely fortunate to find the television aerial to hand, even though there was evidence that the aerial had been seen in the hall of the Goodman's home several days before the murders, wrote Rutter.

The Judge, said Rutter, also ignored the defence's arguments that there was strong evidence that someone other than Danny had moved the mattress and left the bedroom in disarray. He had also dismissed the argument that there was time and opportunity for another assailant to enter the house and kill the Goodmans on the basis that there was not enough time for them to do so without them risk being seen. But, argued Rutter, if there was no time for another attacker to commit the murders, why assume that the same argument did not apply in Danny's case? After all, the defence's case was that Danny knew there was a high likelihood that he would be seen.

Most seriously, Judge Cassels had said in his summing up that Danny did not know whether Leopold was dead or not when he ran away from the house. In fact, Danny had said during his evidence that he believed Leopold to be dead. Rutter argued that the Judge had given a contradictory view of this point in his summing up – at one point he said Danny had sworn that 'I was not sure that he was dead', while a few minutes later he had said that Danny knew he was dead. 'This was prejudicial to the case in that the jury would have false material upon which they could be certain that [Danny] had contradicted himself in the witness box on this vital matter,' wrote Rutter.

Rutter's last point of appeal was more unexpected and concerned one of the jury. 'Bernard Stockman, a practising Jew,' he wrote, 'purported to take the juryman's oath as obligatory upon his conscience while uncovered and upon the New Testament, whereas such jurymen could only be sworn upon the Pentateuch or Old Testament.' The result, argued Rutter, was that Stockman was not tied by his conscience and in effect, Danny had been tried by 11 men rather than 12 – and in the case of murder, a unanimous verdict of 12 members of the jury is required.

On a cold Tuesday morning, 20 December, Danny was taken once again from the condemned cell in Pentonville to the Old Bailey to hear his appeal. Wearing the same brown overcoat he had worn at his trial, he sat in the jury box surrounded by four prison warders and screened from the rest of the court by a green curtain. He listened quietly as John Maude, took almost four hours to complete the arguments for appeal in front of three Appeal Court judges – the Lord Chief Justice Lord Goddard, Mr Justice Humphreys and Mr Justice Hilbery.

'Point after point in Daniel Raven's favour was not presented adequately to the jury,' Maude told the judges. The Crown had presented a formidable case against his client, he conceded, but that meant that the summing up was all the more important. 'In a case where the summing up is adverse to the accused it was of the utmost importance that he should have his case put adequately by the judge to the jury, and that Judge Cassels failed to do,' said Maude.

'The judge is not bound to make a speech for the defence,' replied Lord Goddard, 'nor is he bound to mention every argument put forward by counsel.'

Maude's final point to the judges was the case of Bernard Stockman, the Jewish juryman who had taken the oath on the New Testament with his head uncovered. It was a 'fantastic' idea, said Maude, to allow a practicing Jew to go into a jury box and swear an oath on the New Testament.

The Lord Chief Justice replied with thinly disguised fury. 'When he says "I swear by Almighty God", he is promising that the oath will be binding,' said Lord Goddard. 'You might be opening up the question of whether an atheist or an agnostic should not be sworn in.'

'Let it be quite understood that this court gives no countenance whatever to the suggestion that this court or any court has the right before a juryman is sworn to cross-examine him as to what is his religious belief or whether a particular form of oath is binding or not,' he continued. 'Of course, if you see an obvious Muslim or Chinaman walking into the box to be sworn, as you do in some courts, you would naturally ask him what form of oath he preferred to take; but in the ordinary way there is neither a duty nor, in my opinion, is there a right in the court to cross-examine people as to their religious belief. I can think of nothing worse than it would be for the presiding judge at a trial to say to jurors, in effect, which of you are Jews and which of you are Christians? It has never been done in these courts and I hope it will never be done.'

The clerk of the court handed Maude a letter and the judges waited while Maude read it through. 'I have not seen this before,' he told them. 'But of course my argument will be withdrawn.' The Director of Public Prosecutions, forewarned of the defence team's argument, had contacted Bernard Stockman's synagogue. The letter was from Rabbi Harris Swift, explaining that he had spoken with Stockman and confirmed that he considered the oath he had taken to be binding on his conscience.

Maude's arguments exhausted, it took just 15 minutes for the Lords to deliver their verdict. In almost every case of murder, said Lord Goddard, it was possible to put the judge's summing up under the microscope. In this case, apart from one instance where Judge Cassels had used the word 'some' instead of the word 'all' when talking about the blood found on his trousers, there were no grounds at all for saying that there had been misdirection to the jury. 'The summing up was unfavourable to Daniel Raven because the evidence was unfavourable to him,' said Lord Goddard. 'I would go so far as to say the evidence was overwhelming.'

Danny was the last person to be seen with the Goodmans and he was with them a short time before their death, he continued. When the battered bodies were found, the police had arrived at the house within a minute of being dialed and Danny had made four different statements to different people during the course of the evening. He had later admitted that those statements were entirely untrue. He had burnt his bloodstained clothes to conceal the damning evidence against him. 'What verdict could the jury have returned except the verdict that they did return?' asked Lord Goddard. The Law Lords were unanimous; the appeal was dismissed. A silent Danny was led away from the court and back to Pentonville.

Early the following morning the telephone rang in the hallway of a pub, *Help the Poor Struggler*, in Hollinwood, an unremarkable town outside Oldham. A small man of 44 with thinning hair picked up the receiver. 'Mr Pierrepoint?' asked a voice at the other end, 'would you be available on 6 January?'

Chapter 12 – Days Seventy-two to Eighty-six

In comparison to his time as a remand prisoner, Danny's life in the condemned cell at Pentonville was, ironically, comfortable. Daily newspapers and books were provided, as were a chess set, playing cards and dominoes. Warders guarding a prisoner in the condemned cell were encouraged to play parlour games with him in the belief that it occupied their time and improved their mental state. The stress placed on these warders – who lived so closely with the condemned man for weeks and sometimes months and had to deal with the daily reality of their emotions – was considerable and largely unacknowledged.

The warders could spend many hours talking to a condemned prisoner but were required to make notes of anything they said which might be an admission of guilt or could be constituted as new evidence in their case. Danny said nothing relating to his case but on 28 November one of his guards, FH James, asked to see the Prison Governor and told him that during breakfast that morning Danny had told him that while he was on the hospital ward at Brixton prison, he had been asked to join a planned escape attempt.

Danny said the escape had been planned by Donald Hume, who was in Brixton awaiting trial for the murder of Stanley Setty, and that two other prisoners on the hospital ward were involved. Hume told Danny that only prisoners on serious charges would make the attempt and asked Danny if he wanted to join them. Danny refused.

If Danny was telling the truth it seems he made the right decision because the plan seemed ambitious, to say the least. According to Danny, two of the prisoners intended to ambush the night patrol officer in the hospital bathroom and knock him out with a lump of concrete. The window bars would then be prised apart with a metal floor polisher and blankets used to allow the men could climb down to the ground. The outside prison wall would be scaled using a makeshift rope with a grappling hook at the end, made from the floor polisher. The men planned to steal a car once they made it over the prison wall and drive to Croydon aerodrome, where Hume, a qualified pilot, intended to fly a small plane to North Africa.

The prison Governor wrote a report summarising the conversation but noted that no escape attempt had been made. On 20 January 1950, Hume was found not guilty at the Old Bailey of Setty's murder but was sentenced to 12 years in prison for being an accessory to his death. When he was released eight years later, Hume confessed to a Sunday newspaper that he had, in fact, murdered Setty and had thrown his body from a plane.

In Pentonville, Danny's routine continued. He wrote letters regularly to his parents and sisters, to his aunt and uncle and occasionally, to friends. His meals came as usual from the prison kitchen and he was allowed, if he wished, a pint of beer or stout and 12 cigarettes a day. The prison Governor, the medical officer and chief officer visited him twice a day and he was given free access to the prison chaplain or a local rabbi on request. He was weighed regularly. Perhaps he realised that this was for the executioner's benefit.

The final power to grant a reprieve to Danny lay with the 67-year-old Home Secretary, James Chuter Ede. In the 17 days after Danny's appeal his legal team, his family and even total strangers made desperate efforts to persuade Chuter Ede to grant a reprieve. Their efforts were by no means futile, for history told them that the Home Office had little appetite for execution and was likely to commute a death sentence to life imprisonment if a persuasive enough reason could be found.

Successive Home Secretaries had granted reprieves for a wide number of reasons during the first half of the 20th century. Many condemned men and women were granted an automatic reprieve during the periods when the death sentence was under debate by Parliament, but others were saved for less diplomatic reasons. One man was reprieved because he only had one leg and the Home Office was unsure what the implications would be for the hanging process, while another was granted mercy because he had attempted suicide and it was argued that the old wound on his throat would reopen during the hanging and 'cause an unpleasant mess'. Very young or old prisoners were more likely to be reprieved, particularly if they were women, as was anyone who showed signs of mental illness after their conviction. Conversely, murderers who had used a gun or poison, or women who had displayed loose morals in the course of their crime, were less likely to be shown mercy.

The result was that while the only possible sentence for anyone convicted of murder in 1949 was death, execution was by no means a certainty. Of the 1,485 men and women who were sentenced to death during the 20th century, only 755 (or just over 49%) were executed. Women were far more likely to be reprieved than men and of the 145 women sentenced to death during the century, only 14 were hanged. While the reason behind a reprieve was never made public by the Home Office, reprieves were common enough to persuade supporters of any condemned man that there was still plenty of room for hope.

For Danny's legal team, the hope lay in persuading Chuter Ede that Danny's mental state threw enough doubt on his guilt or on his fitness to be executed to warrant a commutation of his sentence. In the last days of December Sydney Rutter and John Maude bombarded Home Office officials with evidence of Danny's mental fragility – evidence that could have altered the course of his trial had they been allowed to pursue it at the time.

Within hours of Danny's appeal being refused on Tuesday 20 December, John Maude went to the Home Office to meet with Chuter Ede and Sir Frank Newsam, the Undersecretary of State. Maude told the men that he was convinced that Danny was either "dotty" – by which he meant was suffering from a mental abnormality short of insanity – or else innocent of the murders.

Maude was armed with what he and Rutter thought was strong evidence about Danny's mental state, including the results of an EEG examination carried out on Danny just before his appeal, and medical and psychiatric records dating from years before the murders which suggested a long history of mental problems and raised the possibility that Danny could be an undiagnosed epileptic. Maude told Chuter Ede that there was also a history of mental abnormality in Danny's family and that two of his relatives, one on Danny's father's side and one on his mother's, had committed suicide in the past 30 years.

Maude added that he and two of his junior barristers had interviewed Danny for almost two hours about the events at Ashcombe Gardens and while none of them were usually inclined to automatically believe the stories told by the clients, all three had come away completely convinced that Danny was telling the truth. This suggested, said Maude, that he had either not murdered the Goodmans or if he had, had absolutely no memory of doing it. He offered a statement from an eminent doctor, who had suggested that, if Danny was mentally abnormal, the action of the Goodmans in refusing to allow him to stay with them after the birth of his first child could have been seen by Danny as an intolerable insult and thrown him into a frenzy of rage.

Maude's arguments were backed up by Sydney Rutter, who wrote to Chuter Ede to highlight a comment made by the Home Office in a memorandum to the recently appointed Royal Commission on Capital Punishment. The memo, which discussed factors taken into account when granting a reprieve, said: "When a murder is committed without premeditation as the result of some sudden excess of frenzy and the prisoner has previously had no evil animus towards the victim, commutation is often recommended. In cases of this kind it is sometimes necessary to give weight to the consideration that the prisoner, although not insane, is weak-minded or emotionally unstable to an abnormal degree. Account must also be taken of the character of the prisoner, of his relations with the deceased and of all the circumstances."

Chuter Ede told Maude that it was not up to him to retry Danny's case but he felt that the evidence he had offered warranted that a medical examination of Danny, which would assess whether he was sane and fit to be executed under the Criminal Lunatics Act of 1884, would be an appropriate course of action. Chuter Ede would also read a report summarising the investigation, trial and appeal, prepared by a Home Office civil servant, in making his decision of whether the execution should go ahead.

After Chuter Ede's meeting with John Maude, the Home Office appointed three doctors – Sir Norwood East, the Medical Commissioner of HM Prisons, Dr Hopwood, the medical superintendent at Broadmoor, and Dr Desmond Curran – to assess Danny at Pentonville under the Criminal Lunatics Act. The three men examined Danny at the prison hospital on Saturday 31 December and again on the following day. They also questioned the prison doctors who had treated him in Brixton and in Pentonville, the prison Governor and a Rabbi who had seen Danny daily since he arrived at Pentonville, and the team of warders who watched over Danny in his cell.

The conclusion of the three doctors was damning. They found Danny to be defensive and occasionally difficult, but in full control of himself and as far as they were concerned, in no way insane. His accounts of his attacks of sunstroke while in the RAF, they concluded, were 'unconvincing', and they disputed the suggestion that he suffered from epileptic blackouts. In fact, concluded Sir Norwood East in his report to Chuter Ede, Danny seemed to be of above average intelligence and well aware of his surroundings and the situation he found himself in. 'We do not consider that Raven was insane at the time of the crime or that he is insane now. He is probably an anxious and nervous type of man, but we do not believe that he is suffering now, or was suffering at the time of the crime from any minor mental abnormality which would justify us in making any medical recommendation,' he wrote. There were, he added, 'no sufficient grounds to justify interfering with the due course of law'.

On Sunday 2 January, Chuter Ede sat down to read the doctors' report, followed by the summary of the case prepared for him by a Home Office civil servant. The Home Office report was thorough and admirably unbiased, beginning with a summary of the events of 10 October through to Danny's arrest, the trial and the arguments put forward by Danny's defence team that the murders could have been carried out by a burglar or by someone harbouring a grudge against Leopold.

'The defence laid emphasis on the fact that Raven was on reasonably good terms with his wife's parents although he had frankly admitted from the start that there were some differences between them,' added the report. 'He had been taking his meals at the Goodman's house and had, for instance, left his shaving kit there. They had all been talking and laughing together at nine o'clock and what motive could there have been for Raven to have made this violent attack half an hour or so later?'

The report highlighted 'a number of rather odd features' about the case: 'Neither the prosecution nor the defence produced a very satisfactory explanation of the disturbance upstairs. If it was an attempt to suggest that there had been a burglar, it is odd that the money on the table by the bed was left untouched. Presumably this disturbance was done before the murder, since otherwise it seems improbable that the murderer would not have left some trace of blood on the stairs or in the bedroom. It is however odd, so far as bloodstains are concerned, to note that no traces of blood were found between the dining room and the front door, or between the dining room and the back window; even on Raven's own story he must have walked with bloodstained shoes from the dining room to the front door. We do not know definitely how it came about that the back window was open, and indeed it is difficult to suggest any reconstruction of the sequence of events which covers all the known facts.'

In spite of this, the report's conclusion was unambiguous: 'There can be no doubt, it seems to me, that the murders were committed by Raven,' wrote the nameless civil servant. 'The suggestion that there was a mysterious stranger in the house was pure theory and as regards the evidence given by Detective Inspector Hannam, it is to be observed that he said that he had never received information from Mr Goodman which in his view was likely to involve danger to Mr Goodman's life, and he also said that as far as he was aware no other living person knew that Mr Goodman had given him information. If the mysterious stranger came to the house intending to attack Mr Goodman, he did not bring any weapon with him for the purpose, or at any rate did not use that weapon, but made use of the television aerial which happened to be standing conveniently in the hall.

'The fact that Mr Goodman was apparently struck when sitting at the table would suggest that he was not surprised by an unknown person. The time schedule indeed hardly allows for the murder to have been committed by someone else. It is known that the Goodmans did not leave the nursing home until about 9.10pm, and that they were at the very least 15 minutes' drive away from their house. It is known that Alfred, on finding the bodies, telephoned the police at 10.02pm and that he must have been in the house for some minutes before that. In the intervening period, which could not have been more than half an hour and was probably less, it is suggested that an unknown individual, who was in the house for an unknown purpose, murdered Mr and Mrs Goodman by striking each of them a considerable number of blows with a weapon which he found in the house, and that he then washed the aerial, leaving it in the scullery sink, and made good his escape without leaving any trace behind him; and that Raven appeared on the scene and knelt by the bodies at least two minutes after the wounds had been caused and then left the house in a panic, driving away in time for his car to be clear of the scene by the time Alfred and his wife and daughter appeared. Apart from this, it is extremely odd that, if Raven's story is true, he should return to the Goodman's house 15 minutes after they had wished him goodnight and made it clear that they did not want him to stay there for the night.

'It is also odd that he should have made a number of untrue statements to the police, one of them when accompanied by a solicitor, and that he should change his story after he realised that the blood-stained clothing and shoes had been found. Finally, the jury evidently did not accept his explanation that on finding the bodies (Mr Goodman being then still alive) he rushed out of the house, instead of calling for assistance, and burned his clothes. Their conclusion, was that Raven's conduct in making a hurried departure from the house, destroying his clothes, washing his shoes and deceiving the police, was consistent with guilt.'

James Chuter Ede closed the report and after a moment, picked up his pen. He wrote across the front of the file: 'The law must take its course.' The execution would go ahead.

Public opinion on the case remained deeply divided. Chuter Ede's statement issued to the press that he would not grant a reprieve prompted a flurry of letters from the public to the Home Office and to national newspapers. A majority believed Danny was innocent or even if he was guilty, that he should not hang. But a significant minority vented their exasperation at what they saw as the steady eroding of the deterrent of capital punishment.

Between 22 December 1949 and 1 January 1950, thousands of people signed a petition for Danny's reprieve which had been organised by a 39-year-old Jewish mother of four, Fay Schein, whose husband ran a newsagent in St Pancras but who had no previous connection with the Ravens. On Sunday 2 January, surrounded by a small crowd of supporters and several newspaper reporters, Sydney Rutter handed the petition – which contained over 16,100 names – to the Home Office.

The petition was widely reported in the press and forced Chuter Ede to issue another statement, saying again that there were not sufficient grounds to grant a reprieve. 'You have the support of all intelligent people in not reprieving the murderer Daniel Raven,' wrote a Mr Jones from Liverpool in a letter to the Home Secretary the following day. 'The mentality of the

16,000 folks who signed for this mindless reprieve is a blot on our civilisation.'

Neither were some sections of the press impressed. 'A Home Secretary does not ignore public opinion in these cases,' wrote the *Sunday Pictorial*. 'Occasionally one has felt it right to commute a sentence in deference to a widely spread or strong local expression of public opinion. But a petition for which signatures were canvassed on dog tracks, football grounds and among Christmas shopping crowds could not be expected to carry much weight. In our opinion, the Raven petition constituted an emotional plea likely to embarrass an already over-burdened Minister.'

On the morning of Monday 3 January, James Chuter Ede caught a train from Paddington station to Devon, where he had arranged a series of meetings. Later that day John Maude sent a telegram to the Home Secretary, which eventually found Chuter Ede in Torquay. It read:

YOU KNOW HOW DEEPLY I FEEL UPON THE MATTER ABOUT WHICH YOU SAW ME AND I NOW BEG YOU TO GIVE EFFECT TO ALL THE LONG HISTORY OF THE MANS ABNORMALITY STOP SIMPLY CANNOT RID MYSELF OF A PROFOUND BELIEF IN IRRESPONSIBILITY IN THIS CASE WHICH I FOUND OVERWHELMING AND TERRIBLE

Within hours Maude received his reply:

RECEIVED AND CAREFULLY CONSIDERED YOUR TELEGRAPH BUT REGRET I AM UNABLE TO ALTER MY DECISION

The only hope now was that the Home Secretary would bow to public opinion if enough sympathy could be raised for Danny's plight. Late that same evening, Sydney Rutter called several journalists to his office in Great Winchester Street in a desperate attempt to whip up public support.

A *Daily Mirror* journalist described the scene: 'As an ancient London clock boomed out the strokes of midnight, it interrupted Mr Rutter's soft voice as, to a silent audience in his second-floor city office, he read doctors' statements which he claimed proved Raven was mad. Reporters had been invited hastily to his office at 11pm. Mr Rutter arrived 10 minutes later, his black overcoat damp with the drizzle that was falling outside.

'He led us into his office. But first he flicked an ornate table lamp which cast a soft light on his paper-littered desk and reflected from the dark wood-pannelled walls. From a black deed box he brought folder after folder. And then he started to read.'

Rutter spent more than an hour reading through a series of medical reports on Danny, from his time with the RAF to a report from the prison doctor at Brixton and a ground-breaking EEG examination carried out just before the appeal. Rutter spelled out the medical terms for the journalists and building a chain of evidence that, he said, showed that Danny was insane. 'If Raven hangs, I believe a terrible injustice will be done,' he told the journalists. 'From the test made by the EEG and other evidence it is clear that Raven is mentally abnormal. Every endeavour should be made to see that this man does not hang. It would be absolutely wrong.'

The journalists, though, were unmoved and while they were careful to respect Rutter's social standing as a solicitor, his entreaties fell on barren ground. 'Mr Rutter sacrificed a great deal of his valuable time [on Danny's defence],' commented the *Sunday Pictorial* the following day. 'Indeed, if it were possible for a man to be _too_ energetic in the interests of a murderer, Mr Rutter was that man. He made a great deal of noise, and all to no purpose.'

The paper took exception to Rutter's view that Danny's execution would be an injustice. 'It is utter nonsense to suggest that Mr Chuter Ede, a humane and kindly man, would abuse his tremendous and delicate trust,' it said. 'No doubt Mr Rutter did his job right. It is a pity that his protests concerned such a hopeless cause.'

On the afternoon of Tuesday 4 January, Danny was told that the Home Secretary would not grant a reprieve and that his execution was set for 9am on Friday morning. The prison doctor, who saw him every day, recorded in his notes that Danny's mood that day was 'sullen' and that he 'remained seated when visited'.

A few miles away at the Home Office, Sir Frank Newsam was receiving two visitors. The Chief Rabbi Israel Brodie introduced Sir Frank to Rabbi Myer Lew, who had seen Danny regularly at Pentonville since his conviction. The Chief Rabbi told Sir Frank that Rabbi Lew had come to him the previous evening in some distress, saying that he had become increasingly troubled about Danny's case. Rabbi Lew had begged him to arrange a meeting with the Home Secretary so he could put his views across.

Rabbi Lew told Sir Frank that in all the conversations he had had with Danny over the past few weeks, Danny had never given him the slightest reason to suspect that he was aware that he held any responsibility for the murders. It ought to be possible, he added, to find extenuating circumstances to warrant a reprieve. Sir Frank asked him what those circumstances might be. 'Right now, I can't think of any,' replied the Rabbi. Sir Frank thanked the men but explained that the final decision for a reprieve lay with the Home Secretary, who had concluded that there were no grounds to stop the execution.

On Wednesday 4 January, with all other options seemingly exhausted, Betty Raven sent two telegrams, one to King George VI at Buckingham Palace and one to Queen Elizabeth, who was at the Sandringham Estate in Norfolk:

I AM THE MOTHER OF DANIEL RAVEN NOW AWAITING EXECUTION ON FRIDAY MORNING FOR MURDER STOP THE HOME OFFICE DOCTORS HAVE FOUND HIM TO BE AN EPILEPTIC STOP HIS RAF AND OTHER DOCTORS REPORTS AND MEDICAL RECORDS PROVE HIM TO BE WRONG IN THE MIND NO MOTIVE WAS EVER SUGGESTED BY THE CROWN STOP HIS WIFE HAD THEIR FIRST BABY ONLY FOUR DAYS BEFORE THE MURDER STOP PLEASE I BEG OF YOUR MAJESTY AS A MOTHER TO SAVE THE LIFE OF MY ONLY SON AGED 23 STOP PLEASE INTERCEDE STOP I AM ONE OF YOUR LOYAL SUBJECTS

The telegram was passed to the Home Office. The following day Sir Frank Newsam wrote to Sydney Rutter saying that the Home Secretary had again reviewed the circumstances of the case but 'regrets he cannot find any grounds on which he would feel justified in modifying his decision'.

On Thursday 5 January Danny sat down and wrote four last letters: to his mother, to Muriel, to his sister Sylvia and her husband, and one to Sydney Rutter. At 2pm that afternoon he received his last visit from his parents. His mother told him that his photograph, dressed in his RAF uniform, would remain by her bed forever. 'Keep cheerful,' he told her as they led him away.

Chapter 13 – Day Eighty-seven

Shortly before 4pm on Thursday 5 January, Albert Pierrepoint and his assistant, Harry Kirk, slipped quietly into Pentonville. Pierrepoint was dedicated to his unusual profession and took his responsibilities extraordinarily seriously; even so, the time of his arrival at Pentonville was enshrined in Home Office guidelines. These were set out in the 1930s following, the story goes, a number of unfortunate incidents including an occasion when an intoxicated executioner attempted to hang the prison chaplain. The guidelines laid down by the Home Office required Pierrepoint to arrive at the prison no later than 4pm on the day before the execution and to remain there until he had permission to leave. The guidelines also limited him to a pint of malt liquor at dinner.

Pierrepoint arrived on time at Pentonville not because of any legal obligation but because he felt the preparation time was necessary. In a controversial article that appeared in the *Empire News and Sunday Chronicle* on 18 March 1956, that Pierrepoint denied contributing to but which still contained details that could only have come from the executioner or a close confident, he was quoted as saying: 'I still find that I need all that time, for it is on the night before the execution that I make my calculations.' Once at the prison, Pierrepoint and Kirk were taken to a room overlooking the exercise yard, where they could see the condemned man walking below. Danny would never have known that Pierrepoint was watching him and was estimating (generally, with pinpoint accuracy) his height as well as his build and likely muscular strength. With this and Danny's weight, he calculated the length of the rope that he would use the following morning:

The heavier the man, the shorter the drop; the weaker his neck, the shorter the drop.

The entry in Pierrepoint's diary for that day simply says:

Daniel Raven   *age 23*   *height 5'9"*   *weight 144lbs*   *drop 7'9"*

In his autobiography Pierrepoint describes the execution chamber in Pentonville as 'spotlessly clean and trim', which had surprised him on his first viewing as he had been expecting something more 'dark and neglected, like a tomb'. It was set in a three-storey set of cells halfway along Pentonville's A Wing, next door to Danny's cell. The green-walled room on the first floor contained the scaffold with its two hinged doors, measuring eight and a half feet by two and a half feet. A long lever to the side of the scaffold released the bolts and plates that supported the doors. Above the scaffold, two parallel beams ran across the cell at ceiling height, with three chains falling between them. The chains were attached to a much larger beam in the cell on the level above. The noose was attached to the central chain for a single execution, or to each of the outer chains in the event of a double execution. Below the scaffold doors was the ground floor cell, which served as the pit of the execution chamber into which the hanged prisoner would fall.

While Danny remained in the exercise yard outside, Pierrepoint and Kirk set out the rope in the execution chamber, attached it to the chain, tied a sandbag weighing slightly more than the condemned man, to the end of the rope and pulled the lever. It made a heavy clunk as it dropped. The pair left the sack swinging silently in the night.

After a light supper Pierrepoint retired to his room in the gatehouse of the prison overlooking Caledonian Road. Outside, he could hear the faint sound of passers-by and a small number of anti-capital punishment protestors waiting outside. As the executioner slept, Danny's father Edward was making a last, frantic effort to save his life.

At 10pm that evening, a few miles away on Victoria Embankment, Edward, Sydney Rutter and a *Daily Express* reporter, Vargas Gardner, turned up at Scotland Yard demanding to see a senior officer. The men were taken to see Chief Inspector Henry Stoddard, the senior officer on duty, and told him that they had uncovered new information about Danny's case which could warrant postponement of the execution. Stoddard sat down with the three men and took statements from each in turn.

Gardner told the Inspector that he had started his night shift at the *Daily Express* at 6pm and been assigned that evening, by the Night News Editor, to follow up on the Home Secretary's refusal to reprieve Danny. Gardner had been a regular visitor to the Drummond Street flat of Fay Schein, who had organised the petition to save Danny over previous days and he had arranged to meet her and Edward at the flat at 9pm that evening. But while waiting for the meeting in a pub on Warren Street nearby, he had met by chance a contact he knew from another story. He told the man, a used car dealer called Eddie Noble, that he was writing a story about Danny's Raven's execution and was due to meet Edward Raven that evening.

'It's a pity this fellow should swing,' said Noble, before hinting that he knew more about the case than had appeared in the papers. He told Gardner that on the previous Saturday evening, New Year's Eve, he had seen seven letters – he refused to say where – either written by or addressed to Edward Raven that had been sent from the Majestic Hotel in Cannes. Five were demands for payment due on foreign currency transactions and the remaining two were threats relating to the same payments. He added that Edward Raven knew of the existence of the letters and sometime after Danny's conviction in November, had agreed to meet the mysterious holder of them in a pub, but had not kept the appointment. Gardner asked Noble to wait in the pub and he would bring Edward to see him.

When Gardner and Edward returned to the Goat and Compass at 9.30pm, Noble had already left, but Gardner quickly found him in the Marquis of Cornwallis on Warren Street. Noble repeated his story about the letters to the two men and Edward pleaded with him for the name and address of the man who held the letters. Noble was reluctant but, said Gardner, eventually gave a telephone number – North 4165 – and a name, Aron Ellison.

What is particularly curious about the meeting between Edward and Chief Inspector Stoddard that evening is that, even with his son's execution hours away, Edward could not bring himself to be entirely candid about his involvement in the events that were under discussion. Edward backed up Gardner's recollection of the conversation with Noble in the Marquis of Cornwallis but told Stoddard that he knew nothing about the letters or about any appointment that had been made in order for him to see them. When his statement was read back to him by the Chief Inspector, Vargas Gardner turned to Edward and said, 'What about the currency transactions?' But Edward merely shrugged and said, 'There's no need to mention that.'

Just after midnight, Stoddard telephoned Chief Superintendent Peter Beveridge at his home in Edgware and told him of the developments. Beveridge told him that he had already heard of Edward Raven's involvement in currency transactions and had asked Chief Inspector Jamieson of D Division to stand by to make the necessary enquiries. Stoddard telephoned Jamieson, summarising what Edward and Gardner had said, and asked a junior detective to immediately take copies of their statements to him.

Aron Ellison was taken to Albany Street Police Station from his flat in Lorraine Mansions, N7, in the early hours of 6 January. He described himself as a 'manufacturer's agent', who sold property and goods on a commission basis. He told Jamieson that about 18 months previously he had received from an acquaintance he named as Tovey a collection of documents signed by or sent to Edward Raven. These included an IOU for 157,000 French Francs signed by Edward, a number of letters between Edward and a Mr Grey of the Hotel Majestic in Cannes discussing a loan made to Edward, and two copies of the hotel register which showed cash deposits made to Edward, apparently part payments of the Fr 157,000 loaned. Two days after receiving these documents he had contacted Edward for the first time and arranged to meet him at a club in Central London. Tovey, he said, lived in France and gave him the documents while on a short visit to London, asking him to contact Edward and arrange for repayment of the money.

The meeting with Eddie Noble was an astonishing coincidence but ultimately, nothing to do with Danny's case. The most likely explanation is that Tovey and Ellison, realising Edward's connection to Danny from the newspaper reports after the trial, attempted to blackmail Edward with the letters, and failed. Even so, the meeting was more than enough to persuade an increasingly agitated Edward that evidence that could clear his son's name could come to light at any moment. Back at Fay Schein's flat as the time approached midnight, Edward called the night news desks of several papers and summoned as many reporters as possible to the flat, saying that new and important information had come to light.

The reporter from *The Star* described how a dozen newspaper men sat in the room above a newsagent's shop 'in dingy Drummond Street'. Edward looked 'breathless and pale' as he told them of the 'startling, world-shattering evidence' that had come to light. 'We have only a matter of hours to save a life,' he said. Beside him, Fay Schein 'served coffee and biscuits and later paced up and down, dressed in black, hands outstretched with fingers crossed.'

As the reporters watched, Edward telephoned Herbert Hannam, the police inspector who had questioned him about his currency dealings years before. Hannam's wife answered the telephone and Edward told her that he had to speak to her husband 'on a matter of life and death'. Mrs Hannam told him that her husband was away and would not return home until the weekend.

In fact, Herbert Hannam was at home, upstairs in the bath. Hannam said later that he had discussed with his wife the possibility that Edward might contact him before Danny's execution and they had agreed that if he did, she would say that her husband was away in the north of England was not due to return until 7 January.

At 3.25am, his enquiries complete, Jamieson telephoned Chief Inspector Stoddard at Scotland Yard. Eddie Noble and Aron Ellison had been interviewed, he said, and he had concluded that while Ellison did appear to have documents in his possession that related to currency transactions between Edward and a Mr Gray of the Hotel Majestic, he was convinced that the documents had no bearing on the Goodman's murders. Jamieson added that the Assistant Police Commissioner, Hugh Young, had said that Sydney Rutter should be told of his conclusions immediately.

Just before 4am, with only a few reporters remaining at the Drummond Street flat, Edward took the call from Inspector Stoddard which told him that his son's execution would not be postponed. An hour later, Sydney Rutter and Edward left the flat. 'There is nothing more we can do,' Fay Schein told the reporters.

Chapter 14 – Day Eighty-eight

As the sun rose on the morning of Friday 6 January, Danny's mother and sisters sat desolate with a small collection of friends and neighbours in the kitchen of Sylvia's home in Edgware.

In Pentonville, all staff leave had been cancelled. Early in the morning all prisoners in A Wing, apart from Danny, were moved into B Wing or into the prison reception area. All catering staff were locked into the kitchen, the exercise yards emptied, the main gate frozen and all movement between prison buildings was stopped until 10am. A crowd of about 200 people had gathered in the biting wind outside the prison gates, some of them women with shopping bags and a small number of children. A few plain clothes police officers mingled with the crowd, who watched as a prison guard pinned a notice to the front gate, confirming that the execution of Daniel Raven would be carried out at 9am.

With Danny sitting with his warders only yards away, Pierrepoint and Kirk returned silently to the execution chamber just after 7am. They removed the sandbag, closed and secured the trap doors and fitted the safety pin into the lever. A good executioner, in Pierrepoint's view, hardly spoke a word before a hanging. In the pit below the drop, a stretcher had been placed at one side.

Danny was the first of the 18 men who were to be hanged in Britain's prisons in 1950. 'An execution should be a solemn and dignified thing,' said Pierrepoint in 1956. 'It is only by preserving the doomed man's dignity that we can keep our own.'

The importance of speed and efficiency during the condemned man's last moments had been drilled into Pierrepoint during his training at

Pentonville. From the prison's point of view speed was essential since it minimised the chances of the condemned man (or woman, although Pierrepoint always claimed that female prisoners were always braver than men in their final moments) struggling or collapsing. Pierrepoint agreed, but because he felt that the execution should be carried out as humanely as possible. He had been horrified when he was asked to carry out an execution of a US prisoner at an army camp in Oxfordshire during the war by the sight of the condemned man standing with the noose around his neck for nine minutes while the charges against him were read out. In Pierrepoint's view the process should be as quick as possible and, on average, fewer than 10 seconds elapsed between his entering the condemned man's cell and pushing the lever to drop the scaffold doors.

Pierrepoint had quickly perfected the technique that he had learned from his father, his uncle and through his week of extensive training at Pentonville. The prisoner's hands were strapped behind his back and he was led to the scaffold. The white cap was drawn over the prisoner's head, followed by the rope. The 'noose' section of the rope looped through a pear-shaped metal eye at its end. This eyelet was always adjusted to fall to the left of his neck, ensuring that at the drop the noose would turn a quarter circle clockwise, finishing under the chin, throwing the neck back and breaking the spine. If the noose was placed at the right of the neck the rope would tightened at the top of the spine, throwing the prisoner's head forward and resulting in a slow death by suffocation or strangulation. If Pierrepoint got it right, death would be instantaneous and painless, where before, hanging had resulted in a slow and agonising death. In the Middle Ages, wealthy condemned men would pay 'hangers on' to rush forward and pull on their legs with their entire weight in order to speed up their death.

The lever that operated the trap doors, similar to that used by railway signalmen to adjust the points, was to the left of the prisoner and when the doors were closed it sloped towards the drop. Executioners were told to move straight to the lever, pull out the safety pin and push it upwards, rather than take the time to walk around it and pull it from behind. 'Pull down the cap, adjust the noose, dart to your left, crouching to withdraw the safety pin, push lever, drop: Cap, noose, pin, lever, drop.'

At 8.30am Rabbi Lew arrived at Danny's cell and sat with him and two warders for the final half hour. In the remaining three wings the prisoners were at their regular work. The prison clock, which normally chimed every hour, had been disconnected so the execution hour would pass unnoticed by inmates.

Danny's warders entered through the main cell door, direct from the corridor. There was another door in Danny's cell which led to a small, empty chamber. He would use this door only once. A few short steps across this room and through a second door would bring Danny to the scaffold.

At five minutes to nine Pierrepoint was told that the Under-Sheriff had gone to the Governor's office, his signal to make his way to the condemned cell and wait outside, a leather strap in one hand. A few moments later a small party walked slowly along the metal gangway lining the first floor of A Wing – the Governor, the Under-Sheriff of Middlesex George Weston, a prison doctor and a small number of senior prison officers. They paused outside the door next to the condemned cell; the entrance to the execution chamber. At a sign from one of the prison officers, they went in.

The corridor empty, a prison officer unlocked the door to the condemned cell and Pierrepoint, followed by Harry Kirk, walked through.

It was not unusual for the condemned man to instinctively offer his hand to the approaching Pierrepoint in greeting. Pierrepoint did nothing to discourage this as it allowed him to take the arm and quickly draw it to the back of the prisoner's body where he could strap the hands together. Danny was ushered quickly by Pierrepoint and two warders through the second cell door, across the antechamber and onto the scaffold. Pierrepoint made sure Danny's toes were aligned with a chalk 'T' drawn onto the platform, the arches of his feet directly over the crack in the doors. Do what I tell you, Pierrepoint told him, and you won't be hurt. If Danny's weight was incorrectly distributed over the doors, he would be thrown forward or backwards when the traps fell open. If he 'toed the line', as the expression became known, his death would be painless.

Two warders stood on planks placed across the doors of the drop, holding Danny firmly on each side with one hand between his ribs and upper arm. Behind him, Kirk fastened a leather strap around his ankles. In his autobiography Pierrepoint describes these last moments:

> As the executioner, it has fallen to me to make the last confrontation with all the condemned. It is I who have looked them last in the eyes, whether there has been popular agitation for their reprieve, or for the reverse on the boiling-oil principle that 'hanging's

too good for them', or whether they have been entirely abandoned by public opinion so that any grounds for severity or mitigation of treatment have just not been canvassed. And it is at that moment, with their eyes on mine, and all the official witnesses huddled in a corner behind them, that I have known that any previous emotional involvement I may have had with them is to be regretted. There is only a final relationship which matters; in Christianity this is my brother or sister to whom something dreadful must be done, and I have always tried to be gentle with them, and to give them what dignity I could in their death.

Pierrepoint was neatly dressed, with what appeared to be a white handkerchief in his breast pocket. Danny may have noticed it. He may have wondered why Pierrepoint reached for it as he was standing on the scaffold. Before he had a chance to register, the white hood was pulled over his head. Next the rope. Tightened slightly to the left of his chin. Pierrepoint moved away. The doors fell open and it was over.

Chapter 15 – Life and Death

That Danny was hanged at all was, to some extent, a case of unlucky timing. In 1948, only eight executions were carried out after hangings were suspended altogether for eight months while Parliament debated whether the death sentence should remain a feature of the legal system. The debate concluded that the death sentence should remain for the time being and the hangings resumed in November 1948. But the debate continued and even as Danny faced Pierrepoint, a committee of MPs was considering the future of the death penalty in the UK.

Two months after Danny died, the hanging of another man at Pentonville, Timothy Evans, would mark the beginning of the end of the death penalty in the UK. Evans was hanged on 9 March by Albert Pierrepoint for the murder of his wife and baby daughter at their rented flat at 10 Rillington Place in Notting Hill, West London. Evans' conviction was largely based on the testimony of another tenant in the building, John Christie. In 1953, Christie was executed for the murder of his own wife and the investigation revealed that Christie was a serial killer with necrophiliac tendencies, responsible for at least seven murders, including Timothy Evans' wife. Evans received a posthumous pardon in 1966.

By the time Danny met Pierrepoint for the first and last time, a concerted campaign to end capital punishment for murder offences had already been underway for 20 years. The majority of the public supported capital punishment on the basis that they believed it was an effective deterrent but cases such as Timothy Evans' added strength to the growing minority campaigning loudly for its abolition.

In 1930 a House of Commons Select Committee had recommended by a narrow majority that capital punishment for peace-time crimes be suspended as an experiment for five years. The Committee's recommendation was ignored. In 1938 a similar motion was carried in the House of Commons but again ignored and in 1939 a proposed amendment to the Criminal Justice Bill that would have suspended executions was defeated in the Commons.

In April 1948 the Labour MP Sydney Silverman, a long-time campaigner against capital punishment, introduced a private members' bill to suspend the death penalty for five years. The House of Commons voted narrowly in favour, prompting the Home Secretary James Chuter Ede to reprieve all murderers until the future of the Bill was known. 26 condemned men were granted a reprieve between March and October 1948, when the House of Lords rejected the Bill and executions resumed.

In the wake of the Bill, Chuter Ede set up a Royal Commission in 1949 to consider whether capital punishment for murder should be limited or modified. The Commission would not report its recommendation for another four and a half years.

The Commission concluded that while there were ethical objections to capital punishment, it should be retained in the UK unless there was strong public support for its abolition. Executions continued but in gradually reducing numbers. 15 people were executed in the country in 1954 and 12 in 1955. When Silverman introduced his Bill into the House of Commons again in 1955, executions were suspended once more and 49 condemned prisoners were granted a reprieve between August 1955 and July 1957.

In 1957 the Homicide Act was passed into law, which introduced a distinction between capital homicide and non-capital crimes. The Act specified six categories of murder that were punishable by death: murder by shooting or through the cause of an explosion; murder in the course of theft; murder while resisting arrest; murder of a police officer; murder of a prison officer by a prisoner; and the second of two murders committed on separate occasions. The Act also introduced the concept of diminished responsibility as a defence to murder.

The new categories of murder and the introduction of manslaughter reduced the number of hangings even further and between 1960 and 1964, 17 people in total were executed. The last men to be executed for murder in the UK, Peter Allen and Gwynne Evans, were hanged simultaneously, Allen at Liverpool's Walton Prison and Evans at Strangeways in Manchester, at 9am on 13 August 1964.

In 1965 Sydney Silverman introduced his Bill once more and it was voted through by a large majority in both the House of Commons and House of Lords to become the Murder (Abolition of Death Penalty) Act. The Act suspended the death penalty in England, Wales and Scotland for five years, and replaced it with a mandatory life sentence. The Act was made permanent in December 1969.

Pierrepoint kept his opinions on capital punishment largely to himself until his 1974 autobiography, *Executioner: Pierrepoint*, in which he revealed that over time his views had changed dramatically:

> *During my 25 years as executioner, I believed with all my heart that I was carrying out a public duty. I conducted each execution with great care and a clear conscience. I never allowed myself to get involved with the death penalty controversy.*
>
> *I now sincerely hope that no man is ever called upon to carry out another execution in my country. I have come to the conclusion that executions solve nothing, and are only an antiquated relic of a primitive desire for revenge which takes the easy way and hands over the responsibility for revenge to other people.*
>
> *It is said to be a deterrent. I cannot agree. There have been murders since the beginning of time, and we shall go looking for deterrents until the end of time. If death were a deterrent, I might be expected to know. It is I who have faced them last. I have been amazed to see the courage with which they take that walk into the unknown. It did not deter them then, and it had not deterred them when they committed what they were convicted for. All the men and women whom I have faced at that final moment convinced me that in what I have done I have not prevented a single murder.*
>
> *And if death does not work to deter one person, it should not be held to deter any...The trouble with the death penalty has always been that nobody wanted it for everybody, but everybody differed about who should get off.*

Today, murder carries a mandatory life sentence but what 'life' means depends on the severity of each individual case and, to a lesser extent, on the circumstances of the defendant. The extent of the 'life tariff', which sets the minimum time that the convicted prisoner must spend in prison before he or she becomes eligible for parole is set by the sentencing judge, with the help of guidelines provided by the Home Office.

Some very rare cases are considered to be so serious that they warrant a 'whole life tariff' and these tend to include the murder of two or more people where each murder involves: a substantial degree of premeditation or planning; the abduction of the victim; sexual or sadistic conduct; a murder carried out for the purpose of advancing a religious, political or ideological cause; or carried out by someone who had previously been convicted of murder.

If the sentencing judge takes the view that the case does not warrant a whole life tariff, the next starting point is a 30-year sentence. These tend to include cases such as: the murder of a police officer or prison officer in the course of their duty; a murder involving a gun or explosives; a murder carried out for gain, such as during a robbery; a murder intended to obstruct or interfere with the course of justice; a murder that is racially or religiously aggravated or aggravated by sexual orientation; or one that would normally warrant a whole-life tariff but which was carried out by someone under the age of 21. In Danny's case, his offence would fall into this 30-year tariff bracket.

Once the judge has determined the starting point for the sentence, the next stage is to take into account any aggravating or mitigating factors. Aggravating factors include premeditation, the vulnerability of the victim, the degree of suffering inflicted on the victim, the abuse of a position of trust, and concealment, destruction or dismemberment of the body. Mitigating factors that might result in a reduced sentence include: an intention to cause injury rather than kill; a lack of premeditation; provocation that was not serious enough to be a defence to murder; and if the offender suffered from any mental disorder or mental disability which lowered his degree of culpability, although not to the degree that it afforded a defence to murder.

This suggests that the most likely outcome had Danny been found guilty of murder today would be a 'life' sentence of between 20 and 25 years. But there are two questions still to answer: Did Danny do it? And if he did, was it really murder?

Chapter 16 – Beyond Reasonable Doubt

In 1949 the Metropolitan Police investigated 57 murders. In the 12 months to the end of March 2009, Homicide and Serious Crime Command – the division of the Metropolitan Police that deals with most of the murder investigations in the capital – investigated 130 cases. If cases investigated over the same period by Child Protection Command and by Operation Trident, which deals with gun crime in the black community, are taken into account, the figure rises to 156. In the intervening years the population of London has decreased slightly.

There are complex reasons behind the increase in the murder rate in London – gun crime and drug and gang-related incidents are a relatively modern phenomenon, but it is also true to say that advances in pathology and toxicology mean that unexplained deaths that may not have been identified as murder in 1949 are far more likely to be picked up (and added to the statistics) today. But conversely, the advances in medicine and improvements to the emergency services – particularly the introduction of highly-trained mobile paramedics – mean that a victim with a life-threatening injury is more likely to survive today than in 1949.

The success rate of the Metropolitan Police in solving murder cases in 1949 was between 96% and 97%. In 2009, it is 95%. But while many of the procedures involved in a murder investigation have survived, advances in technology and forensic techniques mean that the methods involved have changed considerably. Advanced forensic techniques such as DNA testing make it possible to identify a murderer with far greater statistical certainty. Improvements in pathology and ballistics mean that it is more often possible to identify the weapon used in a crime from the victim's injuries, even down to the exact make of gun or type of knife. The movements of suspects and victims in modern-day London are also much easier to track, thanks to our habit of using mobile phones, smart technology such as Oyster cards on the London Underground, and the prevalence of CCTV and traffic cameras.

These advancements mean that murder investigations are more thorough than in 1949, but also considerably more labour-intensive and time-consuming. The detective work that underpins a modern investigation, though, remains unchanged. Many of the techniques and processes employed by DCI Tansill and his men during the investigation into the Goodman murders can still be seen today, albeit in a more modern guise.

The Goodman murder investigation was run by an extraordinarily small team by modern standards – DCI Tansill led the investigation and reported regularly to his District Chief Superintendent. The next most senior officer, DI Jack Diller, would have been involved in several other cases at the same time but played a vital role in the Goodman investigation, interviewing Danny and discovering his burnt suit while searching his house. Below DI Diller two Detective Sergeants, DS Grout and DS Erskine, were assigned tasks of responsibility such as interviewing potential witnesses and taking charge of exhibits. The team was supplemented by four Detective Constables, depending on who was on shift at a particular time, and PC Eddie Barrett, DCI Tansill's trusted driver.

DCI Tansill's team was small for a reason. Complex investigations such as a murder enquiry generate an enormous amount of information, evidence and paperwork. Modern-day murder teams use computer technology to store, cross-reference and share information. The 1949 team had no such benefit and the success of an investigation depended on a large extent on the senior officers' ability to remember and recall vital pieces of information. The wider the information was spread, as it would be if the investigating team was larger, the more likely it became that important clues would be missed. For this reason, the senior officer, DCI Tansill, played an active part in the investigation, arriving at the scene within an hour of the bodies being discovered and interviewing Danny when he was identified as the key suspect.

A modern-day DCI takes more of a project management approach and is responsible for organising and overseeing an investigation and setting the strategy, but does not play a hands-on role. Typically, a DCI appoints two or three Detective Inspectors to a murder investigation (each will be working on a number of investigations simultaneously), who perform many of the tasks that DCI Tansill undertook himself in 1949. Below the Detective Inspectors, a number of Detective Sergeants will run specific parts of the investigation.

A DCI taking charge of a similar murder investigation today would assign between 20 and 30 officers to the case initially, and after two or three days may reduce or increase that number, depending on the progress of the investigation. In the most complex cases up to 200 officers can be involved and most would have distinct and separate roles compared with the multi-taskers of the 1949 team. One Detective Sergeant, for example, is appointed as office manager and is solely responsible for running the software for the investigation, while another will act as liaison with the forensic specialists and another will be assigned as exhibits officer and he or she alone will have responsibility for recording, storing and transporting exhibits.

The Edgware team all knew each other well and most worked within a small geographical area for most of their police career. PC Charles Hill, the first constable to arrive at Ashcombe Gardens that night, was a few months away from retirement after more than 25 years with the police force in Edgware. DI Diller and DCI Tansill were very well-known faces in the area and, both with 24 years on the force at the time of the murders, had spent the bulk of them at S Division.

This tendency for detectives to remain in the same geographical area throughout their career meant that senior officers stored a huge amount of local knowledge which they were able to pass down to newer recruits. This localised approach to policing has steadily died out in London, partly because high property prices eventually meant that living near a central London police station became an unrealistic option. As recently as the early 1980s detectives working in the central London divisions were required to live within 25 miles of Charing Cross but that has been replaced with a travel allowance that offers free transport within 100 miles of central London. The result is that detectives in a particular division need not live locally, or indeed near each other, and the historical precedent of handing local knowledge down from generation to generation has been broken.

The knowledge held by investigating officers was all the more crucial in 1949 because the success of an investigation could depend on them remembering a comment or spotting a discrepancy in a witness statement. Years before computers would make the managing of large amounts of information relatively simple, detectives had only instinct and memory to rely upon. Police notes and witness statements were taken by hand and typed up in triplicate and all information gathered during an investigation was recorded on a card index system, which were stored in hundreds of filing drawers at each police station. Aside from the storage problems, information overload was a serious hazard for detectives.

Modern technology has greatly reduced the chance of missing a vital link during a large-scale investigation. HOLMES (Home Office Large Major Enquiry System), a Microsoft Windows-based data management program, was introduced in the 1980s in the wake of the Yorkshire Ripper investigation when it emerged that Peter Sutcliffe, later convicted of the murders, had been stopped on several occasions by police in different districts before being arrested. The original HOLMES system, which was used for all major incidents from 1986, was an enormous administrative step forward as it allowed for the easy filing of large amounts of information. It was less useful, though, in mining the data on the system to allow detectives to share information between all police forces in the UK and link separate incidents. In October 1999 an upgraded system that did just this, HOLMES 2, was tested in the field for the first time during the Paddington rail crash, in which 31 people were killed and more than 500 injured.

In a modern-day murder investigation, every relevant action taken and piece of evidence gathered is recorded on HOLMES 2, from witness descriptions and statements to fingerprints and voice recordings. A reasonably straightforward homicide investigation will result in 12,000 separate entries and more complicated investigations easily reach 50,000 entries. Once the information is input into the system it can be accessed in seconds and detectives can also perform detailed searches to identify links between witnesses, suspects or statements. The system will also prioritise actions that need to be taken and generate graphs to illustrate complex trends and information. The system is secure and easily transportable – a detective will take a laptop computer to a trial so information can be double-checked and relevant documents produced immediately. But as with the 1949 card indexing system, HOLMES is only as good as the information gathered by detectives.

Just as the 1949 investigation relied more heavily on the instincts and memories of the investigating detectives, justice also depended to a greater extent on the integrity of the police and their investigation. Compared with today, suspects had relatively little recourse or legal protection and miscarriages of justice did occur (as indeed they do today). In 1949 police officers and detectives followed the Judges' Rules, which were developed just before the First World War and set out best practice guidelines for obtaining evidence, questioning suspects and the admissability of evidence in court. The Rules, which all detectives were required to learn at training school and which were not legally binding, set out among other things, the appropriate way to record a formal written statement.

Since 1949 a range of official legislation has been put in place that is intended to address the balance between the rights of the public and the powers of the police. The most significant of these is the Police and Criminal Evidence Act (PACE), which came into effect in January 1986. PACE is a comprehensive statute dealing with every stage of a criminal investigation, including police powers to search people and property and the treatment of suspects when in custody. Any breach by police of the requirements of the Act can result in a case collapsing in court.

With a few specific exceptions, a search today cannot be carried out without a search warrant issued by a Justice of the Peace or a Judge, but if a suspect is arrested for an indictable offence (such as murder), the police have the power under PACE to search the property where they were arrested or where they were immediately before being arrested. Danny's home was searched by DI Diller just after Danny was taken to the police station at Edgware but before he was formally arrested. The discovery of his burnt suit in the boiler at the house led directly to Danny's arrest. Had PACE existed at the time, the detectives would have needed 'reasonable suspicion' of Danny's involvement in the murders in order to arrest him and search his home.

The cautioning of suspects before they are interviewed by police was formalised by PACE:

You do not have to say anything. But it may harm your defence if you do not mention when questioned something which you later rely on in court. Anything you do say may be given in evidence.

In 1949 DCI Tansill would have followed the Judges' Rules, which said that police officers should caution a suspect when they had reasonable grounds to suspect that they had committed an offence, and to provide a further caution when they were charged. The precise wording of the caution did tend to vary from force to force in the 1940s but the basic format was: *You do not have to say anything but anything you do say will be taken down in writing and may be used in evidence.*

Under the Rules, further questioning was not allowed once the person was charged, unless there were exceptional circumstances. From DCI Tansill's notes it appears that Danny was not cautioned until he was interviewed for the second time by DCI Tansill and DI Diller at Edgware police station. If that had happened today, Danny's defence could have argued that any statement that Danny gave while not under caution was inadmissible as evidence.

DCI Tansill and DI Diller's tactic in their interviews with Danny were exactly the same as they would be today – to ask open questions that encouraged the suspect to tell a detailed story that could then be unravelled and examined for inaccuracies. But whereas a modern-day interview would be recorded and may be videoed, DCI Tansill and DI Diller relied on their own hand-written notes, as the detectives did throughout the investigation. This frequently meant that a detective would spend many hours late into the night writing up their notes while events were fresh in their mind but even so, it was not unusual for a significant amount of time to lapse between a specific incident and the police report. Every officer involved in the initial investigation provided a witness statement detailing what they saw at Ashcombe Gardens and during their contact with Danny, but in DI Diller's case this was written as a single long narrative four days after the murders. Inspector Harvey, the first senior uniformed officer to arrive at Ashcombe Gardens that night, dated his witness statement some eight days after the bodies were discovered. Today, any written evidence is likely to be fiercely challenged by a defendant's barrister and as a result, notes taken by officers during an investigation must be completed as soon as possible after an incident and their Evidence and Action Report Books are made available to the defence.

The evidence against Danny was strong, but circumstantial. While he appeared to be guilty – and the verdict was undoubtedly due to the appearance of guilt – there was no solid, undeniable evidence that disproved Danny's version of events and incontrovertibly denied the theories of an alternative intruder put forward by the defence. Most crucially, no evidence of motive was offered by the Crown during his trial.

If the Goodman murders were investigated today it is, on balance, likely that the weight of evidence against Danny would be enough to convict him. But there would be risks. Modern juries are far more difficult to convince of a man's guilt than they were in 1949, perhaps because the public is bombarded with crime novels, films and television programmes which encourage the amateur sleuth in us all. Danny's jury returned with the required unanimous verdict in just 45 minutes, but were under more pressure than a modern jury to come to an agreement quickly. Danny's jury left the courtroom at just after 4pm and they were expected to keep on discussing the case until they agreed on a unanimous verdict, even if it was late at night. If it became apparent that they would not reach a verdict that night, they would be taken to a hotel under supervision and returned back to the courtroom the next day – and so on until they came to an agreement. The jury would not see their family until the verdict was agreed.

Today, juries tend to end their discussions for the day at 4pm or 4.30pm – a modern-day jury would not have been sent to begin its deliberations as late in the day as in Danny's case – and are allowed home at the end of each day, under orders not to discuss the case with their families.

In order to improve the chances of securing a conviction, a police investigation today would look for a much higher level of proof of Danny's guilt. The burden of proof, as it was in 1949, is on the prosecution; the defendant does not have to prove anything. The standard to which the prosecution must prove its case is so that the jury are *sure* ('beyond reasonable doubt' is no longer used, although there is little practical significance to the change). The process of discharging the burden will invariably entail seeking to undermine any alternative account which might be put forward on the defendant's behalf.

The timeline of the evening of 10 October would warrant much closer investigation, since the defence's theory of an alternative intruder depended very much on the window of time between the Goodmans arriving home and Alfred and his family arriving at Ashcombe Gardens at 10pm. Today, the nursing home would probably have CCTV cameras, and which could pinpoint whether Danny and the Goodmans left simultaneously and whether they were laughing together, as Gertrude had heard. Traffic cameras and other CCTV could also pick up the cars on their journey back to Edgware, establishing the likely time of their arrival at Ashcombe Gardens and perhaps even confirming or disproving Danny's explanation that he went home and then revisited Ashcombe Gardens later. (That said, CCTV cameras are notoriously unreliable since some are set to record at intervals rather than continuously and in other cases, the tapes are reused before it has been established that that they might contain important evidence).

While a modern-day investigation would have been more thorough and certainly much lengthier, the presence of a highly-trained family liaison officer would also have made it significantly less traumatic for the Goodman family, and particularly for Gertrude. Newspaper reporters learned within hours of the murders that Gertrude was a patient in the nursing home in Muswell Hill and a number of journalists and photographers waited outside the building over the following days, hoping for a glimpse of her. But from the newspaper reports it is clear that Gertrude was not told of her parents' death, or that her husband had been arrested, for at least 24 hours after the murders.

Margaret Flett, the matron of the nursing home, told the *Evening Standard* that she and one of the doctors told Gertrude on the morning after the murders that her husband and parents had been involved in a car crash on their way home the previous evening. Later that afternoon, they told Gertrude that her parents were dead but not that they had been murdered, or that Danny had been arrested. Late in the evening of 11 October, though, Gertrude had a visitor – a relative rather than a police officer – who insisted that she be told the truth. Throughout the week the nursing home was plagued with prowlers, onlookers and reporters trying to gain access to Gertrude, and often posing as relatives of patients. When Gertrude and her baby left the home at the end of that week, the photographers were waiting.

While Gertrude had the support of her aunt and uncle – she moved into their home and stayed there throughout the investigation and trial – it appears that most of her contact with the police came through her solicitor.

Today, the police's approach towards Gertrude would be very different. A family liaison officer is assigned to look after the victim's relatives in every murder investigation and one of their main responsibilities is to protect them from unnecessary trauma. They will make sure that any information about the case, such as details of the injuries suffered by the victims or a significant arrest, comes first and directly from them and not from newspapers or any other source. Family liaison officers play an even more vital role in cases like the Goodman murders, where a suspect is a member of the family, as is it often the trust that they build with the suspect that leads to the uncovering of important evidence.

By far the most important element of the investigation, though, would be forensic evidence, which would begin with an exhaustive investigation of the crime scene. In a modern-day murder investigation a crime scene is effectively sealed off as soon as possible by Scene of Crime Officers (SOCOs) in order to preserve any forensic evidence. In the Goodman case, if it was established that both victims were dead, the 'forensic route' between the bodies and the front door of the house would be sealed off and protected from any contamination, detailed photographs of the scene would be taken, and an expert on blood splattering would probably be brought in to examine the scene while the bodies were still in the house. While the 1949 team dusted parts of the house for fingerprints (and no usable prints were found), the forensic examination was largely cursory – photographs were taken but not of key evidence that would later come up in court, such as the blood patterns in the dining room and a bloody footprint near one of the bodies.

Today, the forensic evidence gathered at the scene and a much more detailed and methodical examination of the Goodmans' injuries would attempt to answer not only the question of whether Danny did kill them, but also the unanswered questions of why and how he did it.

Chapter 17 – Forensic Investigation

Forensic investigation was in an embryonic state in 1949 but public and professional interest in the science was beginning to grow. While police and detectives had used techniques for years that were effectively early forerunners of forensic work – a murder case in Warwick in 1816, for instance, was solved when an impression in the ground was matched with the patchwork on a labourer's trousers – forensics did not become an organised element of police work, and recognised as a separate and valuable area of expertise, until the late 1930s.

Reform of policing in the UK began seriously in 1919 when the Police Act introduced many of the recommendations made by the Desborough Committee. The Committee's recommendations would see police pay and conditions improve, as well as the establishment of the Police Federation and a Police Department at the Home Office, with police reformer Arthur Dixon at its head. In 1929 Dixon put forward a proposal for the formation of a police college, which would include a laboratory to provide scientific research. Dixon's long-term vision was for a series of local and regional forensic laboratories that would advise and support the police in their investigative work, using a range of scientific methods to collect and analyse evidence. It would be several years before Dixon was able to gather the necessary support and funding to see his vision realised.

One of Dixon's concerns was that the use of scientific techniques – even as basic as fingerprinting and photography – varied drastically from regional force to regional force. A police laboratory had been open in Cardiff since 1902 and was the furthest advanced in the country in terms of its commitment to applying scientific techniques to investigation work. A small 'criminal research' laboratory was also operating in Bristol by 1934, set up by a police surgeon and a similar laboratory opened in Nottingham in the same year. The Nottingham lab was small and concentrated mainly on fingerprinting and photography, but employed a consultant botanist and physicist and was considering running training courses for detectives in the district.

Dixon believed that detectives could and should be trained in basic fingerprinting and photography techniques, but that the more advanced scientific work had to be carried out by a specialist service. His ultimate aim was a national forensic science service, with a central research laboratory acting as a central information and research resource and a series of regional laboratories under police control, preferably sited in university towns where they could draw on existing scientific expertise. Dixon's view was that regional police forces need only carry the basic equipment necessary to examine a crime scene and collecting evidence.

In 1934, at Dixon's prompting, the Departmental Committee on Detective Work and Procedure was set up by the Home Office and as part of the investigation, a sub-committee was formed to look specifically at the use made by detectives of scientific aids.

On 10 April 1935, after Dixon successfully lobbied the Treasury for £2,000 to help set up a network of forensic laboratories, the first Metropolitan Police laboratory, with a staff of six, was opened at the Police College in Hendon. The existing laboratories around the country were steadily transferred to Home Office control; in Nottingham, Dr Henry Smith Holden became the first Home Office provincial director of a laboratory, on a salary of £1,250 a year. New labs were opened in Birmingham, Preston and Wakefield over the next six years.

In March 1936, the Home Office published its first Forensic Science circular, *Scientific Aids to Criminal Investigation*, which effectively gave the new discipline of forensic science official status. The same year, the Treasury increased the funding for forensic science services to £20,000 a year.

By the outbreak of the Second World War, a three-tier system of forensic science had been established across England and Wales. Individual police forces ran their own small laboratories, dealing with fingerprinting and photography and using relatively basic equipment including UV lighting and binocular microscopes. A series of intermediate regional laboratories, including Bristol and Preston, were available for more complex work and were funded partly by regional police forces and local government and partly by the Home Office. Above them, three expensively-equipped laboratories, staffed by forensic experts, at Nottingham, Birmingham and Cardiff operated independently outside police control but were funded through a rate levied on police forces.

With this structure in place the discipline developed apace in the years immediately following the Second World War. By 1946 demand for the laboratories' services had increased dramatically and their funding was increased to £42,000 a year. The extra funding and official recognition of the growing importance of forensic science had created a new collection of forensic scientists with clearly defined skills and responsibilities. The profession of forensic science had been born.

In 1949, the Metropolitan Police Scientific laboratory, with Dr Holden at its helm, was moved to the Norman Shaw building in Scotland Yard. Dr Holden's examination of the murder scene at 8 Ashcombe Gardens and of Danny's home on Edgwarebury Lane was one of the first he carried out in his new role as head of the forensic service at Scotland Yard.

By modern standards Dr Holden's examination and his conclusions were basic. He established that both Leopold and Esther Goodman had the same rare AB blood group, and confirmed that the blood found on Danny's shoes, his trousers and on the murder weapon was of the same group. As far as the blood found in Danny's car, and in the sink and on the draining board at Edgwarebury Lane was concerned, Dr Holden was only able to confirm that it was human blood of recent origin – by which he meant up to two days old. His identification of the Goodman's rare blood type, which he confirmed at the trial was seen in only 2% of the population, effectively confirmed that Danny had been at the murder scene, which would have been critical had Danny denied being there. But since Danny admitted being at Ashcombe Gardens that evening and even coming into contact with the Goodman's blood, it is questionable whether Dr Holden's evidence brought anything useful to the investigative process at all.

Even so, Dr Holden's work was a forerunner of a process that has become standard procedure in a murder trial today. Blood and DNA matches would be carried out in a case such as Danny's even if he admitted owning and wearing the blood-stained clothes. Dr Holden's work, combined with the lucky chance of the Goodmans' rare blood group, removed any element of doubt that Danny was at the scene. But even so, the trial revealed an undercurrent of wariness about new forensic techniques by Danny's legal team, that no doubt reflected a wider public view.

Dr Holden was called to give evidence for the prosecution on the first day of Danny's trial, as was Dr Teare, the pathologist who had performed the post-mortems on the bodies. Dr Teare spent over two hours on the witness stand and was questioned closely about the blood patterns in the dining room at Ashcombe Gardens, was asked to speculate on how the injuries to Leopold and Esther were likely to be caused, and was even asked his opinion on the blood patterns on Danny's trousers, even though he admitted that he had not closely examined the trousers before they were handed to him in the witness box. By comparison the forensic scientist Dr Holden was on the stand for less than 30 minutes, was not asked his opinion about the injuries to Esther and Leopold or the blood patterns in the dining room and was treated by the defence team at times with barely disguised contempt.

While cross-examining Dr Holden, Danny's defence barrister John Maude attempted to throw doubt on his authority, on his training and on his right to comment on the evidence. At one point he asked Dr Holden to confirm that he was a doctor of science and not of medicine, and that his doctorate had been awarded as a result of research into invertebrates. Later on in his questioning he asked Dr Holden what sort of blood tests he had carried out while a bacteriologist and assistant in the Department of Pathology at the Royal Naval Hospital in Plymouth.

'Were you doing blood tests?' asked Maude.

'Yes, but not tests of this kind,' replied Dr Holden, referring to the tests he had carried out that established the blood groups of Leopold and Esther Goodman.

'Blood tests of what kind?'

'Wassermann tests for venereal disease and differential blood counts.'

'That is quite different?'

'Yes, this sort of thing was not done then.'

'It would be quite wrong for the jury to think that you were trained to do the sort of blood tests you have done in this case?'

'Quite wrong.'

'You have never been trained at all?'

'Yes, I was trained at Nottingham at the Department of Pathology.'

'In blood testing?'

'Yes.'

Maude's intention clearly was to suggest to the jury that they should place less emphasis on Dr Holden's evidence because he was not what they should consider to be a 'proper' doctor. In Maude's view, and no doubt in the view of the jury, the evidence put forward by Dr Teare, a *bona fide* doctor of medicine in the sense that they could understand, held far more weight. Maude was even more blunt about Dr Holden in his summing up to the jury. 'He is not,' Maude told them, 'a distinguished medical man concerned with cutting up corpses and knows what he is speaking of.'

Forensic science has developed rapidly since 1949 and is now one of the most important elements of a police investigation. The discovery of DNA profiling by Sir Alec Jeffreys in 1984 is considered to be the single most important development in forensic science. The first conviction in the UK based purely on DNA fingerprint evidence, of rapist Colin Pitchfork in Leicester, did not take place until 1987.

Forensic investigation would form a major part of the police work had the murders in Ashcombe Gardens happened today. The work would begin as soon as the bodies were discovered and it was established that both victims were dead, with Scene of Crime Officers (SOCOs) called in to seal the scene and protect it from contamination. Particular attention would be paid to the path that the murderer was likely to have taken in the house and these 'forensic routes' – which in this case are the route between the bodies in the dining room and the front door, and between the bodies and the sink in the scullery where the murder weapon was found – would be sealed off and the floor protected with walk boards.

As was the case for the 1949 detectives, the fact that Danny was a frequent visitor to Ashcombe Gardens and admitted being there on the evening of the murders after the Goodmans were attacked, would present a serious problem for a modern-day forensic investigation. If he denied being at the scene, the blood on his clothes and shoes would be enough to convict him, provided DNA evidence could prove that he alone had worn them. But even though Danny admitted that the suit found in the boiler was his and that the blood on it was the Goodmans' the first step for the forensic team would be to establish this beyond doubt.

The blood found on Danny's clothes, shoes, in his car and on the murder weapon would be tested against an 'SGMPlus' DNA profile generated from the bodies of the Goodmans, and from a sample taken from

Danny. A complete match between the blood found on Danny's clothes and the DNA profiles of Leopold and Esther would mean that there was only a one in one billion chance that the blood could have come from someone else. The forensic investigation would also involve the testing of the inside of Danny's shoes (enhanced techniques such as 'Low Copy Number' profiling are able to generate a profile even if the shoes have been washed) and of his suit to confirm that they were his and that only he had worn them. Since DNA profiling requires a much smaller quantity of blood than required by Dr Holden when he established the blood group, it would be possible to establish if the blood found in the car and on Danny's trousers, which Dr Holden was not able to establish as Leopold and Esther's, did come from the Goodmans.

Given Danny's defence was that the Goodmans were killed by an unknown intruder, any evidence of a stranger's DNA or fingerprints at Ashcombe Gardens would be critical to the case. A modern forensic team would seek to identify any traces of DNA found at the house and take samples from known visitors (and any police officers, doctors or paramedics who had been at the house) in order to eliminate them from the enquiry. Particular attention would be paid to the television aerial base and it is possible that a DNA profile could be recovered from it even though it had been washed. But Danny's DNA on the weapon would not necessarily prove his guilt, since the aerial base was already in the house (Alfred testified that he had seen it in the hall a few days earlier) and Danny's defence team would be likely to argue that his DNA could have transferred to it innocently.

A modern forensic team would also look closely for fingerprints and while the fundamental technique for fingerprint recovery remains the same as in 1949, advances in forensic science mean that it is possible that they could reveal prints that were not uncovered in 1949. DCI Tansill and his team dusted the house at Ashcombe Gardens for fingerprints during the two days following the murders, concentrating particularly on the banisters, the area around the open casement window in the kitchen, the murder weapon, and the dining room. They were unable to recover a single useable print, something that was to become an area of contention after Danny's death.

In the days following Danny's execution, the Labour MP Sydney Silverman wrote to the Home Secretary James Chuter Ede asking why no fingerprint evidence at been presented at the trial. DCI Tansill confirmed to the Home Secretary that a thorough search had been carried out of Ashcombe Gardens, but no decipherable fingerprints were recovered. The Home Secretary was not satisfied and wrote to the Metropolitan Police Commissioner asking for a better explanation. 'What are the instructions to police officers investigating serious crimes?' he asked. 'Is it part of the routine that the house is thoroughly searched for fingerprint impressions and that any impressions which are found are compared with the impressions of dead persons and of other persons known to have been in the house?'

DCI Tansill was less than impressed at being asked to defend the investigative skills of his team. 'It is beyond the realm of credulity that Mr Silverman has suggested that police had not adequately searched for fingerprints in this case, as one of the elementary instructions of an investigating officer is the search for and the preservation of fingerprints at the scene of a crime,' he wrote in reply.

'Fingerprint impressions are not left as frequently as imagined, and as in this case, a scene of crime is searched and nothing is found,' he continued. 'It depends to a certain extent on the time of the year, as impressions are left by sweat and without sweat, the ridge characteristics leaving no impression at all. Incredible as it may seem, our experience is that in innumerable cases, no fingerprints whatsoever are found at the scene of serious crimes and this equally applies to minor cases too.'

'In this case the murderer was traced very quickly and we must not forget the summing up of the trial judge that the case against Raven was overwhelming.'

DCI Tansill's argument that it is not always easy to find useable fingerprints was accurate, but developments in forensic technique since then mean that a modern-day investigative team may have had a better chance at finding a useable print. In a case such as the Goodman murders it is likely that investigators would use a specialised technique to look for fingerprints in blood that are not visible to the naked eye. The use of the luminescent chemical Luminol is not standard procedure during a scene of crime investigation since it requires that the crime scene be blacked out, which is expensive and not always feasible. But in the case of the Goodmans, it is likely that the use of Luminol could uncover vital evidence.

If the use of Luminol is deemed appropriate in a particular case, a specially-trained crime scene investigator will spray a solution of the chemical and an activator onto the area under investigation. The chemical reacts with iron in blood to create a luminescence for about 30 seconds that is visible in a dark room. Luminol will frequently identify trace amounts of blood and even finger and palm prints in blood that are not visible to the naked eye. The Goodman case would warrant an examination of the dining room and much of the downstairs of the house using Luminol, and perhaps even the stairs and upstairs bedroom in order to ascertain whether the murderer had gone upstairs after the Goodmans were attacked.

The investigators would also be looking for footprints or evidence of shoe-scuffing at the scene which could show which route the murderer took in the house, as well as Danny's route according to his story. The scratch patterns found on shoeprints are as individual as fingerprints – the way we walk and live means that we each wear down our shoes in a unique way – and the Metropolitan Police today makes frequent use of a shoeprint database that can identify particular makes and brands of shoes.

Given Danny's explanation that he arrived at the house after the murders had taken place and knelt close to the bodies, the aim of a modern forensic investigation would be to test every part of his story and explain, as far as possible, what happened that evening.

At his trial, the critical questions identified by his defence barrister John Maude was whether the blood found on Danny's clothes came from a fresh arterial bleed or from blood that had been outside of the body for a time, and whether the fact that no blood was found above his knees suggested that he could not have carried out the attacks. These points would be considered less important today. It is possible to estimate whether blood found at the scene and on clothing is fresh arterial blood by analysing the level of coagulants found in it, but the result would not be considered convincing evidence on its own.

The blood patterns found in the dining room and on and around the bodies would also be analysed closely, but are more likely to explain the sequences of events than prove or disprove Danny's story. The police did not take close-up photographs of the blood patterns surrounding the bodies in the dining room of Ashcombe Gardens, but some details can be gleaned from John Maude's questioning of the pathologist Dr Teare at Danny's trial. Dr Teare summised that Leopold had probably been sitting at the table when he was attacked and that his head was 'on or near the table' when he had first been struck.

Maude said there were splashes radiating from the pool of blood on the table, showing that blood had spurted out from whatever was the container of the blood (presumably the head). Dr Teare agreed. 'Like a sunburst clock with no hours,' said Maude. Yes, said Dr Teare.

'From this centre mass of blood there are spurts right out, are there not, right across, even to the edge of the table?' Yes, replied Dr Teare. Mr Maude asked if he would describe them as exclamation marks. Pear drops, said Teare. 'And the direction in which the stalk of the pear is pointing is the direction in which the blood is travelling, always?' Yes.

'Was it clear that blood was spurting in every direction from that central point?' Maude asked Dr Teare. 'More than 180 degrees?' Dr Teare agreed: '190, perhaps 200 degrees.' Given the force of the blows that were needed to cause Leopold's injuries, Dr Teare agreed that it would be surprising if the attacker had not got blood on his jacket, and on the collars of his shirt, if they were protruding from the jacket.

'The remarkable thing,' said Maude, 'is that Mr Goodman was not splashed down the front of his shirt.' Dr Teare said he could not draw any conclusion from that. 'His head might either have been well forward or well back to have achieved that, I think.' He added that he would expect the attacker to have had blood over the top part of the body.

'The blood coming out of an artery of a living person may spurt a very considerable distance?' asked Maude. Yes, agreed Dr Teare, between nine and 12 feet. The blood marks found on the crossbar and legs of the dining room table, he added, was 'most suggestive' of blood spurting from Leopold while he was on the floor.

Modern-day SOCOs include experts on blood splatter patterns who would be able to estimate with some accuracy where Leopold and Esther were when they were struck, as well as whether blood drops had come directly from the victims or were cast off from the weapon as it was swung by the attacker. Closer examination of the injuries suffered by Esther and Leopold might also be able to confirm whether they were caused by the same person, at roughly the same time, where the attacker was positioned and even his estimated height. In this case this evidence would be vital since the postmortem and photographs taken of Leopold and Esther that night show that they suffered very different injuries. Leopold was hit 14 times and suffered a series of deep gashes, most following a similar line and angle, which were probably caused by the sharp bottom edge of the aerial base as it slashed across his head and face. Esther was hit seven times and suffered a much more forceful direct blow from a blunt edge to her forehead, which caused a catastrophic skull fracture. This suggests that there was a time delay between the attacks and perhaps that by the second attack, the murderer had worked out how to wield the weapon with maximum effectiveness.

These techniques would help to explain with far greater certainty the sequence of events that evening, and how Esther and Leopold had died. But establishing beyond doubt whether Danny was the culprit is more difficult. Danny's story was that he arrived at Ashcombe Gardens for the second time at around 9.45pm, entered through the front door, found the Goodmans dead in the dining room, panicked and ran out of the house. The forensic investigation would look for evidence that threw doubt on that explanation. The Goodmans' blood found on Danny's clothes, shoes and in his car would not disprove it. He had stayed at the Goodmans' house, so it would not be unusual for his DNA to be found there, and even found on the cloth that was used to wash the television aerial clean of blood. The key – and the potential smoking gun – is the murder weapon.

If Danny's DNA was found on the television aerial his defence team would be likely to argue that it could have transferred there innocently. Simlarly, his fingerprints on the weapon could be explained away because the aerial had been in the house for days and Danny had frequently visited there. But if a fingerprint of his could be found on the weapon *in blood*, that would be far more difficult to explain.

Danny told police that after finding the bodies he had left the house through the front door, which meant he went directly from the dining room through the hall. If he was in a panicked state, he had no reason to leave the dining room and turn right towards the back of the house, through the kitchen and into the scullery where the murder weapon was found. A fingerprint in blood on the weapon (if revealed under Luminol) would prove that he had touched it *after* the Goodmans were attacked. Similarly, other fingerprints in blood or a footprint in the kitchen or scullery would throw doubt on Danny's story.

But we will never know. Danny was condemned by overwhelming circumstantial evidence and not by incontrovertible truth. He lied to police, burnt his suit and changed his story. And ultimately, he died for it. But even if it could be shown that he did wield the murder weapon, the question of why he killed Leopold and Esther that night still remains.

Chapter 18 – A Guilty Mind

Just 88 days after the murders, Danny was dead and the law had taken its course. The speed of the legal process is astonishing by modern standards – his trial began 40 days after the crime was committed and lasted just three days. Had he not appealed against his sentence, his execution would have been carried out on 13 December, two months and two days after the murders. The appeal was heard on 20 December and lasted only five hours.

Today the process would have taken months. In 2008 the average length of time between arrest and trial in the UK is 119 days, although murder cases are likely to take much longer to come to court. Accused prisoners can be kept in custody for a maximum of 182 days – six months – before their trial, unless the Crown successfully applies to the court for an extension (in which case it must show that all due efficiency has been used in the enquiry). If convicted, a prisoner can wait as much as a year to 18 months for an appeal to be heard.

One of the fundamental differences between the legal process in 1949 and a murder trial today is the system of disclosure. The defence is required to provide a 'defence case statement', which sets out the nature of the defence and any specific points with which it plans to take issue. As part of this statement, the defence will ask for material to be disclosed which undermines the prosecution or helps the defence. The prosecution is obliged to comply, except in very rare cases where the information is privileged. In 1949 the prosecution was obliged to disclose all of the evidence uncovered but the defence was not. In practice, the defence generally had a good idea of the evidence against the defendant, but was not required to disclose what its counter-arguments would be – effectively, the defence barrister could turn up at the trial and call witnesses that were a complete surprise to the Crown. The rules surrounding disclosure changed periodically until the Criminal Procedure and Investigations Act of 1996 formalised the process. The modern system of disclosure means that a fair trial is far more likely but is also one of the factors that has led to much longer and drawn-out trials in murder cases today.

If Danny's trial was held today it would probably last around two weeks. Trial days tend to be slightly shorter than in 1949 but many more experts would be likely to be called, particularly if Danny's mental state came under discussion. But there were other reasons for the brevity of Danny's trial. In 1949 barristers were paid by the case, and while (as now) they were bound by strict ethical codes of behaviour, this could encourage them to move quickly from one trial to another if court time allowed. The eagerness of Anthony Hawke, the prosecution barrister in Danny's case, to begin the next trial as soon as Danny's jury retired to consider its verdict, is an illustration of this unusual work ethic.

While there is no doubt that the prosecution's case against Danny was strong, a trial today would take a much more thorough approach to the evidence, possible motive and explanation of what happened in Ashcombe Gardens that night. The police investigation would concentrate to a far greater degree on proving that Danny did commit the murders, calling on forensic evidence such as a DNA examination of the murder weapon, and on debunking his explanation of what happened that evening. The prosecution and defence would also examine closely the sequence of events that evening and attempt to recreate how and when the Goodmans had been killed.

Assuming that modern forensic science would prove with far greater certainty that Danny was responsible for the killings, the next question to answer was why he did it – and that would undoubtedly raise the critical issue of Danny's mental state.

There are several possible counterarguments to a crime as serious as murder that could lead to an acquittal or a partial defence. Acting in self-defence, for example, is a complete defence to murder. Acting under provocation, by contrast, is a partial defence which could lessen a murder charge to manslaughter. Similarly, diminished responsibility on the part of the defendant, if proven, could also reduce a murder charge to manslaughter. *Actus non facit reum nisi mens sit rea* – the act does not make a man guilty unless his mind is guilty – is a basic fundamental of English criminal law.

Danny's defence throughout his trial and appeal was that he didn't do it: someone else was responsible for the murders. It is clear, though, that Sydney Rutter and John Maude would rather have based their defence on an argument of not guilty due to insanity. This would not have been unusual at the time by any means. Until 1957, when the concept of manslaughter by way of diminished responsibility was introduced through the Homicide Act, some 40% of murder cases in England and Wales involved a plea of insanity by the prisoner.

Danny's mental state was identified by the police and by Rutter as an area that demanded close examination soon after he was arrested. Within two days of the murders DCI Tansill, on hearing from Alfred of Danny's nervous breakdown soon after his marriage, attempted to contact Dr Samuel Hirschmann, a doctor in Hampstead who had treated Danny during those months. And on 13 October – the day he was appointed by Edward Raven – Sydney Rutter telephoned DCI Tansill to say that he was planning to call Dr Hirschmann and some of Danny's relatives as witnesses for the defence.

This suggests that Rutter decided immediately on taking the case that Danny's mental condition was a strong possible line of defence. But by the time of the Magistrate's committal hearing less than three weeks later, Rutter had abandoned this option. Instead, the defence took the risky approach at the Magistrate's hearing of attempting to suggest that others, in this case Alfred, had as much opportunity and a better motive for committing the murders. Danny's breakdown and his mental condition were barely referred to again, either during the trial or the appeal. It was only when Danny's situation became truly desperate, in the days before his execution, that the possibility of mental fragility as a basis for reprieve was raised. And by then it was too late.

So what was Danny's mental state? That he was a nervous and highly-strung young man was obvious throughout the investigation and trial and was frequently commented on by people who met or observed him. Jane Block, who worked with Danny at his father's advertising agency in 1947 and 1948 described him as having 'peculiar staring eyes' that often seemed to be staring into space. 'He impressed me as an extremely nervous young man and a super-sensitive person,' she told Sydney Rutter. 'He had a habit of frequently passing his hand across his face as though he had a very bad headache.'

Even though his mental condition was not raised until a very late stage in the legal proceedings, a number of reports from various medical professionals are available. The conclusions point to a young man who had suffered from anxiety since childhood, showing symptoms which became more pronounced as he grew older.

Danny's childhood appeared to be difficult, and not just because he was forced to move from school to school as his family moved around the country. A number of medical professionals observed that he came from a family that appeared to be nervous and highly-strung. Danny's RAF records noted that his father 'is nervous and worries abnormally' and that his mother 'is timid and easily worried'.

Part of the reason behind this nervousness could have been Edward Raven's uncontrollable temper. Betty Raven told Sydney Rutter that Edward had been prone to serious tempers for as long as she had known him and would often lose his temper over small things that did not meet his approval or if he could not get his own way. Danny told Rutter that he was often the target of Edward's rages and that Edward would frequently hit him when he was a child and this continued into adulthood. Between July 1946, when Danny left the RAF, and September 1947, when he became engaged to Gertrude, Danny said that Edward had hit him three or four times during violent arguments.

Over the course of his contact with the Ravens, Sydney Rutter would see proof of this himself. 'I have on a number of occasions during the past two months seen Edward Raven in tempers,' he wrote in December 1949. 'There were occasions when his temper was frightening. On one occasion, because he could not get his own way while he was speaking on the telephone, he flew into a temper such as I have never witnessed before. He screamed and raved to such an extent that I thought he had gone mad. This went on for about five minutes. Eventually I had to take the telephone away from him as he would not stop shouting when I asked him several times to stop. On another occasion when somebody was in the room and said something he did not like he flew into a temper for no good reason which was frightful and became insulting and abusive.'

Danny seemed to have inherited something of his father's temperament. According to his mother, as a toddler Danny showed a 'violent temper' whenever he did not get his own way. The family consulted a doctor in Stoke Newington and after taking his advice, Danny's temper tantrums abated. But as he grew older he would frequently fly into a temper for no good reason.

The brief details of his childhood that Danny gave to Dr Matthews, the prison doctor who examined him when he was first taken to Brixton, suggested that he was a nervous and highly-strung child. Danny told Dr Matthews that he had 'frequent attacks of night terrors' as a child, was afraid of the dark and of heights, and wetted the bed until the age of 10. He also bit his nails. Dr Matthews noted in his report that his family history 'indicates that the prisoner's early environment might have been harmful to him in that the anxious condition of his parents would induce in him a feeling of insecurity, and make him more prone to be abnormally anxious himself.'

Dr Matthews was able to glean some more information on Danny's health from his RAF medical report. Danny passed the required medical at the age of 18, the report only noting a scar on his forehead, which was caused at the age of six when he crashed his head through the glass panel of a door that had been suddenly shut by his father. The wound needed several stitches and as an adult, the resulting scar became more noticeable whenever Danny became agitated.

Danny told Alfred, his wife's uncle, that he had been involved in a serious plane crash while in the RAF and Alfred repeated this story to DCI Tansill after the murders. If true, the air crash would only have increased Danny's anxiety and could, arguably, have resulted in some form of post-traumatic stress disorder. Danny's full RAF file was only seen by the Director of Public Prosecutions and by Sydney Rutter, but it appears from their notes that Danny might have embellished the story. What is more likely is that several air crew who were well-known to Danny were killed in an air crash in Egypt some time in 1945, but Danny was not on the plane at the time. He was, however, deeply affected by the incident.

Danny was discharged due to an anxiety-related illness in the summer of 1946, after less than two years of service. In August 1945, while in Egypt, he complained of a severe headache, dizziness and a throbbing in his head after spending 20 minutes working outside in the afternoon sun. He told the RAF doctor who examined him that he had suffered from sunstroke in the past but the doctor assessed that Danny's sudden illness was down to anxiety and had nothing to do with exposure to the sun. As a result, Danny was removed from flying duties.

Danny was referred to an RAF neuro-psychiatrist, who found no evidence of any disorder in his central nervous system. His view was that Danny was suffering from anxiety and that he had a long personal history of being unduly nervous, adding that Danny was 'an anxious and worrying type of personality with the scales hereditarily and constitutionally loaded against him', and that his state of anxiety had become 'more manifest' while in the Service. Danny was, added the psychiatrist, unlikely to be of any further use to the RAF. Danny was brought before a medical board in 1946, who agreed with the psychiatrist's report and he was invalided out of the service due to 'anxiety neurosis'. Within two weeks of returning to the UK in July 1946, Danny was hospitalised and treated for malaria. He was to suffer a number of relapses until the end of 1948.

In the days before Danny's execution, as Sydney Rutter and John Maude made increasingly desperate efforts to persuade the Home Secretary to grant a reprieve, more detailed information about Danny's mental health emerged. Rutter provided the Home Office with written depositions from Samuel Hirschmann, the Ravens' family doctor, and from Dr Murdo McKenzie, a psychiatrist based in Upper Wimpole Street, who had treated Danny over several weeks in 1948. The depositions were taken in October and November 1949, before Danny's trial.

Dr Hirschmann told Rutter that he had seen Danny on a number of occasions between 1947 and 1949. At the beginning of September 1947, shortly after Danny became engaged to Gertrude, Edward Raven called Dr Hirschmann at home just before midnight and told him that Danny had suffered a blackout. Edward collected Dr Hirschmann in his car and took him to 8 Ashcombe Gardens, where Danny was lying on the sofa in the kitchen. He was sweating heavily and his pulse was racing. Dr Hirschmann concluded that Danny was suffering from 'faintness of a nervous origin' and prescribed a sedative. He saw Danny again a week later at his surgery, when Danny complained of frequent headaches, and prescribed more sedatives.

Dr Hirschmann did not see Danny again until September 1948, shortly after his marriage to Gertrude. Danny was showing signs of acute anxiety and Dr Hirschmann referred him to the psychiatrist, Dr Murdo McKenzie. At Rutter's request, Dr McKenzie released his written notes of Danny's treatment and gave a detailed statement of his meetings with him.

Dr McKenzie said that he had seen Danny for the first time on 24 September 1948. He told the doctor that a few days previously he had been to a show at the Palladium and had suddenly felt as though he were going to pass out. He said he often felt unable to concentrate, was restless, and suffered from headaches and a sense of tightness in the scalp. At times, he added, he felt as though he were in a dream and only barely in touch with the world, and that recently he had been dreaming at night and waking up in the morning feeling scared. Gertrude, who was with Danny at the appointment, added that he talked a great deal in his sleep and kept twisting and turning.

Danny told Dr McKenzie that he had recently found work a strain – he was working for his father's advertising agency at the time – and felt unable to return to the office. Dr McKenzie diagnosed an acute anxiety state, advised sedative medication and said he would see Danny for the next few weeks with a view to giving him psychological advice. 'They seem to be a very decent pair,' Dr McKenzie reported back to Dr Hirschmann, 'and with our united efforts I do hope the two young folk will quite soon settle down into a psychologically satisfactory home life.'

Dr McKenzie saw Danny four more times over the next two weeks. On the first two visits, his symptoms were unchanged. 'He re-complained of a sense of insurmountable panic, especially in relation to meeting people,' said Dr McKenzie. 'He added that on one occasion he had to leave the drawing room because some friends had arrived and he felt unable to cope with them. He also had a vague idea that folk imagined that he looked peculiar.'

During one of these visits, Danny appeared to almost faint. He told the doctor that he felt tightness in his chest and could feel the room closing in. When Dr McKenzie reassured him that he was fine, the attack stopped. At the fourth meeting on 7 October 1948, Dr McKenzie noted that Danny's confidence appeared to be returning and he said he was sleeping more comfortably.

Three days later, on Sunday 10 October, Edward telephoned Dr McKenzie at his home. He said that Danny had visited the family that evening and had behaved in an unreasonable fashion, accusing his parents of favouring other members of the family over him. He had lost his temper, said Edward, and would not calm down. Dr McKenzie made an appointment to see both Edward and Danny the following day.

The pair gave conflicting views of what had happened that evening, but it was clear that there had been a heated argument and that Danny had become so enraged that Edward and Betty were concerned for his health. Danny told the doctor that he had been worried about Gertrude, who had a kidney infection, and his parents had not seemed to take his concerns seriously enough. He agreed, though, with Dr McKenzie's suggestion that he was feeling an overwhelming sense of jealousy and no longer felt himself to be the favoured child of the family. Dr McKenzie spoke separately to Edward, who told him that Danny's behaviour at work was also giving him cause for concern. He had been given a prominent position at the firm, said Edward, but was finding the responsibility difficult and despite being on a good salary, had been far too extravagant over his wedding.

Dr McKenzie decided that while these family tensions continued it would be pointless treating Danny. He suggested a stay in a sanatorium, which Danny resisted, and instead they agreed on the compromise that Danny and Gertrude would go to Bournemouth for a few weeks to allow him to recuperate. When Dr McKenzie saw Danny again – for the last time – in November 1948, the rest had significantly improved his health.

Even so, Danny continued to suffer intermittently from panic attacks and insomnia. Gertrude called Dr Hirschmann to their home in December 1948, saying that Danny had had a nightmare and was frightened. The doctor gave him a sedative and a prescription for sleeping tablets. By September 1949 Danny was again suffering from insomnia and Dr Hirschmann prescribed more sleeping tablets. He saw Danny for the last time on 8 October 1949 at the nursing home in Muswell Hill where he was treating Gertrude, and told Sydney Rutter that he looked 'a little worried'.

Danny's anxiety and nervousness were noted by the prison doctors who examined him at Brixton and at Pentonville, but were never considered to be relevant to his defence. The conclusion of Dr Matthews at Brixton prison was that Danny was sane and fit to stand trial. 'At no time have I observed any indication of insanity nor feeble-mindedness, nor have I observed in him any abnormal state of anxiety,' he wrote in his report to the Criminal Court. 'He has always, I think, been a rather timid, "nervy" person, and he is the type who would readily develop a state of anxiety when affairs did not go just as he wanted them to. I failed to find any evidence of insanity in his past. I am of the opinion that at no time has he been insane.'

Chapter 19 – An Unfashionable Affliction

Sydney Rutter hinted strongly to a number of journalists in the days before his client's execution that, given a choice, he would have pursued a defence of not guilty due to insanity during Danny's trial. That he did not, it seems, was down to the explicit instructions of Danny and his father. Years later, in a conversation with Gertrude's friend Bernard Elliston, Rutter said that the case haunted him because he felt that a plea of insanity would have saved Danny's life, but that Danny and Edward were firmly against it. Neither Danny nor Edward were prepared to accept the stigma of a life spent in Broadmoor – particularly since they both firmly believed that Danny was innocent.

The social, medical and legal attitude towards mental health has transformed over the past 60 years. Depression, anxiety and stress are modern phenomena that received short shrift in the 1940s and mental illness, unless it was an extreme and easily diagnosable case, was viewed with suspicion and often exasperation.

The comments made to Danny by several police officers when he arrived at the murder scene on the evening of 10 October illustrate the clichéd view of the immediate post-war British population taking the 'stiff upper lip' approach to life. Faced with a distressed man, their immediate reaction was to tell him to 'pull yourself together'. As Danny progressed through the legal system, time and again were references made to his nervousness and to the erratic behaviour of his father, who by all accounts was as highly-strung as his son. The assumption was inevitably that Danny was nervous and anxious because he was guilty, even though his medical history suggested that he had been nervous and anxious all his life.

Unable to offer a defence of insanity, Danny's legal team floundered under the weight of circumstantial evidence against him. A week before the trial opened at the Old Bailey, Danny's barrister John Maude approached the Home Office and asked whether the Secretary of State would be likely to allow Danny to undergo an EEG test if he was found guilty and sentenced to death. This was hardly a resounding vote of confidence that their case as it stood would succeed, but it also suggests that Maude already knew that Danny's mental condition was the only thing that could save him if he was found guilty.

What was also clear from the conversation between John Maude and the Home Office official was that it was Danny himself who was preventing his defence team from pursuing a plea of insanity. He had, said Maude, so far refused to undergo an EEG test and was 'anxious that the defence of insanity should not be put forward'. Maude's enquiries to the Home Office, though, indicate that he was reasonably confident that Danny would change his mind about the test if convicted.

Maude was right. On 11 December 1949, nine days before Danny's appeal was heard, the Governor at Pentonville received a request that Danny be allowed to undergo an EEG examination and blood sugar tests. 'This is an unusual request,' noted the Governor in Danny's prison file. 'As far as I can gather no question of his mental state was raised at the trial and the Brixton medical report to the Director of Public Prosecutions revealed no abnormal mental state. It does not appear that this examination can be of any use to the defence in the appeal they are making.' He asked the Home Office for advice on whether the tests should go ahead. The Home Office agreed to the request, noting that 'the information may be of use to the Secretary of State at a later date' – in other words, if the tests show that Danny was sane, his chances of gaining a reprieve from the Secretary of State at his execution would be seriously diminished.

EEG (electroencephalography) tests, the recording of electrical activity in the brain through electrodes placed on the scalp, would become a relatively common feature in the diagnosis of epilepsy, but in 1949 John Maude was stepping into a highly experimental area in both medical and legal terms. Maude's aim was to use the test to show that Danny was suffering from a defect of the mind, using a new scientific technique that, presumably, would hold some weight with the Home Office. Today, an assessment of Danny's mental state during a trial would be based on the evidence of psychiatrists – perhaps as many as four (two for the defence and two for the prosecution) – and an EEG test would not feature at all.

Medically, the EEG test was still a relatively unknown phenomenon in 1949. A British physician, Richard Caton, presented his findings on a crude fore-runner of the EEG test when he described the electrical charges he found in the exposed brains of rabbits in 1875, but the technique was not successfully developed for use on humans until the 1930s. A German psychiatrist, Hans Berger, gave the EEG device its name and published a paper, *On the Electroencephalogram of Man*, describing the 'brain waves' identified during a test performed on his teenage son, in 1929. His work was developed and expanded by others and the first EEG specialist laboratory was opened in the US in 1936. The first international conference to discuss EEG testing was not held until 1947. In this context Maude's request that Danny undergo an EEG test was extraordinarily unusual and it was hardly surprising that the Home Office and the Pentonville Governor saw it simply as a case of the defence clutching at straws.

On 15 December, Danny was taken in secrecy from Pentonville to the Maudsley psychiatric hospital in Camberwell, south London, where the EEG test was carried out by Denis Hill of the Department of Applied Electrophysiology.

Hill attached a series of electrodes to Danny's scalp and the test began. The EEG, wrote Denis Hill in his report, was 'essentially normal' under resting conditions. Danny was then asked to hyperventilate, which resulted in 'slow waves of high amplitude in the pre-frontal areas' combined with 'frequent long-duration sharp waves' This pattern, wrote Hill, was 'suspicious of epilepsy'.

Hill tried a number of further tests to check his initial findings. He asked Danny to look at a flickering light, but this did not trigger any epileptic activity in his brain. He was given a glucose drink to increase his blood sugar level and the overbreathing exercise was repeated, which again did not give an abnormal response. The tests were suspicious enough, though, for Hill to ask for time to repeat them the following day.

On the 16 December Danny was taken again to Maudsley where Hill gave him a dose of the circulatory and respiratory stimulant Metrazol, which in large quantities was known to prompt a seizure. The EEG test recorded a strong spike wave on both sides of Danny's brain. He was then asked to overbreathe again, but Danny was quickly becoming unco-operative. 'The patient was somewhat troubled by the procedure and became aggressive,' wrote Hill in his report.

Hill repeated the test once again after giving Danny a sedative. His verdict was that, with 'a high degree of probability', Danny was epileptic. 'The prisoner is probably an idiopathic epileptic,' he added, although the head injury Danny sustained as a child might have triggered the epilepsy.

Hill added in his report that there was enough in Danny's sparse medical history to suggest that he had suffered from epilepsy for some time. Danny's claim to have suffered sunstroke while in England and in Egypt was, said Hill, 'highly suspicious' of epilepsy. 'Further,' he continued, 'it is reported in the RAF notes that he had a peculiar feeling in the head and an inability to stand straight during the attacks, and that his face was noticed to be twitching on occasions. It is also reported in his RAF notes that he had had attacks of headaches and vomiting since the age of six onwards and the attacks which he described while in the RAF were of sudden onset, occurring without warning and accompanied by dizziness and throbbing in the head. The prisoner reported to the RAF board that these attacks had got worse after going overseas and that during the period of a year preceding his discharge from the service, he had 'partial blackouts' lasting two or three minutes.'

The EEG results suggest that it is likely that Danny did suffer from some form of epilepsy, most likely 'absence' or petit mal seizures, although it is impossible to assess to what degree. If Denis Hill was correct in claiming that the episodes that Danny took to be sunstroke during his teenage years and his time in the RAF were in fact mild epileptic attacks, it is possible that these attacks continued up until his death. Sydney Rutter produced a written statement for the Home Secretary from Jane Block, who worked as a secretary for Danny in Edward Raven's advertising business, which seemed to support this theory. Miss Block told Rutter that Danny had complained of being ill on several occasions while in the office. 'The large scar which he had on his forehead became very red and obvious and he seemed to be in a complete daze and not realise what was going on,' she told Rutter. 'On such occasions he would not, if anybody spoke to him, realise that anyone was speaking and he just looked blankly into space. On several occasions he had to be taken home. These incidents often occurred after he had been upset by trifling things.'

According to Sydney Rutter, Gertrude Raven was also able to confirm that Danny had suffered from regular unexplained blackouts during their time together. She told Rutter that on one occasion she and Danny had argued and she was crying on the bed, with Danny sitting on a chair nearby. When she looked up she saw him panting heavily and rushed to him, asking what was the matter. He seemed startled to hear her voice, as though he was in a stupor and asked Gertrude what had happened. Danny's mind seemed blank, Gertrude told Rutter, and he had no recollection of what had happened.

On another occasion Danny collapsed on the stairs at their home and, thinking that he had hit his head, Gertrude called for an ambulance. Danny regained consciousness just before the ambulance arrived but when the medics tried to examine him he started shouting and fighting against them. He told Gertrude afterwards that he had no recollection of the incident.

Danny's prison medical records also contain some unexplained attacks which could have been the result of mild epilepsy. He was often treated for headaches while at Brixton and on 29 November 1949, while in his condemned cell in Pentonville, the prison doctor was called to see him late in the evening. Danny was in bed and told the doctor that he had suffered a fainting attack while undressing. He also complained of pins and needles in both hands but refused medical attention, saying the problem was his nerves and all he needed was a cigarette.

The results of the EEG test were made known to the Home Office but were not raised at Danny's appeal and indeed, it is difficult to see whether the test, on its own, would have helped Danny's defence at that stage. Sydney Rutter would later discuss the results of the EEG test with newspaper reporters in the days before Danny's execution but their reaction was scarcely less than scathing. The *Hendon and Finchley Times* commented benignly that Danny was the first prisoner in the country to undergo this new 'brain wave test', but the *Sunday Pictorial* was more forthright: 'The encephalograph is not accepted in British law,' it said. 'It has not yet been proved to be more reliable than the brain of a highly-trained mental specialist and the Home Secretary was right to depend on his own experts and not on a chancy mechanical device.'

By the time the EEG test was carried out, the only real hope for Danny was that the Home Secretary would grant a reprieve on the basis that he was unfit for execution, or as an act of mercy. In presenting the medical evidence to the Home Secretary, Rutter called on the M'Naghten Rules, set in 1843, which prevented the execution of a prisoner if, among other things, he was suffering from a mental illness that meant he did not understand the nature of his crime or did not realise that it was wrong. If there was any doubt as to the sanity of a prisoner who was due to be executed, the condemned man was required under the Criminal Lunatics Act of 1884 to be examined by a board of psychiatrists.

The three-man board – Sir Norwood East, the former Medical Commissioner of HM Prisons, Dr Hopwood, Medical Superintendent at Broadmoor, and Dr Desmond Curran – prepared their report between 23 December 1949 and 1 January 1950. During the process the three doctors interviewed the prison Governor at Pentonville, Dr Coates and Dr Quinn, two doctors at the prison who had seen Danny, Dr Matthews, the medical officer at Brixton, the Rabbi Myer Lew who had seen Danny frequently at Pentonville, and nine prison warders who had guarded Danny since his conviction. They also had 'prolonged' interviews with Danny himself.

Sir Norwood East's report was, unfortunately for Danny, definitive in its conclusion that he was sane and fit to be executed. But it is curious in that it leaves absolutely no room for doubt to the extent that, at some points, it contradicts evidence from other quarters.

'The general impression of the lay witnesses was to the effect that the prisoner was rather above the average in intelligence,' wrote Sir Norwood. 'He had neither done nor said anything to lead them to think that he was not in his right mind. He had had no fits. He occupied himself and was not morbidly depressed. He had gained a stone in weight *[this is rather disingenuous since prison records show that Danny lost almost a stone in weight in the month between his arrest and the trial. He regained that weight between his conviction and execution]*. He fully realised his position and the possible consequences of his act.'

Dr Coates, the medical officer at Pentonville, had told the medical board that he considered Danny to be 'above the average in intelligence. He found no evidence of insanity, epilepsy or minor mental disorder. He had been rational in conduct and conversation.' Dr Coates was on duty at Pentonville on 29 November when Danny suffered a fainting attack and had been called to see him, but Sir Norwood was quick to dismiss the incident. 'Throughout this attack the prisoner did not lose consciousness and stated this fact to us,' he wrote. 'The officers on duty stated that he was talking sensibly throughout. The general impression was that the attack was probably not genuine. *[This is a little unreasonable since Dr Coates' report of the incident says that Danny said he did not need a doctor and asked him to leave – if he was faking the attack, it made little sense to send the doctor away]*. Dr Coates thought it was an emotional upset. We understand from the prisoner that this attack was similar to the attacks to which he had referred. It clearly was not a demonstration of epilepsy.'

The most damning section of the report was Sir Norwood's assessment of Danny's behaviour at the trial. He described him as 'alert, composed and confident', although the trial transcript and numerous newspaper reports suggest that he was emotional, nervous and cried frequently while giving evidence. Event worse, Sir Norwood described Danny's replies to questions from counsel during the trial as 'shrewd, relevant and appeared to be well thought out'. The implicit assumption was that Danny's answered were calculated lies.

'At our interviews with Raven he was alert and clearly on the defensive,' continued Sir Norwood. 'He implied that he does not know now whether what he said in court about the crime was true or not. His memory, attention and perceptive faculty, as well as his reasoning and judgment, are good. He is above the ordinary intelligence of the general population.'

The conclusion was that Danny was fit to face Albert Pierrepoint: 'We do not consider that Raven was insane at the time of the crime or that he is insane now. He is probably an anxious and nervous type of man, but we do not believe that he is suffering now, or was suffering at the time of the crime from any minor mental abnormality which would justify us in making any medical recommendation.'

The report of the medical board was a fatal blow to Danny's family. Sydney Rutter's last attempt to save Danny came three days before the execution, when he called several journalists to his office in Great Winchester Street and made public the medical and psychiatric evidence that Danny and Edward had been so keen to keep quiet.

Rutter spent more than an hour reading through the results of the EEG examination, Danny's RAF medical records and reports from Dr Hirschmann and Dr McKenzie, spelling out the medical terms for the journalists and building a chain of evidence that, he said, showed that Danny was insane. 'From the test made by the EEG and other evidence it is clear that Raven is mentally abnormal,' he told the journalists. 'Every endeavour should be made to see that this man does not hang. It would be absolutely wrong.'

If Rutter was hoping to whip up public sympathy, he was disappointed. The reaction of the journalists suggests that a defence of insanity against the brutal murder of two innocent people in a London suburb would have been a difficult one for the public – and by association a jury – to accept. Rutter's press conference, said the *Daily Mirror* reporter the following day, was 'an unprecedented gesture by a lawyer. It was sad. But against the picture of the tragedy in an Edgware home – it was not impressive.'

Chapter 20 – Defect of Reason

The insistence of Sydney Rutter and John Maude that Danny undergo the EEG examination suggestions that they were considering the idea that if Danny did suffer from epilepsy, it might be possible to plead insanity based on the argument that he was suffering from a 'defect of reason' cause by a disease of the mind. If that was the case, Rutter and Maude were well ahead of their time. It would not be until 13 years after Danny's death that the question of whether epilepsy could successfully be used as a defence to murder under the M'Naghten Rules would be seriously tested.

The M'Naghten Rules were established by the 1843 case of Daniel M'Naghten, who attempted to shoot Sir Robert Peel, the Prime Minister. He missed Sir Robert but hit his secretary, Edmond Drummond, in the back and he died five days later. M'Naghten was found not guilty of murder at his trial on the grounds of his insanity. After a public outcry the House of Lords asked a panel of judges to establish clear guidance that could be used by juries in a case where the defendant pleads insanity. The result was the M'Naghten Rules, which since then have established the definition of legal insanity. When Danny was examined before his execution by the three Home Office-appointed psychiatrists, they were essentially assessing whether he was fit to be executed under the M'Naghten Rules.

The House of Lords explained that juries should be told in all cases that every man is presumed to be sane unless proven otherwise and that in order to establish a defence on the grounds of insanity, 'it must be clearly proved that, at the time of committing the act, the party accused was labouring under such a defect of reason, from disease of the mind, as not to know the nature and quality of the act he was doing; or, if he did know it, that he did not know he was doing what was wrong'.

The M'Naghten Rules can be broken down into three stages: the defendant must prove on the balance of probabilities that he is suffering from a defect of reason; that the defect is caused by a disease of the mind; and that the defect meant that the defendant did not know what he was doing or if he did, that he did not know it was wrong. The Rules have been tested intensely by case law over the past century and layers of complexity – not all of them helpful – have been added, particularly when it comes to assessing what sort of medical condition could legally be defined as 'a disease of the mind'.

In 1960 in Northern Ireland a young woman, Josephine Fitzsimmons, was found strangled to death with her stockings. George Bratty, an epileptic who had given a lift to Josephine the previous evening in his car, was arrested and questioned by police during which he said he had been overcome by 'some terrible feeling and then a sort of blackness' while with Josephine. He said he had grabbed Josephine and thrown her over the seat into the back of his car. 'I didn't mean to do what happened,' he said. 'Nothing like that happened until last night. I apologise for what happened. I don't think it would have happened only that terrible feeling came over me at the time. I don't really know what caused it at all.'

At his trial, Bratty's defence team put forward three possible verdicts: That he was not guilty on the basis that he was in the aftermath of an epileptic attack and therefore not master of his own actions, or in a state of 'automatism'; that his mental condition was so impaired that he was not capable of forming the necessary intent of murder and so was guilty of manslaughter; or that he was guilty but insane under the M'Naghten Rules on the grounds that he did not know the nature or quality of the act. The trial judge refused to allow the jury to consider the first two defences and Bratty was convicted of murder when the jury rejected the defence of insanity. Bratty appealed but the conviction was upheld by the Court of Appeal and later, the House of Lords.

The House of Lords appeal in the case of Bratty set the legal definition of 'automatism' as 'the state of a person who, though capable of action, is not conscious of what he is doing. It means unconscious, involuntary action and it is a defence because the mind does not go with what is being done.' In other words, said the Lords, it was an action with no consciousness of doing what was being done. Their Lordships added that 'any mental disorder which has manifested itself in violence and is prone to recur is a disease of the mind – at any rate it is the sort of disease for which a person should be detained in hospital rather than be given an unqualified acquittal.'

The Lords ruling in Bratty suggested strongly that if the mind was absent during an epileptic attack, any action carried out was automatic. Medically, it has been shown conclusively that an epileptic attack can cause a 'clouding of consciousness' during or immediately after an attack, during which the sufferer can carry out quite complicated movements and acts without being aware of what is happening, although the level of awareness depends on each individual case.

It is doubtful whether Rutter had the ability to successfully form an argument along these lines, or whether his arguments would have held any weight in 1949. In their report to the Home Secretary before Danny's execution, Sir Norwood East and the other psychiatrists went to great lengths to debunk the theory that Danny's epilepsy, if he suffered from it at all, could explain his actions on the night of the murder. 'Raven's various accounts of the crime are opposed to the possibility that it was due to epileptic automatism,' wrote Sir Norwood. 'The events as stated by Raven occurred in orderly and connected sequences and in none of his statements has it been suggested that there was any loss of consciousness during the relevant period. Nothing was elicited at our interviews to lead us to believe that any such dissociation occurred.'

Sir Norwood conceded that the results of Denis Hill's EEG examination were consistent with the findings in many epileptics, he added that this did not mean that Danny was not criminally responsible for his actions. Support for this argument came from a surprising source – Dr Hill himself. 'Dr Hill has previously stated as regard criminal responsibility,' noted Sir Norwood, 'that the EEG test "cannot indicate what is or what has been in a person's mind at any time. It can give no indication of a person's sanity or insanity. Even if the test proves that the individual tested is epileptic, it cannot alone produce evidence of past automatism, or of a person's thoughts, awareness or intentions at any time in the past."'

'Moreover,' continued Sir Norwood, 'we should perhaps add that it has always been accepted that an epileptic, as such, cannot be considered immune from punishment unless the crime is definitely attributable to that disorder. We have no reason to think that the present crime was due to any other form of epileptic disorder than that already discussed.'

Had Danny's case come to trial today, the issue of his epilepsy, had the defence had sufficient evidence to mount a defence of automatism, would have been far more complicated.

The legal treatment of epilepsy, and particularly of the concept of automatism, has grown more complex since the Bratty ruling in 1963. In May 1981 Mr Sullivan, a 51-year-old man with no previous convictions and described by the appeal judge as having a 'blameless reputation', attacked and seriously injured an elderly neighbour during an epileptic attack. Sullivan had suffered two serious head injuries in the past, resulting in brain damage, and had suffered grand mal seizures since the age of eight. He had been treated at the Maudsley Hospital for years with some success and had not suffered a major seizure for four years before the attack. He continued to suffer petit mal attacks at a frequency of about twice a week, but had no memory of them or of the events immediately afterwards.

Sullivan had been visiting an 86-year-old neighbour and another friend, an 80-year-old man, Mr Payne, when he suffered a seizure. Mr Payne got out of his chair to help but Sullivan pushed him to the ground and kicked him in the head and body. Sullivan was charged with grievous bodily harm and the prosecution at his trial accepted that Sullivan had been suffering an epileptic attack at the time. Sullivan put forward a defence of 'sane automatism' – that he was not insane but was not in control of his actions at the time of the attack – and pleaded not guilty. The trial judge, though, ruled that the plea must be not guilty with a defence of automatism due to disease of the mind. The ruling was confirmed by the House of Lords, which effectively meant that Sullivan was ruled to be temporarily insane at the time of the attack.

This ruling meant that the law was effectively distinguishing between non-insane and insane automatism. Non-insane automatism is the result of an external event, which could mean anything from a reaction to drugs or alcohol, a knock to the head or even a reflex reaction to an insect bite or bee sting (although the law tends to distinguish between self-inflicted events and others – in Sullivan, for example, the court held that non-insane automatism, the result of an external event, could entitle a jury to deliver a not guilty verdict provided the impairment was in no way self-induced). Insane automatism is the result of an intrinsic underlying condition that results in a disorder of the mind, even if it is temporary, which leads to a situation that could recur and which is prone to violence. This covers a wide range of medical and psychiatric conditions, including epilepsy. But it also leads to unhelpful arbitrary distinctions – for instance, if a diabetic commits an offence after an injection of insulin it could be argued to be non-insane automatism, while if the same offence was carried out during a natural hyperglycaemic attack, it would be insane automatism.

This distinction is crucial because if a defendant successfully pleads non-insane automatism, in theory it would be possible for him to walk free from the court. The facts of the case are tried and if the accused is found guilty, a number of outcomes are possible. If it is established that the crime was the result of non-insane automatism, the defendant is entitled to be acquitted. If the accused is ruled to suffer from insane automatism (which resulted from a disease of the mind), he must be sentenced under the Fitness to Plead and Insanity Act 1991 which could result in detention in a secure mental hospital, depending on the discretion of the judge.

Had Danny's case come to the courts today and he had chosen to plead not guilty to murder due to automatism, psychiatric experts for both the defence and prosecution would be called on to assess whether, if he did attack the Goodmans, it was done during or in the aftermath of an epileptic attack. In order to successfully prove epileptic automatism the defence would have to convince the court on a number of key points.

First, it would have to proven that Danny had previously been clinically diagnosed with epilepsy, or at least that he had suffered from epilepsy for some time. A court would be unlikely to accept the argument that the offence occurred during his first ever seizure. Whether Danny would have been diagnosed as epileptic by modern medicine before he reached adulthood is impossible to say.

Second, the defence should show that the criminal act was out of character and inappropriate to the circumstances. A vicious physical attack was clearly out of character for Danny – while his family conceded that he had a temper, he was generally seen as a non-aggressive and harmless man. Whether his actions were appropriate in the circumstances is difficult to establish as the police investigation in 1949 failed to pinpoint what had happened that evening and why Danny would have suddenly attacked the Goodmans.

Third, the epileptic should have no memory of the attack, but should remember events immediately before it. This is impossible to assess in Danny's case since his defence was that he did not attack the Goodmans at all. Even so, comments made by his barrister, John Maude, to the Home Office in the days before Danny's execution suggested strongly that even if he had committed the murders, Danny firmly believed that he had not.

Finally, there should be no evidence of premeditation or concealment. This would be a tricky task for the defence in Danny's case. It is possible that they could successfully argue that there was no premeditation but clearly Danny attempted to conceal his actions afterwards. The law assumes that after an automotive event, an epileptic would be unlikely to fully register what had happened once they regain full consciousness, and that their natural response would be to seek help rather than to conceal the crime.

Danny's version of events that evening would warrant close examination by both the prosecution and defence, but while the fact that he changed his story during the course of the investigation was one of the most damning elements of the case against him in 1949, his lies to the police would be treated with more circumspection in a modern-day trial.

Danny was effectively condemned at his trial because he had lied to the police about his movements on the night of 10 October. He initially told DI Diller that he had left the Goodmans alive and well at 9.30pm and had gone home to have a bath. He told two similar versions of this story to other detectives, before telling DCI Tansill, after his burnt suit had been found in the boiler, that he had returned to the house later, found the bodies, panicked and ran. The fact that he had lied and changed his story was used heavily against Danny in the prosecution's summing up and was brought up by both the trial judge and the appeal court judges.

Today, if the prosecution relies at any point in a trial on the fact that the defendant has lied – to the police or anyone else during the course of the investigation – in order to suggest or prove his guilt, the judge is generally obliged to give what is known as the Lucas Direction to the jury. In effect, the Lucas direction reminds the jury that people lie for many reasons and not necessarily because they are guilty of something. In the case of a Lucas direction the jury is told by the judge that the lie is only evidence of guilt if it is made deliberately, and that the lie alone is insufficient evidence and the jury should look to see if other evidence corroborates guilt. The judge will also remind the jury that people might lie to protect someone, to cover up shameful behaviour, or out of panic.

In 1949 Danny faced a bleak outcome. His best hope – however unlikely – was that he would be found not guilty by the jury. If he was convicted there were only two options: death by hanging or life in Broadmoor. It was not until 1957 that a legal distinction was introduced between capital and non-capital homicide through the Homicide Act, but since Danny was accused of a double murder it is likely that, had he been tried after the introduction of the Homicide Act, he would still have faced a death sentence if convicted.

Given his mental state, though, the 1957 Act would have offered a lifeline to Danny in its introduction of the concept of diminished responsibility as a defence to murder. Section 2 of the Act says that a killer cannot be convicted of murder 'if he was suffering from such abnormality of the mind (whether arising from a condition of arrested or retarded development of mind or any inherent causes induced by disease or injury) as substantially impaired his mental responsibility for his acts or omissions in doing or being a party to the killing'. The responsibility for proving that the accused is not guilty of murder lies with the defence but it must be proved on the balance of probabilities rather than beyond reasonable doubt, which is a lesser standard. If the defence is successful, a conviction of manslaughter rather than murder applies.

The definition of 'an abnormality of the mind' was established through the 1960 case of Byrne, a sexual psychopath who murdered a young woman and mutilated her body, as 'a state of mind so different from that of ordinary human beings that the reasonable man would term it abnormal. It appears to us to be wide enough to cover the mind's activities in all its aspects, not only in the perception of physical acts and manners, and the ability to form a rational judgment as to whether an act is right or wrong, but also the ability to exercise willpower to control physical acts in accordance with rational judgments'.

In other words, abnormality of the mind is not enough. The defence would have to show that the abnormality – in Danny's case, his blackouts – were enough to substantially impair his mental responsibility. The defence would have to show that Danny suffered a blackout at the time of the attack, that the blackouts constituted an abnormality of the mind, and that the effect was enough to substantially impair his responsibility at the time.

Danny's defence would depend on the skills and judgment of the psychiatric experts called by the prosecution and defence.

In arguing diminished responsibility, the key evidence would undoubtedly be that of Dr Murdo McKenzie, who treated Danny for symptoms of anxiety a year before the murders. After he saw Danny for the last time in November 1948, Dr McKenzie wrote to Dr Hirschmann, detailing his conclusions. The case was not an easy one, he wrote, and he warned that while Danny's symptoms of anxiety could be treated, there seemed to be serious underlying problems that could reappear without warning in the future: 'His sense of doubt from time to time about the good intentions of anybody, and the defined sense of unreality left open the possibility that, in addition to recoverable anxiety, a dissociating illness of a paranoid schizophrenic type lay latent to become manifest at a later date.'

Dr McKenzie warned that Danny's 'unreasoning sense of jealousy with his parents' had boiled over into a rage a few weeks previously, seemed to be triggered by a mild illness in his wife. Bearing in mind that Danny was under considerable stress in the week his child was born and that on the day of the murders, Gertrude was suffering from the painful infection mastitis, Dr McKenzie's words seem prophetic.

After the murders, Dr McKenzie gave a detailed deposition to Sydney Rutter, which expanded on this theory. 'On the assumption that the Goodmans were murdered by Daniel Raven and that there was no motive for the crime,' he said, 'I am of the opinion that his act was as a result of illness of the mind. From the facts presented to me the most likely condition would be paranoid schizophrenia.'

Dr McKenzie added that his opinion was based on his assessment made in October 1948 that Danny's feelings of jealousy, isolation and persecution were triggered by Gertrude's illness. 'In the current situation the strain experienced was much more considerable and involved his wife's pregnancy, labour and post-parturition breast infection. The effect of these events may well have been to have precipitated an acute recrudescence of the symptoms of persecution similar in kind as on the previous occasion, but much more severe in degree.

'These facts should be made known to the appropriate authorities because in my opinion, viewing the situation as a whole, these facts indicate that the question of a mental illness of paranoid schizophrenic type merits serious consideration.'

Dr McKenzie's opinion was never heard by a jury and by the time it was drawn to the attention of the Home Office, time had run out for Danny.

Dr McKenzie's assessment suggests strongly that Danny had an underlying condition that could make him prone to unpredictable and perhaps violent behaviour, particularly when under stress. Whether this medical evidence, combined with Rutter's arguments about Danny's undiagnosed epilepsy, would result in a verdict of manslaughter due to diminished responsibility today is arguable, but seems possible. If Danny was convicted of manslaughter due to diminished responsibility today, there could be a number of possible outcomes. If the court ruled that he had on-going mental health problems he could be sentenced under section 37 of the Mental Health Act 1983 and sent to a secure hospital for an indeterminate period for treatment. If it was considered that he was a danger to the public he would be sentenced to an indeterminate period in a secure institution under section 41 of the Act and could not be released without a ruling from the Home Secretary.

Given the evidence and arguments presented to the Home Office by Sydney Rutter and John Maude in the days before Danny's execution, it seems extraordinary that he was not granted a reprieve by the Home Secretary. On 22 December 1949 Rutter wrote to Chuter Ede, drawing attention to the depositions obtained from Dr McKenzie and Dr Hirschmann, and pointing out a memo outlining the standard Home Office practice for reprieves, which had recently been sent to the Royal Commission on Capital Punishment. The memo said:

> *When a murder is committed without premeditation as the result of some sudden excess of frenzy and the prisoner has previously had no evil animus towards the victim, commutation is often recommended. In case of this kind it is sometimes necessary to give weight to the consideration that the prisoner, although not insane, is weak-minded or emotionally unstable to an abnormal degree. Account must also be taken of the character of the prisoner, of his relations with the deceased and of all the circumstances.*

With the exception of Samuel Vosper, who bought stolen goods off Danny and told police that he was jealous of Leopold's wealth, and Danny himself, who told police that he got on well with Leopold but not so well with Esther, many other witnesses said that Danny was fond of the Goodmans and behaved kindly towards them. Gertrude Raven herself confirmed this to Sydney Rutter, saying that she knew of no reason why Danny would have wanted to harm her parents. She told Rutter that her parents were always kind and good to Danny and he appreciated that, and often told her so. Dr McKenzie and Dr Hirschmann also said in their depositions that he always spoke well of the Goodmans and seemed to be very fond of them.

Ultimately, it was the fact that Danny was convicted of killing *two* people that condemned him to death. Had there been only one victim it is possible that the Home Secretary may have felt the new medical evidence presented by Rutter in the days before his execution would be enough to warrant a reprieve. But a double murder in a quiet London suburb was something else entirely. An article in the *Sunday Pictorial*, two days after Danny's death, put the point bluntly:

> *The uproar over the hanging of Daniel Raven has been quite out of proportion to the facts of the case. In the general hubbub one grim fact seemed to have been forgotten. Daniel Raven was found guilty of the particularly brutal killing of his father-in-law and assumed guilty of the murder of his mother-in-law. So long as hanging remains, few men have deserved it more.*

Chapter 21 – Why and How?

Danny was buried in the grounds of Pentonville three hours after his execution, in a grave marked only by an identification number. The crowds wandered away from outside the prison and, for many, life returned to normal. The execution justified only a short note in some of the national newspapers, most of which had turned their attention to the attempts to track down the film star Ingrid Bergman, who was in hiding following rumours of an affair with Roberto Rossellini, the director of her latest film.

For others, though, and particularly the local press and residents of Edgware, there remained many unanswered questions. 'At Pentonville prison today will end one of the most widely discussed and controversial murder stories of recent years,' said the editorial of the *Hendon and Finchley Times* on the day of Danny's execution. 'A question which will now never be answered is why he seized the television aerial base in his father-in-law's home and battered him to death. Was there a motive? Was the murder committed in a sudden fit of rage, or was it premeditated?'

The paper was not alone in its search for answers. A steady stream of letters from members of the public continued to arrive at the Home Office in the weeks after the execution, questioning whether Danny was guilty. 'I notice that where there is no motive the Crown always stresses that it is not essential to produce a motive,' wrote Donald Dickinson from Wiltshire. 'Yet when the Crown can produce a motive it pedals it for all it is worth. It's quite clear why – a double murder without motive is so unlikely that a jury must be persuaded into giving a verdict which when looked at without bias is somewhat perverse.'

The inability of the police investigation to identify a motive for the murders, as well as the apparent lack of interest by the prosecution in even putting a possible motive forward at the trial, meant that doubt continued to surround the case. Even today in Edgware, the many people who remember the murders still wonder why Danny did it. In an explanation there is security. If the murders were a random act of madness then they could happen to anyone. If a satisfactory explanation could be found – that Danny killed the Goodmans for money, or that an argument had erupted over something specific – then it becomes easier to detach yourself from the possibility that it might just as easily happen to you.

In the absence of an explanation for Danny's actions a number of rumours and counter-rumours tore through the local community, many of which are still discussed today. One of the most popular theories is that Danny had been presented with a large bill for Gertrude's stay at the private nursing home on the evening of 10 October, which he was unable to pay as he had no regular income. He had asked the Goodmans for money that evening, they had refused and in a rage, he lashed out and killed them.

There are several problems with this theory, not least that Gertrude was a much-loved only child of the Goodmans and it seems reasonable to assume that they would pay the nursing home bill if asked. It is also clear that Gertrude would not have left the nursing home until several days later – according to newspaper reports she discharged herself against medical advice four days after the murders. And no-one at the nursing home mentioned anything about a bill during the police investigation (although it is very possible that they were not asked).

The police officers investigating the case had a different theory. DCI Albert Tansill revealed a few weeks after Danny's execution that many of the investigating team believed that he had left the nursing home that evening believing that the Goodmans were heading straight from Muswell Hill to another appointment and would not be home for a while. He drove straight to Ashcombe Gardens and broke into the house through the scullery window, with the intention of stealing any money he found in the house – given the burglary problem in Edgware at the time, it would be easy to blame the break-in on a random intruder. The police believed that Danny was upstairs in the bedroom when the Goodmans returned home unexpectedly and, finding himself 'in a serious dilemma', he killed the couple when they discovered him in the house. 'Whether that supposition is right or wrong we shall never know,' Tansill said later, 'but the circumstantial evidence was so overwhelming that the officers had no difficulty in arriving at the conclusion that he was the murderer.'

Again, there are problems with this theory. Neither Gertrude nor anyone at the nursing home suggested that the Goodmans intended going anywhere else that evening. Alfred had spoken to the Goodmans just before 8pm and had arranged to come to the house as usual at about 10pm – if Leopold and Esther intended to go out after visiting Gertrude, they either neglected to tell Alfred, or made the decision while at the nursing home and after they had left Gertrude. Danny knew their routine well and it seems unlikely that he would pick that moment to burgle the house unless he knew for a fact that they would be out for a while – which leaves the unlikely explanation that the Goodmans told only him of their plans.

An added complication is the safe. It was never established if Danny knew about the existence of the safe under the stairs at Ashcombe Gardens. The safe was never tested for fingerprints because the police believed that it had not been touched that evening, so it was not possible to ascertain whether Danny had ever been near it. It held a great deal of money and, as the defence team pointed out at the trial, anyone who knew Leopold's business could reasonably assume that there would be bounty in the house. If Danny intended to rob the house and knew about the safe, why would he waste time looking anywhere else?

What is clear is that Danny was short of money. He had seen his income dwindle from earning £20 a week – a handsome sum – when working for his father, to £8 a week when he worked for Leopold. The bill of sale he took out on his furniture and his dealings with Samuel Vosper, to whom he sold stock he had stolen from Leopold, suggest that he was willing to take risks to boost his 'income' but is also a reflection of his father's long-standing, fly-by-the-seat-of-your-pants approach to business. Danny had lost his job with Leopold as a result and had no regular income, as well as the added responsibility of a new baby, at the time of the murders. He was dabbling with a new venture, his recording studio, but as his finances were not investigated it is impossible to say whether that was bringing in any income at all.

Danny was, in other words, a man in desperate financial straits with increasing responsibilities and, most likely, a deep-rooted feeling of inadequacy in providing for his family. His home and some of his furniture had been provided by his parents-in-law. Until recently, his job had also been provided by Leopold. If he had gone to the house that night to ask for money – perhaps a loan to fund his new business – and Leopold had refused, perhaps his frustration boiled over into unexpected violence.

Aside from motive, there remain a number of unexplained elements at the crime scene, most of which were identified in the Home Office report on the murders that James Chuter Ede read when deciding whether to grant Danny a reprieve.

First, why was the casement window in the scullery unlocked and open when Alfred and his family arrived at the house? Alfred told police that the Goodmans were very security-conscious and always closed the window if they left the house. There was no sign that the lock was broken which leaves two possibilities – either Leopold or Esther opened the window when they returned or it was open when they left for Muswell Hill. Perhaps they simply forgot to close it, which would have left an easy entry point for an opportunistic burglar. Or perhaps Danny did plan to stage a burglary at the house and took the window off the latch while he was at the house earlier that day.

Second, who went upstairs that evening and why? The disorder in the Goodmans bedroom was discussed at the trial but never explained. Esther's coat and hat, which presumably she wore to the nursing home (although that was never established), were on the floor of the bedroom and the mattress on the bed nearest the door had been pushed diagonally aside. The bedding was also on the floor, while the other bed was neatly made. The money on the side table, though, was untouched. The police were unable to find any traces of blood on the stairs, the banister or in the bedroom, which suggests that the murderer did not go upstairs after killing the Goodmans.

Third, was the light in the dining room ever turned on? Because Leopold and Esther were discovered in the dining room and the light was turned off when Alfred arrived at the house at 10pm, the prosecution assumed that the murders must have been carried out by someone who knew the house well. The assumption was that Leopold had been killed when the light was on and that the murderer had turned out the light when he left – and since the light switch was positioned five inches from the floor and behind the door, it would have been almost impossible for a stranger to find it. But as John Maude said during his summing up, to ask who turned the light off you must first assume that it was once turned on. And no blood marks were found on the switch.

Fourth, why were the Goodmans in the dining room at all? And were they together when attacked? Evidence from family members suggested that they spent most of their time in the kitchen, which was large and comfortable with a sofa and table and chairs. The fact that Leopold was in the dining room when attacked could suggest that a formal discussion was taking place.

And fifth, where was the murder weapon that evening? Alfred told police that he had seen it a few days earlier propped against a wall in the hallway. There was no aerial attached to the base, so it is unlikely that Leopold was using it for his own television set. But if it was still in the hall that night, and if Danny had flown into a rage while in the dining room with Leopold, he would have had to go into the hall to pick it up and return to the dining room before striking Leopold.

As the Home Office report pointed out, it is almost impossible to come up with an explanation for what happened that evening that answers all of these points.

Alan Wall, a North London accountant who began writing a book about the Raven case in the 1990s, came to the conclusion that Danny followed Esther into the house when they arrived at Ashcombe Gardens that evening, while Leopold was putting his car in the garage. As Esther went upstairs to put her coat and hat away Danny followed her, perhaps pleading increasingly desperately for money. In the bedroom he lost his temper and pushed the mattress aside, looking for money. Frightened, Esther ran downstairs chased by Danny, who by now was wild with rage. He grabbed the television aerial base from the hallway and, in the doorway of the dining room, hit her seven times. At this moment Leopold came into the house from the side door next to the garage, and found Danny leaning over his wife. Danny turned on Leopold and as the older man raised his hands to protect himself, Danny hit him with the aerial base in a frenzy, landing 14 blows.

Alan Wall's theory certainly explains the disorder in the bedroom, the lack of blood on the stairs and the fact that Leopold was struck many more times than Esther. But since Leopold was found in the centre of the dining room, between the table and the fireplace, and Esther was found in the doorway, Leopold and Danny would have had to step over Esther at some point as she lay dead on the floor, which seems unlikely. Neither does it explain why Leopold's coat was hanging on a peg in the hallway.

DCI Albert Tansill's explanation of the events of that evening, which he set out in his report to his Chief Superintendent a week after the murders, are perhaps the closest to the truth:

> *In our view the crime was carried out in this way. Raven arrived at the house at 9.30pm. He went inside, [Leopold] Goodman removed the jacket he was wearing, and went into the dining room with the prisoner. Simultaneously Mrs Goodman went upstairs to her bedroom. While the prisoner and Mr Goodman were in the dining room a quarrel developed. In a raging temper the prisoner got the aerial base and attacked his father-in-law, who shouted out. On hearing the noise downstairs Mrs Goodman, who had put on her indoor shoes, leaving her coat and handbag on the divan bed, which was then made, rushed downstairs. The prisoner continued to batter the man. Hearing Mrs Goodman coming downstairs he stood behind the door and, as she entered the dining room he struck her a blow on the head and continued to rain blows on his victims with the aerial base. Having done this he went to the sink in the scullery, washed the instrument and his hands. He returned to the dining room and switched off the fluorescent lighting.*

Tansill's explanation for the disorder in the bedroom of the house, though, is less convincing given that no blood was found on the stairs or in the bedroom. It also suggests that Danny was fully in control of his actions that evening:

> *To make it seem that a burglary had occurred he went upstairs, entered the front bedroom, disarranged the bed, threw the eiderdown and other property on it onto the floor. He then switched off the light in the bedroom and closed the door. He left the house through the front door by pulling the lever of the Ingersoll lock. The attempted disposal of the suit and the washing of his shoes followed immediately on his arrival at his house.*

If Danny did enter the house with the Goodmans at around 9.30pm that evening, rather than leave them after having a conversation at the front gate as he told police, perhaps he went into the dining room with Leopold to talk about money or about Gertrude's health, while Esther went upstairs to put her coat and hat away. An argument broke out and Danny flew into a violent rage as predicted by Dr McKenzie a year earlier, shouting and striding in a fury from the dining room to the hall, where he picked up the television aerial base and flew at Leopold as he raised his hand to protect himself, striking him unconscious. Hearing the commotion Esther dropped her coat and hat on the floor, perhaps falling against the bed in her shock. Or maybe she began searching frantically and vainly under the bed and mattress for a long-forgotten weapon that Leopold had once hidden there in case they ever needed to defend themselves against a burglar. She ran downstairs into the dining room, where she was struck hard by Danny, who was standing just behind the door as she entered the room. In a daze, he staggered into the kitchen, washed the aerial base and ran out of the house.

We will never know exactly what happened in Ashcombe Gardens that night, or why it happened. Perhaps Dr McKenzie was right and Danny attacked the Goodmans in a psychotic rage, triggered by the sudden responsibility of being a father and worry about Gertrude's health, but had no recollection of his actions afterwards. John Maude's insistence that Danny was utterly convinced of his own innocence is some support of this theory. Or perhaps the defence team was right all along and the Goodmans were killed by a burglar who fled the scene before Danny arrived. Whatever happened, the only certainty is that 88 days later, Danny died for it.

Chapter 22 – What Happened Next

Three weeks after Danny's death and under a new name organised for them by the Home Office, Edward, Betty and Muriel Raven left London behind and with the last of their money, bought three tickets to Australia. Edward had not worked since the day his son was arrested and had sold the family's home in Gurney Drive, along with most of their possessions, in order to pay for Danny's defence. When the family arrived in Australia at the beginning of February 1950, they had £44 to their name.

The family rented a house in Double Bay, New South Wales and after a few weeks of recuperation, Edward found work as a travelling salesman.

Back in London, Gertrude cut herself off from her friends and her old life in Edgware. Bernard and Netta Elliston recall seeing her on the street in central London a few weeks after the trial, but she ducked into a doorway when she saw them. Another friend was convinced that they saw her in the South of France late in 1950, but again she quickly turned and walked away. Shortly after Danny's execution she made a legal application to change her name.

Leopold's radio dealership carried on under Alfred's guiding hand for a few months, before being wound down and liquidated in 1951. The house at Ashcombe Gardens was put on the market with Gordon Hudson & Co, an estate agent on Mowbray Parade near Edgware Station, on the instruction of Gertrude's solicitor. There was strong demand for family homes in the district at the time but, unsurprisingly given the history of the house, a buyer was difficult to find. Eventually the house was sold to a doctor who, as a man of science, rated a much reduced selling price well above what had taken place there.

Gertrude was adamant that her child should be spared any contact with Danny's family and in the first few months of 1950 her solicitor Alfred Bieber embarked on a plan that he was sure would guarantee that the Ravens would remain in Australia – he filed a bankruptcy order against Edward.

A court in Bloomsbury heard Beiber's application on 16 March 1950. An unpaid debt of at least £50 was required before a court order could be made and so Bieber, on behalf of Leopold's business, filed a petition against Edward for £52 plus costs. When Edward failed to respond – he was, after all, in Australia – a judgment was entered against him and the bankruptcy proceedings began.

The bankruptcy petition lists three creditors besides Leopold's company that, it said, were owed money by Edward: British Motor Trust of North Finchley was owed £1,055, the National Westminster Bank in Kingston Upon Thames was owed £659 and Eastern Electricity was owed £20. Edward was required, as part of the bankruptcy process, to provide detailed information on the debts and his finances and he was eventually tracked down to New South Wales in 1951, where he filled in the required form and returned it to the Official Receiver. Years later he would say that he had no recollection of completing the form.

This is not so difficult to believe when presented with the original document. Edward's writing is loose and erratic and his answers become increasingly exasperated as he worked his way through the numerous questions. He crossed through many sections with violent strokes of his pen. In answer to the question, What do you believe to be the total amount of your unsecured indebtedness and the number of your creditors? Edward wrote: 'Do not know. Can only accept information you give'. Later, when asked to give the names and addresses of the creditors he wrote: 'Not known. Have not been informed of anything.'

Edward wrote on the form that he had not been served with a bankruptcy notice and that all of his possessions, including his clothes, had been sold to pay the costs of defending his son. At the bottom of the form, though, is a note added later by Edward in different coloured ink. The writing is neat and controlled, with two words underlined several times. The question asked: What are the causes of your insolvency? Edward wrote: 'I absented myself from business from October 11 1949 and never returned. My time was occupied in making a futile attempt to save my innocent son from capital punishment – for a crime he did not commit. I do not know what happened to the business except that any claims I had were perhaps not admitted or included.'

Bieber's application was successful and Edward was declared bankrupt in November 1950. A month later Gertrude remarried at the Savoy Hotel in London, with Alfred Bieber acting as a witness. Ashleigh Brilliant recorded the event in his diary: 'We read in the evening paper that the wife of Daniel Raven has married again. The wedding was a surprisingly large affair, with about 180 guests.'

Gertrude and her new husband, a 28-year-old Jewish company director, went on to have three more children.

The police and CID team investigating the murder of Gertrude's parents were singled out for praise by the trial and appeal judges, and by the Director of Public Prosecutions. DI Jack Diller's 'intuition and quick thinking' in shutting down the boiler in Danny's house was particularly noted and, on the recommendation of his Chief Superintendent, he was highly commended for his initiative and ability displayed during the case by the Metropolitan Police Commissioner. Eight other officers involved in the case, including PC Charles Hill, Inspector Harvey, DS Grout and DS Erskine, also received commendations. DCI Tansill, who could not receive a commendation because of his rank, was described as 'a tower of strength and a splendid example of efficiency to his subordinates,' by his superior officer. 'Seldom have I seen a better team in action,' wrote Chief Superintendent Beveridge in his report

Edward and Betty Raven returned to England in July 1953 and continued with their chaotic lifestyle. In October of the same year, a company, Slide Publicity, was set up in Betty's name. The company was meant to exploit the relatively new idea of projecting advertising slides and films onto buildings. Betty signed a seven-year lease on a first-floor studio in Coventry Street in Central London at a rent of £750 a year and bought projecting equipment worth about £800.

Perhaps predictably, things did not go well. Late in 1953 Slide Publicity was prosecuted for causing an obstruction when a crowd gathered on a pavement to watch one of its adverts. In its first four months of trading, the company recorded a loss of £1,286 and by June 1954 it was forced to hold a meeting of its creditors when it became clear that it would not be able to pay its bills. All but one of the creditors agreed to a partial settlement of their claim. The remaining creditor applied for and was awarded a court order for his debt of £379, which Betty failed to pay. She was declared bankrupt in December 1954, but told the Official Receiver that Edward controlled the company and she was the director in name only.

The following year Edward and Betty separated and they later divorced. Edward remarried and he and his new wife, Sylvia, embarked on a colourful career, forming and liquidating a string of companies over the next 15 years. Between 1957 and 1972 the couple were listed as directors of 15 different companies, including two advertising and publicity agencies, a number of oil and petrol dealerships, a building contractor and several laundrettes.

In February 1972 Edward, then aged 65, turned up at the Official Receivers' office in London with his solicitor. He told the office that he had recently discovered that a bankruptcy order had been made against him more than 20 years previously and asked how he could apply for the ruling to be discharged. The official on duty told him that he would have to supply details of his finances at the time bankruptcy was declared, as well as his business activities for the past 22 years, and that he would be given an appointment to be interviewed by the Assistant Official Receiver, Mr Jenner, over the coming weeks.

Five appointments were arranged for Edward's interview between February and May 1972 but he failed to turn up on each occasion. At the end of May his solicitor Lewis Cutner, frustrated by Edward's reluctance to talk about how his debts in 1950 had come about and under pressure himself from the Official Receiver, wrote to him and urged him to agree to an interview. 'I hasten to assure you that Mr Jenner has no intention whatever of prying into your personal affairs,' he wrote. 'Let me assure you that I am not in any way whatsoever intending to browbeat you into doing something that is abhorrent, as against trying to make you see sense in a sensible way.'

Edward reluctantly took Cutner's advice and was interviewed by Jenner on 13 June 1972. The session did not go well and Edward refused to answer any questions in much detail. Jenner wrote in the margin of his notes that Edward was 'unco-operative and belligerent'.

It would take another eight months for the Official Receivers office to coax enough information out of Edward for the bankruptcy discharge process to continue. In February 1973 Edward, with enormous reluctance and the same belligerence he had displayed from the beginning, attended a public examination by the Official Receiver, James Tye, in front of a judge at the Royal Courts of Justice. In a setting that must have brought back painful memories of his son's trial, Edward was questioned under oath by Tye for three hours in a frequently bad-tempered exchange. Edward's answers show that, 23 years after his son's execution, the emotional scars were still raw.

Tye asked him why he could not remember filling in the bankruptcy forms while in Australia. 'I left this country under tragic circumstances, and if you knew those circumstances you would not ask the last question,' Edward snapped back.

Tye noted that the 1950 ruling was the second time that Edward had been declared bankrupt. Surely, he said, he would therefore be more likely to understand the consequences of the forms he was sent in Australia. 'The tragic circumstances so clouded my mind that I could not remember,' said Edward. 'I could not remember. I was not in a fit state to remember, mentally.' Increasingly agitated, he said he could not remember filling in the form or signing it. 'I was not in a fit state of health. At the time when I signed it I knew nothing of what I was signing and I was not to be relied upon. I was still suffering. I am a fit man today mentally but at that time I was not.'

The judge interjected as Edward became more upset: 'You are not doing yourself justice by getting yourself excited,' he told Edward.

Edward's solicitor told the judge that Edward was not anxious to talk about what passed before 1950 and had asked that he be allowed to write down the circumstances under which he left England in 1950 for the court. Edward wrote a short note on a piece of paper, which he passed to the judge. 'Your Honour having seen that, your Honour may be able to understand my client's attitude,' said Cutner.

'I see,' said the judge. 'I can better appreciate why he has adopted the attitude that he has.'

James Tye would later describe Edward as 'of a highly excitable nature – belligerent – and at times, almost incoherent'. He had a point. Edward's attitude and unco-operative behaviour made the process much more difficult and long-winded that it could have been. The Official Receiver had traced all of the creditors named on Bieber's 1950 petition and almost all had either gone out of business or had no record of the claims at all. The remaining debts were paid by Edward's wife. Even so, it would take two more tortuous hearings before enough information was coaxed out of Edward for the bankruptcy discharge to be granted. His reluctance could be partly explained by the messy state of his current business interests – during the process he eventually revealed that the majority of the companies he had set up since 1953 were either dormant or had been dissolved, that a co-director in one of his businesses owed over £50,000 to a bank, and that a partner in another business had defrauded the company of another £50,000.

The fact that Edward had acted as a company director while an undischarged bankrupt, however, was problematic as it laid him open to criminal charges. After a short investigation, though, the Official Receiver agreed not to press charges against him on the grounds that while Edward's behaviour had not been entirely satisfactory, 'further proceedings against him are almost certain to give rise to a revival of the unwelcome publicity to which he was subjected in 1950. The person most likely to suffer from the publicity which criminal proceedings against the bankrupt would inevitably attract would be the bankrupt's grandchild.'

Edward died in December 1974 of a brain haemorrhage exacerbated by hypertension. He was 67.

DCI Albert Tansill remained at S Division in Edgware for three years after the murders and retired from the force on 31 August 1952 at the age of 48. He had served 26 years, 8 months and 18 days with the Metropolitan Police. He died in July 1985 at the age of 81.

DI Jack Diller was promoted to Detective Chief Inspector of the murder squad in 1952 and Detective Chief Superintendent in 1953, moving from his base in Edgware to Islington and later to the divisional headquarters in East London. He retired from the force on 30 June 1955 at the age of 52 after more than 30 years with the Metropolitan Police. He died in November 1985 at the age of 82.

DS Philip Grout transferred from Edgware to Hendon and later to Scotland Yard, where he was promoted to Detective Inspector in 1957 and Detective Chief Inspector in 1960. Between 1957 and 1960 he was a lecturer at Hendon Detective Training School, before returning to CID. He was commended nine times by the Commissioner of Police during his 32-year career with the Metropolitan Police. By the time he retired from the Met in

1968 he was a Detective Chief Superintendent and was in charge of the Criminal Records Office at Scotland Yard. He died in 2002 at the age of 85.

In 1953, Detective Inspector Herbert Hannam was put in charge of the investigation into the infamous Teddington Towpath Murders, later described as 'one of Scotland Yard's most notable triumphs'. Alfred Whiteway was charged with the murder of two schoolgirls on the towpath with an axe and was hanged at Wandsworth Prison on 22 December 1953. In 1956 Hannam took on another high profile investigation, that of the suspected serial killer Dr John Bodkin Adams, a wealthy GP working in Eastbourne. More than 150 of Dr Adams' patients had died over the course of the previous five years, and more than 130 had left him a legacy in their will. After a lengthy investigation, Adams was eventually charged with the murder of two of his elderly female patients but was found not guilty.

Hannam was promoted to Commander but left CID in 1960 to work as a security adviser. He died in 1983.

Gertrude is alive and well. She has no memory of the terrible events of 1949.

* * * * *

Significant Participants

Leopold Goodman – murder victim
Esther Goodman – his wife, also murdered
Gertrude Raven – their daughter
Daniel Raven – Gertrude's husband

Alfred – Leopold's brother-in-law

Edward Raven – Daniel Raven's father
Betty Raven – his mother
Sylvia – Daniel's elder sister
Muriel – Daniel's younger sister
Esther – Daniel's aunt
Dennis – Esther's son and Daniel's cousin

PC **Charles Hill** – the first constable on scene at 8 Ashcombe Gardens
PC **Nabbs** – his wireless operator

Inspector John Harvey – senior uniformed officer at Edgware police station on the night of 10 October 1949
Sergeant Worth – his driver

The CID team:

District Chief Superintendent **Peter Beveridge**
Detective Chief Inspector **Albert Tansill**
Detective Inspector **Jack Diller**
Detective Sergeant **Philip Grout**
Detective Sergeant **Erskine**
Detective **Thomas**

Detective Inspector **Herbert Hannam** – Golders Green police station

Chief Inspector **Henry Stoddard** – Scotland Yard

Dr **Henry Smith Holden** – head of forensic science at Scotland Yard
Dr **Donald Teare** – a pathologist appointed by the Home Office
Dr **Matthews** – police surgeon
Dr **Cairns** – an Edgware GP, Alfred's family doctor
Dr **Samuel Hirschmann** – the Raven's GP
Dr **Murdo McKenzie** – a psychiatrist
Dr **Coates** – medical officer, Pentonville Prison

Sydney Rutter – Daniel Raven's solicitor
John Maude KC – defence barrister
Gerald Howard – junior member of Maude's team
Victor Durand – junior member of Maude's team
Anthony Hawke KC – barrister for the prosecution
Henry Elam – his assistant
Mr **Justice Cassels** – judge at the Old Bailey

Maurice Arram – Gertrude Raven's solicitor
Alfred Bieber – Alfred's solicitor
KS Lewis – officer of the Director of Public Prosecutions

James Chuter Ede – Home Secretary
Sir **Frank Newsam** – Undersecretary of State

Sir **Norwood East** – Medical Commissioner of HM Prisons
Dr **Hopwood** – medical superintendent at Broadmoor Prison
Dr **Desmond Curran** – Home Officer-appointed doctor

Linda Thomas – a nurse at Strathlene Nursing Home, Muswell Hill
Phyllis Conquest – a nurse at Strathlene Nursing Home
Vargas Gardner – a reporter with the *Daily Express*
Eddie Noble – a second-hand car salesman
Mr **Grey** – a currency dealer, based in Cannes
Aron Ellison – a manufacturer's agent
Samuel Vosper – a radio equipment dealer
Fay Schein – 39-year-old mother of four

Photographs and Diagrams

8 Ashcombe Gardens

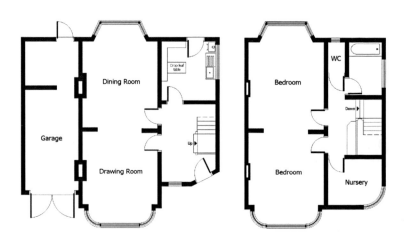

184 Edgwarebury Lane

8 Ashcombe Gardens, today

184 Edgwarebury Lane, with extension, today

Leopold Goodman

Esther and Leopold Goodman (centre)

Police crime scene photograph of Leopold's body

Where the murder weapon was cleaned

Daniel Raven as a school boy

Where Daniel burnt his suit

MRS. GOODMAN'S BROTHER-IN-LAW KNEW NOTHING OF £2518 SAFE

Raven is charged with murder of father-in-law

'CHARRED
SUIT
IS VITAL'

Evening Standard Reporter

Daniel Raven, 23, of Edgwarebury Lane, Edgware, pleaded not guilty at the Old Bailey to-day to murdering his 49-year-old father-in-law, Leopold Goodman, at Ashcombe Gardens, Edgware, on October 10.

newspaper cutting from Tuesday 22 November 1949

Opened window at the rear of the Goodmans' house

Exhibits presented to the court

Edgware police station, today

Bibliography and References

The Murders of the Black Museum 1870-1970 by Gordon Honeycombe
Bloomsbury Books, London 1982

Austerity Britain 1945-51 by David Kynaston
Bloomsbury 2007

Barnet: The Twentieth Century by John Heathfield and Percy Reboul
Sutton Publishing, Stroud 1999

Barnet, Edgware, Hadley and Totteridge: A Pictorial History
by Pamela Taylor and Joanna Corden
Phillimore & Co Ltd 1994
Copyright Barnet Libraries, Arts and Museums

Old Edgware in Camera by Alf Porter
Quotes Ltd 1991

The Eighth Veil by Ann Todd

Executioner: Pierrepoint by Albert Pierrepoint
Eric Dobby Publishing 1974

A Very English Hangman: The Life and Times of Albert Pierrepoint by Leonora
Klein
Corvo Books 2006

Purchasing Power of British Pounds from 1264 to 2007 by Lawrence H Officer
Measuringworth, 2008

Index

A

Abu Suier, Egypt, 43
anti-Semitism, 33
anxiety/anxiety neurosis, 17, 41,
    43, 166–171, 186
appeal, 96, 105, 108, 110–116,
    118–120, 125, 163, 165, 172,
    175, 180, 182, 184, 199
Ashcombe Gardens, 16–24, 28–
    30, 32, 38, 45, 51–52, 55–57,
    61, 63–64, 66, 69, 73–74, 80,
    82–83, 85, 93–96, 99–100,
    120, 143, 146–147, 153–158,
    160, 164, 168, 190–191, 193,
    195, 197, 204, 206–207
Atlee, Clement (Prime Minister), 14
Australia, 46, 197–198, 201

B

bankruptcy, 44, 198–202
BBC, 15, 65
Beveridge, Chief Superintendent
    Peter, 130, 199, 204
Bieber, Alfred (Bieber & Bieber
    solicitors), 61, 198–199, 201,
    205
blood clotting, 102
blood group, 56, 73, 153–154, 156
blood patterns, 70, 149, 154, 158
Brilliant, Ashleigh, 51, 199
Brixton Prison, 52, 61–62, 65, 93,
    111, 117, 121, 125, 167, 170, 172,
    175–176
burglary, 18–19, 29, 47, 60, 78,
    190, 192, 194

C

Cairns, Dr, 18, 20, 53, 63–64, 69,
    99, 205
Cassels, Mr Justice, 66, 75, 81,
    84–85, 87, 98–101, 103, 111,
    113–116, 205
cautioning, 28, 31–32, 145–146

Chief Rabbi, 125
Christie, John, 137
CID, 7, 22, 24, 52, 199, 202–204
condemned cell, 115, 117, 135, 175
conviction, 47, 97, 106, 110, 119,
    125, 129, 137, 147, 155, 176,
    180, 182, 185
court, 13, 38, 46, 52, 59, 61–63,
    65–66, 68–69, 72, 75, 83–85,
    87, 89, 91–92, 98–99, 102–
    103, 107, 110, 115–116, 145,
    149, 163–164, 170, 177, 180,
    182–184, 187, 198, 200–201,
    211
Court of Appeal, 180
Curran, Dr Desmond, 120, 176,
    205
currency transactions/dealing,
    89, 129–131

D

Daily Express, 36, 52, 65, 128–
    129, 205
Daily Mail, 37
Daily Mirror, 83, 87, 89, 91, 98,
    102, 124, 178
death penalty, 137–139
defence (opening argument,
    witnesses, closing argument),
    59, 63–64, 66, 69, 77, 89–91,
    99–101, 109, 111, 113–116, 121,
    125, 138, 140, 145–147, 154,
    156, 158, 160, 163–165, 170–
    173, 175, 178–180, 182–185,
    191, 195, 197, 205
Dick Barton: Special Agent, 15,
    40
Diller, DI Jack, 22–31, 52–55, 64,
    67, 73, 99, 110, 142–143, 145–
    146, 184, 199, 202, 204
diminished responsibility, 138,
    164–165, 185–187
Director of Public Prosecutions,
    60, 62–64, 116, 167, 172, 199,
    205

Dixon, Arthur (police reformer),
  151–152
DNA testing/profiling/profile,
  141, 153, 155–156, 160, 164
Durand, Victor, 66, 111, 205

E

East End (Whitechapel,
  Spitalfields, Petticoat Lane),
  14–15, 33–34
East, Sir Norwood (Medical
  Commissioner, HM Prisons),
  120–121, 176, 181, 205
Ede, James Chuter (Home
  Secretary), 118–125, 138, 156,
  187, 192, 205
Edgware (development of,
  Underground line extension,
  station, Station Road, shops,
  population, Jewish
  population, history of), 7–9,
  13–16, 19–20, 22, 24–26, 29,
  33–39, 41, 45–46, 51, 53, 55,
  62, 65, 67, 74, 82, 106, 109–
  110, 130, 133, 143, 145–146,
  148, 178, 189, 190, 197, 202,
  204–205, 211, 213
Edgware and District Post, 62
Edgware police station, 20, 22,
  25–26, 67, 74, 146, 204, 211
EEG examination, 119, 125, 172–
  175, 177, 179, 181
Elam, Henry, 66, 205
Elliston, Bernard, 41, 51, 171, 197
epilepsy, 119, 121, 172–176, 179–
  184, 187
Erskine, DS, 22–23, 25, 142, 199,
  204
escape attempt (from Brixton
  prison), 117–118
Evans, Timothy, 137–138
Evening Standard, 148

F

family liaison officer, 148
fingerprints, 60, 144, 149, 156–
  158, 160, 191
forensic evidence, 99, 149, 164

G

Gardner, Vargas, 128–130, 205
Goddard, Lord (Lord Chief
  Justice), 115–116
Golders Green, 14–15, 34–36, 38,
  57, 204
Goodman, Esther, 7–8, 16–20,
  24–25, 29, 31–32, 34, 38, 40,
  45, 51, 54–56, 59, 62, 68–70,
  73, 78, 82–84, 92, 153–154,
  156, 159–161, 188, 191–193,
  195, 204, 208
Goodman, Leopold, 7–8, 13–20,
  25, 29–34, 38–40, 45–48, 51,
  53–54, 56–59, 61–64, 66, 68–
  70, 72–73, 79–80, 82–83, 89,
  93, 97, 101, 113–114, 121, 153–
  154, 156, 158–161, 187, 191–
  195, 197–198, 204, 208–209
governors, prison, 106, 111, 117–
  118, 121, 135, 172–173, 176
Grout, DS Philip, 7, 9, 52, 54–55,
  61, 109–110, 142, 199, 202,
  204

H

Handel, George Frideric, 14
hanging/execution, 17, 29–30,
  56, 108, 118–120, 123, 125–
  129, 131, 133–135, 137–139,
  156, 163, 165, 168, 171–172,
  175–177, 179, 181, 184–185,
  187–190, 194, 197, 201
Hannam, Inspector Herbert, 30,
  57–58, 80, 89–90, 113, 122,
  131, 203–204
Harvey, Inspector John, 19, 21–
  23, 64, 99, 146, 199, 204
Hawke, Anthony (KC), 66–67,
  69, 72–74, 78, 85–89, 94, 96–
  98, 102, 164, 205
Hendon and Finchley Times, 22,
  48, 175, 189
Hendon Magistrates Court, 66
Hilbery, Mr Justice, 115
Hill, PC Charles, 19, 66, 72, 143,
  199, 204

Hirschmann, Dr Samuel, 165, 168–170, 177, 186–188, 205
HOLMES (Home Office Large Major Enquiry System), 144
Home Office, 58, 69, 108, 111–112, 118–121, 123, 125–127, 140, 144, 151–153, 168, 172–173, 175, 179, 184, 187, 189, 192–193, 197, 205
Home Secretary, 109, 118–126, 129, 138, 156, 168, 174–175, 181, 187–188, 192, 205
Homicide Act, 138, 165, 185
Hopwood, Dr, 120, 176, 205
Hotel Majestic, Cannes, 129–131
House of Lords, 138–139, 179–180, 182
Hume, Donald, 117–118
Humphreys, Mr Justice, 115

I

Immigration (of Jewish families), 33
insane automatism, 182–183
insanity/insane, 8, 119–121, 125, 165, 170–172, 176–183, 187
insomnia, 170

J

Jewish Chronicle, 38
Jose, PC Claude, 19
jury, 66–69, 73, 77–80, 84–85, 91–92, 95–102, 107–109, 113–116, 123, 147, 154–155, 164, 178, 180, 182, 184–185, 187, 189

K

King George, 92, 126
Kirk, Harry, 127–128, 133, 135

L

Law Society, 112
Lew, Rabbi Myer, 54, 63, 125–126, 134, 176
life sentence, 139

Luminol, 157, 160

M

malaria, 43, 168
manslaughter, 138, 164–165, 180, 185, 187
Maude, John, 66, 68–75, 77–85, 87, 89, 91–97, 101, 111, 115–116, 119–120, 124, 154–155, 158–159, 165, 168, 172–173, 179, 184, 187, 192, 195, 205
Maudsley Psychiatric Hospital, 173, 182
McKenzie, Dr Murdo, 168–170, 177, 186–188, 195, 205
mental state (Danny's), 46, 117, 119, 164–165, 172, 185
Metropolitan Police, 7, 38, 141, 152–153, 157–158, 199, 202
mitigation/mitigating factors, 136, 140
Morden-Edgware Underground line extension, 38
motive, 8, 59, 63–64, 66–67, 78, 92–93, 98, 108, 121, 147, 164, –165, 186, 189–190, 192
Murder (Abolition of Death Penalty) Act, 139
murder weapon (TV aerial base), 30, 53, 57, 59–60, 63, 68–70, 72–73, 97, 101, 114, 122, 141, 153, 155–156, 159–161, 164, 189, 193–195, 209

N

Nabbs, PC, 19, 204
naturalisation (Leopold's application for), 58, 89
nervous breakdown, 46, 165
News Chronicle, 81
News of the World, 91
Newsam, Sir Frank (Under secretary of state), 119, 125–126, 205
Noble, Eddie, 129–131, 205
non-insane automatism, 182–183

O

Official Receiver, 198, 200–202
Old Bailey, 64–65, 77, 91, 105,
115, 118, 172, 205

P

PACE (Police and Criminal
Evidence Act), 145
Pentonville Prison, 105–106,
110–111, 115–118, 120, 125,
127–128, 133–134, 137, 170,
172–173, 175–176, 189, 205
petition (for Danny's reprieve),
123–124, 129, 198, 201
Pierrepoint, Albert, 116, 127–128,
133–137, 139, 177, 213
police laboratory (or forensic
laboratory), 27, 30, 56, 100,
151–153, 173
post mortem, 69
premeditation, 98, 120, 140, 184,
187
Premeditation, 189
Premier Advertising, 11, 42, 44
prison warders, 105, 115, 117, 121,
133–135, 176
prosecution (opening argument,
witnesses, closing argument),
63, 66, 68, 77–78, 89, 92, 94,
96, 98–99, 121, 147, 154, 163–
164, 173, 182–184, 186, 190,
192, 205
psychiatrist, 43, 168, 173, 205

Q

Queen Elizabeth, 126

R

rationing, 11, 13–15, 19, 41, 45
Raven, Daniel, 8, 23, 27, 40, 42,
54–55, 58, 65, 69, 79, 81, 87,
89, 91, 93, 103, 109, 113, 115–
116, 123, 128, 133, 179, 186,
188, 199, 204–205, 210
Raven, Edward, 26–27, 32, 42–
44, 46, 52, 57, 62, 89, 103,
106, 110, 128–131, 165–166,
168–171, 174, 177, 197, 198–
202, 204
Raven, Gertrude, 13, 16–18, 23,
34, 40–41, 44–46, 48–49, 51–
55, 61, 63, 69, 82–83, 87–88,
90–91, 98, 106, 148, 166, 168–
171, 175, 186, 188, 190–191,
195, 197–199, 203–204
reprieve, 109, 118–120, 123, 125–
126, 129, 135, 138, 165, 168,
172, 175, 187–188, 192
Ritz cinema, 15, 19, 36, 41, 55
Royal Air Force, 42–43, 53, 59,
77, 121, 125–126, 166–168,
174, 177
Royal Commission on Capital
Punishment, 120, 187
Rutter, Sydney, 32, 62–64, 105,
110–114, 119–120, 123–126,
128, 131, 165–168, 170–171,
174–179, 181, 186–188, 205

S

S Division, 24, 143, 202
scaffold, 128, 134–136
Schein, Fay, 123, 129–131, 205
Scotland Yard, 7, 18–19, 30, 73,
85, 89, 109, 128, 131, 153,
202–205
Scotland Yard Information
Room, 18–19, 85
Setty, Stanley, 51, 117–118
Silverman, Sydney (MP), 138–
139, 156–157
Smith Holden, Dr Henry
(forensic laboratory), 30, 53,
56–57, 64, 73, 99, 152–156,
205
South Bank (construction of), 14
Stoddard, Chief Inspector, 128–
131, 204
Strathlene Nursing Home, 49,
54–55, 67, 205
Sunday Pictorial, 124–125, 175,
188
sunstroke, 43, 121, 167, 174

T

Tansill, DCI Albert, 24–25, 27–
    32, 52–54, 56–62, 64, 66, 74–
    75, 95, 100, 142–143, 146,
    156–157, 165, 167, 184, 190,
    194, 199, 202, 204
Teare, Dr, 31, 32, 69–72, 95, 102,
    113, 154, 155, 158–159, 205
television, 9, 11, 15, 18, 21, 25, 30,
    40, 44, 53, 57, 63, 65, 68–69,
    83, 114, 122, 147, 156, 160,
    189, 193, 195
The Star, 131
Todd, Ann, 65, 213
trial, 8–9, 64–65, 77, 91, 93, 102,
    109–111, 113, 115–117, 119–
    121, 130, 144, 147–148, 153–
    154, 156–158, 163–165, 168,
    170–172, 176–177, 179–180,
    182, 184, 190–192, 197, 199,
    201

V

verdict, 43, 66, 96, 102–103,
    106–110, 113, 115–116, 146–
    147, 164, 174, 180, 182, 187,
    189
Vosper, Samuel, 11, 46–48, 54,
    59, 187, 191, 205

W

Wall, Mr Alan, 193
Wealdstone Magistrates Court,
    52
witnesses, 9, 24, 26, 47, 53, 54,
    63–64, 67–69, 72–74, 81, 84–
    85, 87, 89–93, 99–100, 107,
    109, 114, 136, 142, 144, 146,
    154, 164–165, 176, 188, 199
World War I, 33, 145

Y

Yorkshire Ripper, 144

Lightning Source UK Ltd.
Milton Keynes UK
15 October 2009

145030UK00002B/13/P